D0961869

THE
OVECHKIN
PROJECT

THE
OVECHKIN
PROJECT

A BEHIND-THE-SCENES LOOK AT HOCKEY'S MOST DANGEROUS PLAYER

DAMIEN COX & GARE JOYCE

John Wiley & Sons Canada, Ltd.

Copyright © 2010 Damien Cox, Gare Joyce

All rights reserved. No part of this work covered by the copyright herein may be reproduced or used in any form or by any means—graphic, electronic or mechanical without the prior written permission of the publisher. Any request for photocopying, recording, taping or information storage and retrieval systems of any part of this book shall be directed in writing to The Canadian Copyright Licensing Agency (Access Copyright). For an Access Copyright license, visit www.accesscopyright.ca or call toll free 1-800-893-5777.

Care has been taken to trace ownership of copyright material contained in this book. The publisher will gladly receive any information that will enable them to rectify any reference or credit line in subsequent editions.

Library and Archives Canada Cataloguing in Publication

Cox, Damien, 1961–
    The Ovechkin project : a behind-the-scenes look at hockey's most dangerous player / Damien Cox, Gare Joyce.

ISBN 978-0-470-67914-2

    1. Ovechkin, Alexander, 1985-. 2. Hockey players—Biography. I. Joyce, Gare II. Title.

GV848.5.O95C69 2010   796.962092   C2010-901895-8

Production Credits
Cover design: Ian Koo
Cover photo credit: The Canadian Press Images/Nick Wass.
Interior design and typesetting: Natalia Burobina
Printer: Friesens Printing Ltd.

Editorial Credits
Executive Editor: Karen Milner
Production Editor: Pauline Ricablanca

John Wiley & Sons Canada, Ltd.
6045 Freemont Blvd.
Mississauga, Ontario
L5R 4J3

Printed in Canada
1 2 3 4 5 FP 14 13 12 11 10

Mixed Sources

Cert no. SW-COC-001271
© 1996 FSC

FSC

ENVIRONMENTAL BENEFITS STATEMENT

John Wiley & Sons - Canada saved the following resources by printing the pages of this book on chlorine free paper made with 100% post-consumer waste.

TREES	WATER	SOLID WASTE	GREENHOUSE GASES
264 FULLY GROWN	120,853 GALLONS	7,337 POUNDS	25,093 POUNDS

Calculations based on research by Environmental Defense and the Paper Task Force. Manufactured at Friesens Corporation

Contents

To Frank Cooke and Kim Nossal,
Teachers distant but not forgotten who inspired and believed.
—Damien Cox

To my friend, Jim Kelley, the most honest and decent guy in
the business.
—Gare Joyce

ALEXANDER OVECHKIN was lounging in his suite at the Mandarin Oriental hotel, forty floors above Central Park on a glorious late summer day. Caviar, blini, and splits of champagne were on the nighttable. There was enough for both of them—Ovechkin and Cheyenne Tozzi, a blonde model from Australia, who was currently wearing only a sheet from the bed and a practiced come-hither look, though her attention seemed to be divided between him and the Washington Capitals sweater thrown over the end of the bed. Ovechkin had his back turned to her. He was in a simple white shirt, undone down the mid-chest, and pin-striped pants—whose clothes he was wearing he couldn't keep track of because there was a full rack of designer items for him to select from. He was looking at the camera, trying to ignore the stylist charged with bed-head maintenance and the photographer's assistant bouncing the flash so that it would light his blue eyes just right. Ovechkin was staring into the lens with a brooding expression that seemed to have lifted from a Calvin Klein billboard or, more likely, a scene out of *Zoolander*.

Okay, it wasn't an intimate moment, just a recreation of the everyday life of a sports superstar—or, at least, an imagining of what it's like to be Alexander Ovechkin, age 24. How fans imagine his life must be and how he imagines his life should be.

Ovechkin later rifled through the rack, trying to find the right look. Ms. Tozzi was a little easier to fit—one shot would capture Ovechkin looking admiringly at her as she emerged from the bathtub wearing only a discreet lather of bubbles. She'd later don his Capitals sweater— okay, don isn't quite the right word—she strategically draped it over herself to cover the bare minimum required to keep the September issue of *Men's Journal* on the magazine racks of suitable-for-family news-stands.

A fashion shoot is a good measure of celebrity. They ask you to pose and look natural in the most unnatural positions. They ask you to submit to inane question-and-answer sessions (**Q:** "Jessica Alba or Megan Fox?"? **A:** "Definitely both." **Q:** "What bores you more than anything?" **A:** "This. [Smiles.] Most boring thing ever.") That's when you know you've made it or, at least, are making it.

It was hard to imagine any other player in the NHL circa 2009 doing this. Some had a sense of fashion. Henrik Lundqvist, the New York Rangers' goaltender, is ranked among the best-dressed athletes, and probably one of the best-dressed New Yorkers of any stripe, but his tastes run to the high formal. Other NHLers look good when they wear suits to the arena. But Ovechkin's fashion in this *Men's Journal* spread was nothing that Lundqvist would wear and nothing that most players in the league have hanging in their closets. The look was more rock star than hockey player, that of a jet-setter who was looking to burn his way through his millions as quickly as possible, a celebrity rebel thumbing his nose at authority.

His face said hockey. It always had and, short of getting work done by a surgeon to the stars, it always will. His crooked nose, his uneven hair looked like it had been sitting under a helmet. The rest of him said hockey, too. He was as thick through the chest as any two size-44s. Never mind suits, any shirt he put on looked like it had padded shoulders. His bare feet, visible in one shot, looked like something that you'd find in the dinosaur wing of a museum. But this fashion spread didn't say hockey at all. It said star.

Four years before, when he came to North America, to begin his NHL career, he was a kid who just couldn't get enough. When he went to the NHL's draft combine, he already had the top slot in the NHL entry draft locked up, but just for the fun of it, attacked the most grueling of stations of the physical testing and posted the biggest numbers of the 100 prospects who tried it—it was like a new video game was being passed around. When he first joined the Washington Capitals months later, he had been like a kid on his first visit to Disneyland—a kid with millions in his pocket. Back then he was just 20, a man-child, seemingly determined to soak up every bit of a new culture at every opportunity. When he met his future employer, Ted Leonsis, Ovechkin ate a whole cantaloupe over the course of a short conversation—his family was one of the few he knew that was able to get fruit during the winter, but he had never had a cantaloupe and went through it like it was an oversized orange. In Leonsis's pool, Ovechkin did lap after lap underwater for up to two minutes at a time—"like a torpedo," the Capitals' owner said. When Ovechkin stayed over at George McPhee's, the Washington general manager let him borrow a bicycle to go out for a ride—which seemed like a good idea until Ovechkin pulled away from him on the hilly country roads and faded from view well up ahead. McPhee, a former player still at his playing weight, was beat by the time he got back to the house but Ovechkin was already there, playing hockey in the driveway with his hosts' kids.

He was almost desperate to fit in with his new teammates. In the dressing room after the first practice in his first training camp, he walked up to the erasable board, copied down the names from the nameplates over the players' stalls, and then tried to say them. He was stuck on one name of one player, Steve Eminger. "I walked into the room and the players were howling," said Glen Hanlon, Ovechkin's first coach with the Capitals. "He just couldn't pronounce Eminger. The harder he tried to say it the funnier it got. I realized this is no little shrinking violet here. A 20-year-old kid had taken control of the room."

When it came time to head out on road trips, Ovechkin asked for an English-speaking roommate, a journeyman from Canada named Brian Willsie, rather than Dairius Zubrus, a Russian-speaking center. Zubrus, Ovechkin's linemate, might have been able to help him with the routine on the road but Ovechkin thought it would be better to do a language immersion. He did the usual rookie-dinner rite of initiation and picked up the tab for the team—and a few other times he was left with the check on a draw of credit cards that might not have been completely on the up-and-up. The veterans taught him to play poker and he joined in games on flights, using all the accessories of the TV poker pros (hats pulled down, headphones, reflecting shades) before he had command of the rules, never mind the odds. Even though his fractured English limited some joke-playing, he strung along credulous reporters—when one asked him if he had any nicknames, Ovechkin told her, "Sexbomb."

His was a charmed life. The first time he ever picked up a baseball he was throwing out the first pitch at a Washington Nationals game at RFK Stadium, a strike over the plate that drew an ovation from the crowd and had fans chanting his name. Even less likely, five days later, the first time that he ever played golf, he got a hole in one on a 160-yard par-three with a borrowed 4-iron. Captured on video, Ovechkin pretended the club was a guitar and then, not knowing the game's etiquette, ran around the Springfield Golf and Country Club course and yelled to his teammates on other holes, "I swear to Gaaa-a! I swear on my mom!" In those first days the biggest miracle might have been not getting into an accident while driving around Washington in his Cadillac Escalade or BMW M6 with his head out the window to take in the sights—it might have been that the 120-decibel Eurodisco pounding out of the sound system gave drivers enough of a heads-up to clear the road, thinking that the presidential motorcade was approaching.

His was, if anything, an even more charmed life on the ice. That's not to say that he needed much luck on the ice. He was an unprecedented mix of skill, size, and toughness. Mike Knuble, who became a teammate with the Caps in 2009, has a frame of reference, having been a linemate of Hockey Hall of Famers Wayne Gretzky and Steve Yzerman, as well as former league MVPs Sergei Fedorov and Peter Forsberg. "Mash them all together in a bigger body and that's Alex," Knuble said. Bobby Carpenter, Washington's hockey hero back in the early '80s, called Ovechkin, "a bigger, faster Gordie Howe." Carpenter played with Hockey Hall of Famer Cam Neely, a legend in Boston for his strength and toughness, but he says Ovechkin eclipses him. "This guy is so much faster and has so much skill," Carpenter said. "No of-fence to Cam but Ovechkin can do so many things that Cam couldn't."

Or anybody else. And in the 43rd game of his NHL career, Ovech-kin scored a goal that left those who watched it, including Wayne Gretzky, speechless. Barely halfway through his first season he scored The Goal—there have been hundreds of thousands of goals scored in the NHL, but mention The Goal, just those two words, to hockey fans and they'll know exactly what you're talking about.

The Capitals were playing the Coyotes in Phoenix in an unremark-able game that the visitors led by a lopsided score. It was a situation where most NHLers move into a lockdown mode—not going through the motions, per se, but certainly not pushing the boundaries and tak-ing big risks. About 12 minutes into the third period, Ovechkin started down the right wing, his off wing, and was facing Phoenix defense-man Paul Mara, who would play a supporting role in a YouTube video watched by millions over the next four years. It looked like Mara had Ovechkin stopped, tackling him as he crossed in front of the Coyotes' netminder Brian Boucher. Neither of Ovechkin's skates was on the ice when he caught the puck in the bend where the shaft of his stick meets the blade. He was airborne but falling, with his back turning to the net. Twisting like an Olympic diver, he swept the puck 30 feet past and through Mara and Boucher into the Phoenix net, blindly, with one hand. The Capitals' announcers couldn't even start to describe the play. "Alexander Ovechkin. When it looked like it was no longer possible, he still got it done." The crowd didn't boo, as you'd expect when a visiting player scored with the home team being run out of the building. No, though there were several thousand ticket-holders in attendance, a hush fell over the arena. Ovechkin wasn't sure how the puck went in until he skated back to the Capitals' bench, watching the replay over his shoulder. And when the screen showed the puck going in, his wide smile revealed his missing teeth while Gretzky, the Coy-otes' coach, watched, expressionless.

"As he fell, he had the presence of mind to change the angle of his hand and his stick so that he could kind of shoot with the stick be-hind his head," Olaf Kolzig, the Capitals' veteran goalie said. "Unless you've played hockey, you don't understand how difficult that is. Once we saw that on replay, we all lost our minds on the bench . . . A talent like his only comes by once in a lifetime."

Usually a goaltender who is victimized on a landmark goal will be touchy when the subject is raised, but Brian Boucher has made his peace with his place in this bit of hockey history. "Now, looking back, it was a helluva goal by him," Boucher said. "I guess I'm proud to be a part of it. He's a world-class player. You know, my son certainly gets a kick out of looking at it on YouTube."

Everyone got a kick out of Ovechkin. His rookie season was a spontaneous, almost immediate legend and it just took off after The Goal. When the Capitals played in Montreal he received an ovation, a once-in-a-generation tribute from the Canadiens' fans for a visiting player, something unheard of for a rookie. When he got up on stage to announce the Capitals' first-round draft pick at the NHL draft in Vancouver in June 2006, the fans there also gave him an ovation.

But it wasn't the rookie Ovechkin who was posing with Cheyenne Tozzi. By then, Alexander Ovechkin was different than the young man who came to America five years before.

He had happily promoted local Washington businesses, seemingly unaffected or maybe unaware of his burgeoning stardom. For example, he endorsed The Hair Cuttery, a modest hairstyling outfit, even though his mother cut his hair and it frequently looked like she used garden shears. His gregarious manner inspired a parody in McDonald's commercials: Sergei Puckizen, an animated antic character who, though he didn't even come up to his teammates' shin pads, skated rings around pros, giving his own play-by-play in broken English. But by the time the commercials aired in 2009, the real-life comic wasn't seen so often.

Asked at age 24 how he had changed in his time in Washington, he said not all. "I am still the same," though the way he said it—flat, subdued, disengaged—suggested that he was very different than he had been at 19. It wasn't that he had lost his sense of humor but he did seem to take things more seriously. And when he tried for laughs it often fell flat. In April 2009, Ovechkin scored his 50th goal of the season during a game in Tampa Bay. To celebrate, he laid his stick on the ice and pretended to warm his hands over it—his stick-on-fire bit. To many it crossed the line and amounted to taunting. "It doesn't bother me that much but some of the veterans on the team didn't like it," Tampa Bay's young star Steven Stamkos said.

Ovechkin had won the Calder Trophy as the NHL's top rookie and he collected two Hart Trophies as the league's most-valuable player. He was voted to the First All-Star team in each of his first four seasons, the first player to do that since Montreal goaltender Bill Durnan in the early '40s. Still, going into his fifth NHL season, he had yet to win a championship with the Capitals. Patience is not part of his game or his personality and, clearly, he had tired of losing. He also had his eyes on an Olympic gold medal—one to match those won by his mother with Soviet basketball teams in 1976 and 1980. And, more than that, he aspired to be a star. In Washington he was. "Last year it was Ovechkin and Obama," Capitals publicist Nate Ewell said. "Now, it's just Ovechkin."

But by 2010 he was looking to reach beyond the Capitals' home market and beyond hockey's fan base. That was going to take something more than The Goal and variations on it. That was going to take more than stick-on-fire celebrations—in fact, it might require the snuffing of all the pantomimed pyrotechnics. That was going to take more than fashion spreads in men's magazines, no matter how enjoyable the process. That was going to take winning.

chapter 1

Vancouver

"It's a Dangerous Game and He's the Most Dangerous Guy"

ALEXANDER OVECHKIN'S visor blocked out his eyes but in no way concealed his identity. Razor stubble lined his oversized jaw. His underbite gave the impression that he was biting his lip. His abundant black hair looked like it was trying to escape his helmet through any available gap. Just an inch or so of his nose was visible below his visor, but you could tell it had been knocked out of line. Even if you couldn't see his face, even if you couldn't make out his name and number on the back of his sweater, even though there were no individual player introductions, you could have picked him out among his Russian teammates standing on the blue line. He was instantly recognizable in nothing more than a silhouette. He's the rare player whose athleticism is not contained by standard hockey equipment. He dons his uniform and then looks a threat to rip right out of it. Muscles seem to bulge through his sweater. The inseams of his hockey pants are unzipped to give him an unconstrained range of motion. Even the tongues of his skates flop over the laces, like they're panting, trying to keep up with him. And he wears his emotions not on his sleeves but on his gloves, the names of his late grandfather and late brother in Cyrillic lettering magic-markered on the cuffs.

It was Vancouver, but it wasn't the gold-medal game of the 2010 Winter Olympics; it was just the quarterfinal. Still, it was arguably the most anticipated hockey game in the modern history of the sport. Other nations were involved, other nations posing threats of varying degrees. But for a couple of years leading up to the Games, there was the belief that Canada and Russia, the two nations with the longest-standing hockey histories, were going to collide in Vancouver.

Both countries had stars dressed for Olympic collision. At the moment of the opening face-off, the entire hockey world was watching Alexander Ovechkin. Those who were watching him closest were on the ice or within spitting distance of it. They were the best known, the ones with the most at stake in this game.

Rick Nash was the closest to Ovechkin at the opening face-off, lined up directly across the red line from him, bumping elbows and shoulders. The captain of the Columbus Blue Jackets, Nash entered the NHL three years before Ovechkin and yet had played in only four playoff games in his entire career. Only in international games did Nash get a chance to show the hockey world his talent, and in them he had established himself as one of Canada's top scorers. Many figured that Nash was going to end up on Canada's first line—with his height and strength, he had the ability to shed the very best defensemen in the game to get to the net and finish plays. There wasn't anyone on the Canadian team who was better at cutting through heavy traffic. In this game, however he was on the checking line. He wasn't expected to cut through traffic—he was supposed to create it, slowing Ovechkin to a crawl. *In front of him, never behind him.*

From his spot behind the Canadian bench, Mike Babcock saw Ovechkin's and Nash's backs when the puck dropped from the referee's hand and hit the ice. At 6-foot-2½ and a solid 230 pounds,

Ovechkin looks physically imposing when he stands across from most NHLers, but he was giving away almost two inches to Nash, who just about matched him pound for pound. Nash was just part of a plan that Babcock and his assistant coaches had come up with the day before the showdown with Russia. *The Russians are giving us a present, putting him out there against Nash right off the hop.*

Sidney Crosby was leaning forward on the Canadian bench, in front of a pacing Babcock. He and Ovechkin had been the faces of their Olympic teams, the subjects of an hour-long documentary that had aired across Canada and a feature spread in *Sports Illustrated.* Crosby had previously chosen his words carefully when talking about Ovechkin publicly—he had wanted to avoid giving his rival any bulletin-board material. That changed on the eve of the Vancouver Games, when Crosby had spoken more plainly about Ovechkin. "When we started to play each other, it was more like people were celebrating two players," Crosby said. "But it seemed like, with each game, he was just trying to line me up. So we start having run-ins, and the media is watching. Then, with it getting stirred around off the ice, it built into more of a hate relationship." *Everyone knows it.*

Ovechkin wasn't a concern of just those on the ice or near it. Elsewhere in the arena, in the seats and the exclusive suites, others had a stake in the outcome, a stake in Ovechkin's tournament. Casual fans of the sport might know their names but not necessarily their faces and maybe not their connection to Ovechkin.

Most fans would have recognized Gary Bettman, and many of them would have booed him at some point or called in to a sports talk-radio show demanding he get the boot from his $7.2-million a year job. The National Hockey League commissioner since 1993, Bettman has been criticized more than any major sports executive not named Bud Selig. He has been blamed for, among other things: the failure of the NHL to gain a stronger position in the American sports market; the league's failure to attract a major network television deal like the NFL's, the NBA's, or major-league baseball's;

and what is perceived as a game watered down by overexpansion. The NHL's participation in the Olympics started in 1998 under Bettman's tenure, and the league's fan base almost unanimously approves of it, yet he came to Vancouver insisting that the 2010 Games might be the NHL's last. *The owners don't like it. We haven't had enough of a bounce.* His skin has thickened to the criticisms over the years, but what doesn't sit well with him is Ovechkin's vow to go to the 2014 Winter Olympics in Sochi, Russia, with or without the league's approval. *We can't have an insurrection led by the league's top player.*

Slava Fetisov was watching from VIP seating reserved for officials of the Russian Olympic Committee. Others wore stiff dark suits, but he was more casual than the rest in a baby-blue windbreaker bearing the logo of the 2014 Winter Games. One of the greatest defensemen of all time, he had won gold medals with the Soviet Union's Big Red Machine in the '80s and Stanley Cups with the Detroit Red Wings in the late '90s. Fetisov had not just delivered in his prime but done so imperiously. Many Russian players who had come over to North America to play in the NHL stayed on. Fetisov had gone home with the intent of building a hockey program in the new Russia that would equal the U.S.S.R.'s. *It's a different time. I don't know if it will be better.*

Don Meehan had a good seat in the arena and, as usual, the agent with the longest list of NHL clients had rooting interests on both sides of the ice. In the Canadian lineup, Meehan's Newport Sports agency represented Jarome Iginla and Scott Niedermayer, two holdovers from the Olympic gold-medal winners in 2002. On the Russian side of the ice, Newport handled the business affairs of Andrei Markov, the Montreal Canadiens' top defenseman, and Maxim Afinogenov, a winger with the Atlanta Thrashers. Both Russian goaltenders dressed for this game were Meehan clients: the starter, Evgeni Nabokov, and the backup, Ilya Bryzgalov. Others in the seats around him might have been as emotionally invested in the game but none were so deeply financially invested. Then again,

Meehan wasn't as deeply financially invested as he would have liked. He wished he had Ovechkin as a client. Ovechkin signed a 13-year $124-million contract two years before, becoming the highest paid player in the sport. An agent with a standard commission would have been looking at a minimum of $400,000 a year, maybe more. Then there would have been a slice—a larger slice on a percentage basis—of Ovechkin's off-ice income. But neither Meehan nor any other NHL certified agent was getting a single dollar of it—none was involved in the negotiations. Agents in the hockey business can't afford to dwell on what might have been. Waiting for the face-off, another of Meehan's clients, defenseman Shea Weber, was lined up directly behind Nash. *Shea will do a good job against him.*

George McPhee, the Capitals' general manager, was watching the game in a suite with other GMs. He wasn't going to stick around for the gold-medal game—he wanted to head back to the office because the NHL trading deadline was looming and he thought a couple of deals could push his team over the top. He had five players in the tournament: three Russians, Ovechkin, winger Alexander Semin, and Semyon Varlamov, a third goaltender who practiced with the team but would only dress in the event of injury; center Nicklas Backstrom with Sweden; and forward Tomas Fleischmann with the Czech Republic. McPhee wanted all of them to play well, but he was thinking about getting them back safely to the Capitals. He was sure the Canadians were going to go after his franchise player. *They'll go after him and he'll go back harder, and something's going to give.* And he didn't think that the Russian team was deep enough to give Ovechkin the support he needed to make it a contest. *A loss would be tough on him.*

It seemed like David Abrutyn had a rooting interest at every venue at the Vancouver Games. As the head of global consulting at International Management Group (IMG), he was fame manager and strategist to the stars. On the slopes it was American skier Lindsey Vonn. On the ice at Pacific Coliseum it was another American, figure skater Evan Lysacek. And in the half pipe for snowboarders it was yet another American, Shaun White (aka the Flying Tomato). Abrutyn's role was to maximize the celebrity and the financial rewards that were there for the victors to claim. Abrutyn's rooting interest in hockey wasn't an American ready for a Wheaties box. It was Ovechkin. IMG had dropped hockey as a going interest a few years earlier—just not enough in it for either the company or the client on the endorsement side of the sports business. Abrutyn, however, got IMG back in the game, and he had identified Ovechkin as the player with the greatest commercial upside. *A gold for Russia will cement it.*

Others weren't in Vancouver but they watched the game just as closely as those who were. Some had skated beside him. Others had never been in the same arena, had only ever seen him on television. Some had known him all his life and watched him grow up from an energetic kid at practices at the Moscow Dynamo rink. Others had never met him and, beyond their fleeting and indirect roles in his career, knew nothing more about his life than they gleaned from reading stories in newspapers or watching broadcasts of games.

Ted Leonsis, the Capitals' billionaire owner, had decided to go home early from Vancouver. He had had enough of the Olympics. *Had it up to here.* Like other NHL owners, he had to put his team on hold for three weeks while the Olympics played out. Worse, he felt like the Olympics had distracted his Capitals—they had been on a run of 15 consecutive victories, but went into the Olympic break losing their last three games on the road. *It was like they checked out for the Olympics a week early.* He felt like his franchise and the league as a whole were not going to have a lot to show for their participation in the Olympics. *Two tickets, that's all I got. And lineups, no express lines for VIPs.* Some owners are content to stay in their skybox suites, but Leonsis likes to go down to the dressing room to rub elbows with his players, to be part of the scene. That wasn't going to happen at the Olympics. He couldn't even get his star player on the phone. So Leonsis flew home to his mansion in McLean, Virginia. He was watching the game on high-def in his den. He was going to write in *Ted's Take*, a blog that he updates with his innermost thoughts a couple of times daily: "We are all blessed to watch him every game. We are all blessed to call him a friend."

Bruce Boudreau, the Capitals' coach, was watching the game at his home in Alexandria, Virginia. It was the House That Ovie Built, a home afforded Boudreau by the sort of talent he never imagined he'd get a chance to coach. Somehow the last guy they ever thought of as an NHL coach turned out to be the perfect fit with Ovechkin and the Capitals. Boudreau's thinking was along the same lines as Leonsis's when it came to the days before the Olympics. *Playing so bad the Olympics couldn't get here soon enough.* And it was along the same lines as McPhee's when it came to the priority for the rest of season. *No injuries. Want him to feel good about himself, about the team.* But while McPhee sensed that Ovechkin might be in the weeds against Canada, Boudreau didn't put anything past him, including making it a long night for Canada. *Alex is a machine.*

Dean Evason, one of Washington's assistant coaches, was also watching the game at home in the D.C. suburbs. Evason wasn't getting a big-ticket salary like Boudreau's but he was making a good living in the game. Watching Canada line up against Ovechkin and his Russian teammates, Evason thought back to his own experience playing for Canada at the 1997 World Championships in Helsinki. In 1997 he was the only player in the Canadian lineup who wasn't playing in the NHL at the time—his NHL career had wound down and he had spent the winter playing for Hockey Canada's national team in exhibitions and lesser tournaments. As a tribute for his commitment to that program, Evason was named the captain of the Canadian team. Proving that the hockey world is a small one, two of Evason's teammates from that championship team, Jarome Iginla and Chris Pronger, were in the Canadian lineup in Vancouver. Back in '97, Evason went on to be the unlikeliest captain to raise the world championship trophy, but only after Canada had beaten Russia 2–1 in the semifinal and then Sweden by the same score in the game that decided the gold medal. *The games that matter most can be that tight, right down to a lucky bounce or a bad break.*

You half-expected that Mike Knuble would have been lined up with or against Ovechkin at the opening face-off in Vancouver. He's like hockey's Zelig, a decent but far from sensational player who just happens to be around greatness, Hall of Famers, scoring champions, record holders. He came by his professional modesty honestly. *Ovie makes everyone better. I don't make anyone better.* Knuble had signed as a free agent with Washington over the summer. McPhee figured that he offered championship experience to a Capitals team led by young talent. Knowing that his top line would need some toughness, someone to work the corners, Boudreau threw Knuble on with Ovechkin and center Nicklas Backstrom early in the season and ran with it as the Capitals became the highest scoring team in the league. Knuble was another guy in his living room in a suburb of Washington, watching the game. He saw Ovechkin's linemates, Evgeni Malkin at center and Semin, another talented young Russian, on right wing. *Three skill guys. Three guys to drink the water, no one to carry it.*

Attention was also focused on Ovechkin far beyond commuting distance of D.C. Jamie Heward was in his den in Regina, Saskatchewan watching the game alone in the heartland of hockey. He hadn't watched a lot of hockey in the weeks before the Olympics—he was decompressing, getting the game out of his system. He had some hard luck in his NHL career and some memories haunted him. But he had no memory of his worst moment, the play that ended his career, or the whole day it happened. He had been on the Capitals' roster when Ovechkin arrived. He had befriended him. And when Ovechkin ended his career, Heward had no grievance. *It's a dangerous game and he's the most dangerous guy.*

Farther north and to the east, in Thompson, Manitoba, Mel (The Mangler) Angelstad was watching the game in a rec room with a few old photos from his playing days on the wall and more stuffed in drawers. Ovechkin had never met Mel Angelstad, had never spoken to him. Ovechkin would have only ever seen him if he had looked through video libraries of old hockey fights. Angelstad had played for 20 teams over his career and only has rough counts on broken bones he had suffered and stitches sewn into his face. His hockey career had ended a couple of years earlier after a stint in Europe, and he had gone from mangler to healer, working as a paramedic in his hometown. Angelstad had never seen him play in person, but since Ovechkin's arrival in Washington he had been Angelstad's guy. Like a lot of very modestly talented players, Angelstad had a small and virtually unknown role in Ovechkin winding up with the Capitals. *Not a brush with fame. A near-brush with fame.*

In Moscow, Ovechkin's hometown, the viewership numbers for Russia versus Canada might not have been as big as they were in Regina and Thompson. The game was played in the wee hours of the morning, and broadcasts were available only on a pricey pay-per-view service. Still, many of those watching there knew Ovechkin best. They knew him when he was a schoolboy skating at the Dynamo arena.

Vladimir Mochalov thought about the days when he had played against Ovechkin at age 12. So did a bunch of 24-year-olds who had played with him on Moscow Dynamo's youth teams, the '85 birthdays. *Back then he wasn't the best. We were better than him.*

Alexander Kirillov thought about his late father, Vyacheslav. A father he barely remembers. He was too young. When he thinks of his father, he thinks of family photographs. The closest thing to a hockey legacy for his father is Ovechkin. *When he skates, my father lives.*

Watching Ovechkin line up for the opening face-off in Vancouver, Ramis Valiulin was transported back to the days when he and Vyacheslav Kirillov worked with the Dynamo '85s, the group of players born in 1985. Back then, Ovechkin and his teammates, 11 and 12 years old, came to practice after school and then would head home to do homework. Valiulin took Ovechkin and his teammates on their first trips to invitational tournaments in other European countries. *In 12 years, he's bigger but nothing much else has changed. Same Sasha. Same hunger.*

Mikhail and Tatiana Ovechkin were in Moscow. Four years earlier they had been in the stands for the Russia-Canada quarterfinal game in Torino at the 2006 Winter Olympics, and their then-19-year-old son had scored the goal that knocked the defending gold medalists out of the tournament. In Vancouver the expectations for him were different. Tatiana knew all about these expectations from her time with the Soviet Union's Olympic basketball teams. *He will have a gold medal like mine. And that will lead to even greater things. He will be the greatest player in the world. He will get everything he deserves.*

chapter 2

Dynamo

"If You Won't Become a Player, I Don't Know Who Will."

IN THE COLD WAR YEARS, the athletes from the Soviet Union seemed stoic, even robotic, no matter the excellence of their performances. There was no joy, no anger, no expression whatsoever. They seemed unwilling, like soulless drones, pawns coerced into competing for the Kremlin's propaganda goals. That was because those in the West didn't know their stories, stories like Tatiana Ovechkina's.

Ovechkina wanted it as much as any athlete you'd find anywhere. Through force of will, she brushed aside injuries suffered when she was hit by a car as a grade-schooler. She heard the doctors tell her that she might lose her leg, that she'd have to learn how to walk again, and that she'd never play sports. She didn't listen. She invented ways to train and make her damaged leg stronger. She lifted bricks to turn weakness into strength. Just on will, she overcame the limitations of a withered leg and played through pain, becoming an elite point guard, first on Moscow Dynamo's team and later on the U.S.S.R.'s national basketball team, winning two Olympic gold medals. Indeed, at the 1976 Summer Games in Montreal, the giant 7-foot-2 Juliana Semenova had been unstoppable, but it was the speedy Ovechkina, playing every minute of every game, who was running the show. She was not going to be denied.

Ovechkina was as motivated, dedicated, and passionate as any athlete in the West. It wasn't just love of country and love of the game. Her desire was also fuelled by material wants and needs. The state offered privileges to elite athletes: apartments, money, cars. Sport offered her a way of providing for her family, for her husband and three sons. She could jump the bread lines. Her family could have fruit in the winter, unlike their neighbors. Her boys could have chewing gum and soccer balls, things their friends envied.

Her two older boys weren't up to athletic stardom. Sergei, the oldest, was an amateur wrestler, but he wasn't an elite athlete. He was never a candidate for national teams. Mikhail, the middle son, was quiet and not competitive at all. He walked away from sports in his early teens. But Tatiana Ovechkina found a willing vessel in her third son, Alexander. She called him Sasha, which was a little more endearing than Sergei's nickname for his kid brother, Toad. The youngest of the Ovechkins was something out of the ordinary right from his arrival; he was 12 pounds at birth. His physical gifts as a child were obvious to his mother.

"From his early childhood, Sasha had talent towards sports," his mother said in a 2007 interview with *Sovetsky Sport*. "Obviously, it is in his genes. Our son could make a name for himself in any sport. When he started playing basketball, he immediately began catching the ball the proper way. In soccer, he demonstrated nice technical skills in the field and even he was able to play as a goalkeeper very well. Many principals from various sports-related schools back home kept asking me to send Sasha to their place."

In a lot of ways Sasha seemed unexceptional. He went to school, but he wasn't much of a student—one time he playfully bribed a teacher with flowers for a passing mark. He wasn't much for homework, but he could spend hours with his Nintendo. He played games with his friends in the hallways and stairwells of the apartment where they lived—a favorite was called The Demons, a game of tag up and down a darkened stairwell with The Demon ambushing and frightening other players when they went to step out of the elevator. It was mischief that scared the old ladies in the building who were caught in the middle of the game, which only made it better.

It was inevitable that he gravitated towards what he did best: sports. He had the size and strength. His mother taught him the lessons, blunt and uncompromising, about physical sacrifice. She nurtured him. She conditioned him. "Never stop," she would say to him. "You stop and you'll be nothing." Tatiana wanted Sasha to play basketball, her sport. His father, Mikhail, had played soccer, a game the boy also liked. He was a goalkeeper, a position where his raw athletic ability and reflexes served him well. Sergei wanted Toad to play hockey at the Moscow Dynamo school. Sasha followed Sergei's lead.

"I first tried on a pair of skates when I was seven," Ovechkin told the *Vancouver Sun* in a 2002 interview. "I tried skating for a while and I took some lessons but after four months I'd had enough. I decided I didn't like it."

He was the furthest thing from a prodigy in the beginning. He got a late start. When he first went to the Dynamo rink, the other boys had a head start on him and had been skating for years. Vladimir Mochalov was the star player among the 1985 birthdays, but others weren't that far behind him. Their parents were already talking about them going on to play for Dynamo and becoming stars like Sergei Fedorov and Pavel Bure. The other boys knew what to do in the drills, but Ovechkin struggled to stay standing and not be embarrassed. In those first practices, the coaches had the kids skating figure eights and Sasha struggled to do crossovers, but it only got worse when the coaches blew the whistles and had the players do the drill skating backwards. When the coaches saw him struggle, they were prepared to give him a pass and let him sit out the drill, but he felt humiliated in front of his teammates and parents.

Games were no better than practice. The coaches wouldn't put him in games until the end of blowouts—and Dynamo didn't have a strong team for players in Sasha's age-group, so his team was often on the wrong end of a lopsided score. When time wound down and Sasha thought he was going to be sent out, he'd try to hide on the bench. But sometimes, when his team was down by seven or eight goals, the coaches still didn't put him into the game, and afterwards they'd tell the Ovechkins that they couldn't get him on the ice while there was still a chance to catch up.

Other kids would have been chased off, but Sasha was motivated to work on it. He wouldn't stop. Not just an hour or two a day but every spare hour—he set down his Nintendo and had grown too old for The Demons. Some days he'd be on the ice five or six or even seven hours. Because of his mother's reputation and her position on the Dynamo board, he always had equipment—he had the run of the sports organization. More than that, the Ovechkins had money that they could spend on expert coaches.

Vyacheslav Kirillov was the first to work with Sasha in private lessons, $10 a session. "Kirillov taught him the ABCs of the game of hockey," said Mikhail Ovechkin, the father, in a 2007 interview with *Sovetsky Sport*. The lessons caused some jealousy around the arena—other parents thought the Ovechkin boy was getting preferential treatment because he was Tatiana Ovechkina's boy. But Kirillov pushed his young student hard. He had the boy skate lengths of the ice with his stick in a heavy tire, teaching him how to position his body properly. Mikhail Ovechkin came up with the idea to cut Sasha's stick short, less than chest height, to make him bend his knees to improve his skating.

Other hockey phenoms skated on frozen ponds or, like Wayne Gretzky, backyard rinks. Some had access to neighborhood rinks where they could play unsupervised for hours on end. That wasn't the experience for Sasha Ovechkin—there was nothing bucolic or old-fashioned about his hockey education. It was hard work, not recreation. On a good day he'd get in three practices: one at 7 a.m., one in the afternoon after school, and one at night. Before the morning practices, and sometimes before the evening workouts, he'd sleep in his father's old Lada 6 on the drive to the arena and then change in the front seat before stepping on the ice. Mikhail would give Kirillov rides to and from the practices, and the coach would give him updates on Sasha's progress.

Kirillov always encouraged the youngster, but his mother took the opposite approach. "I tried not to praise him," Tatiana Ovechkina told the *Washington Post* in a 2006 interview. "After a win . . . the next morning over breakfast I could tell him, 'You know, you did okay. But right there you made a mistake. And there, you didn't skate hard enough. And there you didn't get all the way to fight for the puck. And you were lazy in that episode, so work on that.'"

Sasha toughed it out and improved. When Sergei came out to games, Toad was able to hear him from the ice, and he tried to play tougher than usual, giving opponents facewashes after whistles.

• • •

On his 10th birthday, September 17, 1995, Sasha was off with the Dynamo team for a tournament in Yaroslavl. That morning, he got a phone call from his parents—Sergei had been in a car accident. Though he was in hospital with a broken leg, it didn't seem to be too serious. Sasha played on his birthday and then came home on the 18th and visited Sergei with his parents and his brother Mikhail. Sergei was already up and around, hobbling on crutches but seemingly ready to go home.

The next morning he died at the hospital from a blood clot that had formed in his leg. Sergei was 24.

The impact on the Ovechkin family was devastating. Alexander had a game scheduled for the day after his brother's death. He played. "His brother wasn't even in the ground yet," said his father,

Mikhail, in a 2006 *Washington Post* interview. "We decided he shouldn't skip the game. He played while tears were flowing down his cheeks. He cried the entire game, but he played. He wanted to play. We were obviously not thinking about hockey that day. I don't even know what the score was. We didn't really think of it as a lesson. We didn't want him to sit at home and dwell, and to cry and poison himself with his thoughts."

Tatiana tried to keep up appearances. Her hair went gray in just a matter of weeks. She would dye it black, only to see it turn gray again. In another interview with the *Post*, Tatiana recalled going to Alexander's hockey games soon after the death of Sergei. "He looked up at the stands where I'm sitting and he saw my eyes were bloated with tears and he ran up to me and told me, 'Mama, don't cry.'"

Sasha was in a fog, his world was shaken, but he kept going. He kept playing the game that his brother encouraged him to play. Soon, he donned No. 8, the same number his mother had worn for the Soviet Union. Everything was in place. The necessary DNA. The perfect athletic role model. The mental toughness. The motivation supplied by tragic circumstances. Alexander Ovechkin was ready to take his dreams to places where heroes of Dynamo in the Soviet era hadn't dared to imagine.

Like a lot of kids in other countries, 10-year-old Sasha collected hockey cards. Unlike kids of his parents' generation, he collected cards of Russian players in the NHL. By the mid-'90s, more than 40 Russians were playing in the NHL. Pavel Bure was electrifying fans in Vancouver, Detroit's Sergei Fedorov had been named the league's most valuable player, and Alexei Kovalev had won a Stanley Cup in New York. His parents' generation had looked at the Olympics as the pinnacle of sport. But by the mid-'90s in Russia, the NHL was accepted as the best hockey league in the world, something a 10-year-old card-collector could dream of while lining up his cards on the floor of his family's two-bedroom, 10th-floor apartment in Moscow.

He had no idea what it had taken for them to get from Russia to the NHL.

• • •

Nick Polano shivered when he walked past the soldiers with the machine guns and suspicious looks. He walked behind two Russian fixers he didn't know into a military hospital that he shouldn't have been in. They told him not to speak English and that meant saying not a word because he didn't speak any Russian. A KGB informant eyeballed him from a neighboring bed as Polano finally met the teenager he had traveled around the globe to meet. And the kid had almost been killed in a car accident, disfigured beyond recognition.

Polano left a mining town in northern Ontario to play hockey when he was in his teens. By his late 40s he was an old-school hockey man who took on tough jobs behind the bench, on the road scouting players, and, for a time in the 1980s and early '90s, smuggling players through holes in the Iron Curtain, first from Czechoslovakia and later from the Soviet Union.

He even looked the part of a smuggler. With a broad, battered, and often broken nose, he could have been an extra in *The Untouchables*, running bootleg booze across the Detroit River. He knew how to get business done. He could carry bags of Detroit Red Wings owner Mike Ilitch's money through the Moscow airport without raising more than the usual suspicions. He could bribe border guards with packs of Marlboros as easily as he could pay for parking. "A lot of people thought we were bad to do it illegally," he says. "But we were taking players who wanted freedom, who wanted to play in the best league in the world. I wanted to help them."

Polano was old school, but he had an open mind. He'd never despised the Russians as many of his generation had, at least never as hockey players. In 1980, as the general manager and head coach of the Erie Blades of the old Eastern Hockey League, he convinced the Soviet national team to play an exhibition against his team prior to the Lake Placid Winter Olympics. "When it was announced we were playing the Soviets, I had people calling, threatening my life," says Polano. "So we turned it into a patriotic night. Lots of flags, singing the national anthem." Polano was just playing along. "I loved their talent. I was inspired by the way they trained, with their skill level." The Blades lost, but they might have taken something out of Viktor Tikhonov's crew, for they went on to lose that famous Olympic showdown with Herb Brooks's Miracle on Ice team in Lake Placid.

In those days, the stars of the Soviet Union were unavailable to the teams of the west. NHL clubs would draft them, but nothing would ever come of it. It took a historic franchise on hard times, the Detroit Red Wings, to disrupt the status quo. By 1982, they had missed the playoffs in 11 of the previous 12 seasons. At that point the Norris family sold the franchise to Little Caesars pizza magnate Mike Ilitch. Ilitch shook up the organization. "He was very aggressive," said Jimmy Devellano, who was hired by Ilitch in June 1982 to run the club. "The team we had inherited had 4,000 season tickets. We were bound and determined to get better on the ice. That would get more asses in the seats, and then business would get better." The 1981–82 Wings had won only 21 games and picked up 54 points while surrendering 351 goals. The next season, with Polano hired to coach the Wings, the club won 21 games again. With the fourth pick in the draft they landed the player who would define their franchise for the next two decades, Steve Yzerman. Devellano used other picks to draft three future NHL enforcers in Bob Probert, Joey Kocur, and Stu Grimson. Already, however, Devellano had realized that his promise of building through the draft was flawed.

"I was finding that in the later rounds of the draft the players didn't seem to have much NHL potential," he said. "I thought, 'How the heck can we build through the draft if we're only getting one or two guys per draft?' I talked to our scouts and they kept telling me there were 18- and 19-year-old Russians and Czechs with NHL potential. There was this old standard that if you drafted one of those players, you were wasting your pick. Well, I reversed that. I thought we were wasting our picks in the fourth and fifth rounds by taking North Americans."

Devellano tested his theory in the fifth round of the '83 draft when he selected talented Czech forward Petr Klima, who most assumed would be a star for his national team for years to come and therefore like Soviets unavailable to the NHL. The Czechs had seen the Stastny brothers escape to the West in 1980 and in general seemed more open to dealing with NHL clubs, but they weren't letting young stars like Klima leave. In the 1984 draft, after another lamentable Detroit season, the Wings took Canadian prospects Shawn Burr and Doug Houda with their first two picks. In the third round, higher than most teams were willing to take Eastern bloc players who hadn't yet defected, Devellano picked defenseman Milan Chalupa, a 30-year-old defenseman from the Czechoslovakian national team. That summer, the Wings negotiated the release of Chalupa and his teammate, forward Frantisek Cernik, and both came to Detroit for the 1984–85 season. It was a disaster. Cernik played only 49 games, while Chalupa played just 14.

"One night we were playing Chicago and Behn Wilson, a pretty tough guy, yelled at Chalupa, 'You Communist prick, touch the puck again and I'll rip your fucking head off,'" Polano said. For the rest of the season, Chalupa hid away in the trainer's room with one mysterious injury after another. "Once in a while I'd see him and I'd say, 'Okay, ready to play tonight?'" said Polano. "And he'd smile and say, 'Not me, mister.' After that, we decided we better go after young guys."

That meant taking dead aim at Klima, who had seen his best friend, Petr Svoboda, bolt to the West and join the Montreal Canadiens. "Klima showed us the things we would have to do," said Devellano. In the summer of 1985, using $50,000 of Ilitch's pizza money, Polano and Wings executive Jim Lites spirited Klima away from the Czech national team while they were training in West Germany and later reunited him with his girlfriend after she was smuggled across the Austrian border in the trunk of a car. The Wings were officially in the business of smuggling talent from behind the Iron Curtain. "It prepared us really well for dealing with the Soviets," said Lites.

Soon, they'd be back for more.

• • •

While the Wings contemplated other ways to procure Eastern European talent, the rise of reform-minded Mikhail Gorbachev to the position of General Secretary of the Communist Party in the Soviet Union meant there were new stirrings within both the political establishment and hockey structure. Many Soviet stars, from Vladislav Tretiak to Igor Larionov, Sergei Makarov, and Viacheslav Fetisov, had already been drafted by NHL teams, but none had been allowed to leave. Gorbachev's rise to power and a cratering economy gave some hope that the Soviet sports authorities would be willing to start making older players available to the NHL in exchange for desperately needed hard currency.

In April 1987, Lou Lamoriello, the New Jersey Devils' general manager, was just about as desperate for talent for his team as Jimmy Devellano had been in Detroit. Fetisov, regarded as equal to any NHL blueliner, had been drafted by the Devils under Lamoriello's predecessor, Max McNab, in 1983. Lamoriello, American-born, didn't see the political differences between his country and the U.S.S.R. as a reason to write off Soviet players. "We weren't in a war," he said. "I never looked at it that way. My parents came from overseas [Italy]. That just wasn't the thought process in my mind."

Lamoriello went to Calgary for the 1988 Winter Olympics where the Soviets would capture the gold medal, and he was able to forge a contact with officials from Sovintersport, the government agency that had started to release national soccer team stars to teams in the European leagues.

"I made an appointment to go over to Russia. Fetisov was their captain, so if there was any player they were going to let go, it was going to be him. There was almost a tentative agreement that we were getting him. I went over alone, and they had an interpreter for me. We went to this building and into a room, and Fetisov came in. There were generals there, lots of smoke. I wasn't nervous then, but I am today looking back. Then they said he couldn't come. It was the first time [Fetisov] had heard that. He had just come back from the Black Sea and had just received the Lenin Award, the highest award. I was shocked. I went down the stairs, and Slava was there. I had never really met Slava. We made eye contact at the bottom of the stairs and I said to myself, 'I'm going to hear from him.' That night, at my hotel room, there was a knock on the door. He was there with an interpreter. And that started the relationship. He wanted to come. And he would do everything he could from the other side."

For two years, Lamoriello made it his mission to get Fetisov out. Fetisov, meanwhile, felt that he had been lied to and began to agitate for his release. "They began to follow me all the time, put pressure on my parents, my wife. It wasn't pleasant," said Fetisov. "I met the minister of defense, he was a powerful person, and he told me they could send me to Siberia, not put me in jail, but send me in my army uniform to Siberia. He said they could do the same thing to my wife and parents. I remember talking to my mother. She said, 'Son, maybe you can apologize.' I said, 'No, mum, I have to try to do what I'm supposed to do.'" Defection was, to Fetisov, out of the question. Instead, he resigned from the army in protest. "It was for principle. I had played 13 years for the national team. It was a fight for my life almost. I said, 'No, Lou, I cannot run from my country, from my family.' If I was to run, they would close the border for everyone else. I wanted it to be legal."

Unable to get Fetisov to toe the line, the Soviets decided to embarrass him by taking away the distinction of being the first Soviet national team player to be officially released to play in the

NHL. In March 1989, the Calgary Flames received the surprise release of winger Sergei Priakin. He was no star, but he was a bona fide national team member, having played for the Big Red Machine since the early 1980s and as recently as the 1988 Canada Cup. "They tried to show us that if we weren't going to work with system, they would let everybody go except us," said Fetisov.

Two months later, however, any pretence that the Soviets were going to be able to control the flow of players to the West was destroyed by 20-year-old Alexander Mogilny. Mogilny's impressive play in international tournaments prompted Buffalo Sabres GM Gerry Meehan to draft him in the fifth round of the 1988 draft, but everyone believed he'd be a fixture on Soviet teams for years. As it turned out, everyone had underestimated Mogilny's rebellious nature—that was a bigger factor than any yearning for a lucrative career in the West when he defected at a world championship tournament in Sweden and joined the Sabres. "I did it for freedom," said Mogilny in a 2009 interview with the International Ice Hockey Federation's (IIHF) magazine. "If the bird can fly and the fish can swim, you have to be able to move around the world and be free and not watched constantly. If a human being doesn't have freedom, that's not life."

Mogilny's defection, along with the political and cultural forces unleashed by Gorbachev's concepts of *glasnost* and *perestroika*, forced the Soviets to give releases to their older players, although they still tried to retain younger players. Within a few weeks it was announced that seven Soviet national team players would be allowed to leave, a list that included Helmut Balderis, goalie Sergei Mylnikov, defenseman Sergei Starikov, the entire KLM line of Vladimir Krutov, Larionov, and Makarov, and, finally, Fetisov.

When he arrived along with Starikov for the 1989–90 NHL season, the 31-year-old Fetisov found the atmosphere "miserable," anything but welcoming. "Everything was hard," he said. "I had tried to be democrat, to do something for people, and they called me a Commie. Even in dressing room, I couldn't speak English, people laughing at me. There was only me and my wife. I ask myself, 'Why fight against one system then get here for this?' I just sucked it up."

While the Soviets were reluctantly opening their doors, the intrigue wasn't over. The Red Wings, four years after the Klima escapade, still had their eyes on Russian talent and were spurred into action by Mogilny's defection. With the 74th pick of the 1989 draft, less than two months after Mogilny had left for the West, the Wings drafted Sergei Fedorov. Then, 147 picks later, they selected defenseman Vladimir Konstantinov. "Jimmy D. said, 'Now it's your responsibility to get these guys out,'" Polano said.

Fedorov was single with no children and a private in the Soviet military, but Konstantinov was married and a captain. Both players skated for Central Red Army, and deserting the army was not an option either man would embrace. Lites used Detroit sportswriter Keith Gave, who spoke Russian, as a go-between and sent bags of Red Wings goodies to both players. Through Gave, the Wings knew both Soviet stars were cautiously interested.

After waiting until his military service was completed, Fedorov walked away from the Soviet national team at the 1990 Goodwill Games in Seattle. "We had him in Detroit before they even knew he was missing," Polano said. Konstantinov, meanwhile, was a more difficult case because he had signed up for a 10-year hitch in the military. A plan was hatched. In exchange for $30,000 in bribe money and a late-model American station wagon, Konstantinov would be granted a medical discharge from the Soviet military. In the summer of 1991, the Wings officials received a call. "Konstantinov was in a military hospital getting his discharge," said Polano. "They had bribed six people on a medical tribunal with $5,000 each to say Konstantinov had inoperable cancer." A month later, he was in Detroit at training camp.

There was still one more name to come, the ultimate test of Polano's nerves. It was the assignment that took him into a Soviet military hospital, with machine guns on one side of him and KGB informants on the other.

In the third round of the '90 draft, the Wings drafted Viacheslav Kozlov, a small but skilled Red Army winger. The following winter, however, Kozlov was driving in Moscow when a bus struck his car, instantly killing his teammate, Kirile Tarasov, and leaving Kozlov badly injured. When Polano visited the 19-year-old Kozlov at that military hospital, he knew he had to get the young star to a U.S. hospital for treatment if the Wings were to ever realize their investment.

Through a series of bribes, the Wings managed to get a medical visa for Kozlov to go to the United States for treatment. They had no intention of ever letting him return to Russia. It would take months for his body and mind to heal. At his first training camp in Detroit, Kozlov was a shadow of the puck wizard he had been years before. "Shawn Burr said to me, 'I don't mind getting these Russians, but this one can't play,'" said Polano. "I said, 'He's been hurt, Shawn. Give him some time.'"

• • •

Though he was no student of history and didn't give a thought to politics, young Sasha Ovechkin knew things were changing. He was too young to remember the Hammer and Sickle being lowered with the collapse of the U.S.S.R. He did know something was going on the day in 1993 when Boris Yeltsin brought tanks into the street to shell the Russian Parliament Building. Usually he walked home from school and his mother watched him from the balcony. On that day, though, the Ovechkins picked up Misha and Sasha at school and drove straight home. They were scared for their lives.

Affairs of state were going to open doors for Ovechkin and other young players, doors that had been shut until the early '90s. As it turned out, Polano's most chilling assignment, spiriting Kozlov out of the hospital and through the Iron Curtain, was his last piece of hockey espionage. For hockey, at least, the Cold War thawed almost overnight.

Within three years of Kozlov's departure, Mogilny had scored 76 goals for the Sabres and Fedorov had won the Hart Trophy as the NHL's most valuable player. An era had ended. There was no longer any need for people like Lites and Polano to secretly get players out from behind the Iron Curtain. Lites left for the Dallas Stars in 1993, but when the Wings won the Stanley Cup in 1997 with Fetisov, Konstantinov, Fedorov, Larionov, and Kozlov playing as a five-man unit, Ilitch made sure Lites received a Stanley Cup ring.

• • •

While the supposed future stars of the motherland were fading around him, Sasha Ovechkin blossomed with Kirillov as his coach in the late '90s. He broke Pavel Bure's goal-scoring record for 12-year-olds. He had 53 coming into the last game of the season, against Vympel. Alex's father approached him and said that the record belonged to Bure who had 56 goals in a season. Vympel was a weak team and would often lose by double-digit scores, so Sasha saw his chance. He ended up scoring six times.

It's the way of the hockey world: wherever there's a young scoring sensation, parents of teammates are bound to be ticked off. Sasha Ovechkin's success predictably caused hard feelings. The parents of his teammates, those who imagined their sons were the next Bures and Fedorovs, complained loudly about what they thought was the special attention he received because of his mother's status in the Dynamo sports organization. While there were age-group coaches in Russian youth leagues who were prepared to be paid off, Kirillov had no interest in anything like that. Despite their parents' problems with Kirillov, the boys enjoyed playing for him. All that didn't matter—rival parents of young Dynamo players filed a letter of complaint, and management fired Kirillov.

When Kirillov said goodbye to the team, he told Sasha Ovechkin, "If you won't become a player, I don't know who will."

Kirillov recognized the boy's talent, but he'd never see his prediction come true. The coach died of a heart attack at age 29, about a year after he had been fired as a Dynamo youth coach and not long after he'd named a newborn son Alexander after his favorite pupil.

After Kirillov's firing, the Ovechkins placed Sasha in the hockey program of Dynamo's arch-rival, CSKA. He had been spotted by Viktor Tikhonov, the former coach of the Soviet Union's Big Red Machine, and he suggested that the boy join CSKA, the former Central Red Army program. He stayed only one practice with CSKA and then went back to Dynamo. Changing teams didn't feel right. It felt too much like surrender.

In his teens, Alexander Ovechkin came under the guidance of Ramis Valiulin, a 53-year-old coach who had played for Lokomotiv Moscow during the 1960s. Valiulin coached Ovechkin for the next three years until, at the age of only 16, he began playing for Dynamo against professionals in the Russian elite league. At that point his family's focus on his career became total, and his father quit his job as a taxi driver to dedicate himself to his son's preparation for hockey stardom.

Valiulin might have thought this was rash on the part of the father. "Sasha was much better than the rest of his class but I couldn't have predicted his immense success at that time," Valiulin said. "Actually, I remember now, most of the kids from that group weren't all that good. It was a weak year, in terms of their hockey skills." The only other player with a future in that group was Ivan Khomutov, who played junior hockey in Canada and minor pro in the United States before returning to play for the Kontinental Hockey League's (KHL) Automobilist Yekaterinburg. "The way Sasha approached the game of hockey, even in that age, his approach on the rink, it was something special," Valiulin said. The best of the teenage Dynamo players Valiulin had previously coached was Alexei Kovalev, one of the stars whose hockey cards Ovechkin had collected. Kovalev emerged as a star with the Stanley Cup champion New York Rangers in 1994, but Valiulin soon realized that Ovechkin was surpassing his former pupil. "Sasha was faster and more determined [than Kovalev] at that age," Valiulin said.

Alexander Ovechkin was about to join what seemed to be an emerging class of young Russian players. It seemed only a matter of time before they were going to make millions and get their names on the Stanley Cup, just like Kovalev. Ovechkin was 14 when the NHL's interest in Russian players spiked dramatically. At the 2000 NHL entry draft in Calgary, 44 Russian-born players were drafted, a 52 percent increase from the year before. Most were teenagers born from September 15, 1981, to September 14, 1982. The top Russian picked was Nikita Alexeev, a towering forward with the Erie Otters of the Ontario Junior League. Tampa Bay drafted Alexeev eighth overall. At Nos. 10 and 11, Chicago selected forwards Mikhail Yakubov and Pavel Vorobiev, and Anaheim followed up those picks with left-winger Alexei Smirnov. With the 15th pick, Buffalo selected center Artem Kryukov, and two picks later the Edmonton Oilers made it six Russians picked out of the top 17 selections by calling out the name of forward Alexei Mikhnov, Kryukov's teammate with Yaroslavl in the Russian elite league.

The 2000 entry draft seemed to mark the day when Russians were accepted into the mainstream of the NHL culture. It didn't work out that way.

chapter 3

Selkirk, Stonewall, Piestany, Halifax, Moscow

"Like a Wild Stallion"

ALEXANDER OVECHKIN'S conquest of North America began just after New Year's Day 2002 in the steel towns of Selkirk and Stonewall, Manitoba, both about a 40-minute drive northeast of Winnipeg. If it wasn't quite the middle of nowhere, it was a long way from the hockey mainstream—the nearest NHL team was almost 400 miles away in St. Paul, Minnesota, and even the nearest major junior team was over 100 miles away in Brandon. The international sports media didn't descend on the event—the under-17 World Cup isn't on their calendar. But that's not to say that Ovechkin escaped notice. Those who braved the frigid temperatures to get to the arenas left shaking their heads after games. That included scouts who filed breathless reports back to their NHL teams—the people who could first have any impact on his career went home thinking: *Who was that No. 8 on Russia, and how the hell do we get him?*

It wasn't Ovechkin's first trip outside of Russia—he had played age-group tournaments in Finland and Quebec the season before.

But the under-17 World Cup was a significant step up from those events. The tournament in Manitoba brought in all-star teams from regions across Canada as well as some international sides.

Fans filled the 3,000-seat Selkirk Arena for games played by the host Canada West team and the neighboring Canada Pacific and Ontario teams but only a couple of hundred made it out for Russia's first game of the tournament, a contest against the Finns. Thus, Ovechkin's international debut took place in virtual obscurity. No video, no photo, no program. His was just another name on the officials' game sheet. It was even misspelled: *Alexandre Overchrine.* Even if those in attendance didn't quite know his name, he gave them a clear idea of things to come.

Russia won 9–6, Ovechkin potted four goals and scouts went to their thesauruses for superlatives. One scout for a team in the NHL's Western Conference filed this scouting report: "Passionate . . . unbelievable speed and strength . . . could use his linemates . . . four goals and could have had more."

If few saw the game in Selkirk, even fewer made it out the following day to the game between Ontario and Russia in the 400-seat Stonewall Arena. The Ontario squad featured a bunch of future NHL stars, including Mike Richards and Jeff Carter of the Philadelphia Flyers, Nathan Horton of the Florida Panthers, and Corey Perry of the Anaheim Ducks.

The same scout who filed a report from the Finland game stood behind the glass at ice level at one end of the rink. The rhapsody continued though, as he admits now, he strained for words. "Like a wild stallion . . . just a great game . . . looks to score and shoots a ton . . . definitely passionate." In retrospect the scout thinks that his files from the tournament might have been taken with a grain of salt by the executives back at the office. "I wish I could have put it all in bold type or something, just to let them know that I hadn't gone soft and was exaggerating," he says.

Despite two more goals from Ovechkin, the Russian teenagers lost the game 6–3, and their chances of advancing to the medal round grew slim. They grew slimmer, even after a one-sided 11–2 victory over outmanned Team Atlantic.

Ovechkin scored five goals against the Maritime squad and they came in almost every fashion imaginable—power play, shorthanded, unassisted, breakaway. Scouts figured that he could have easily had a couple more. So did those on the other team. "We had heard about what he had done in the other game but we hadn't seen him," says Stephen Dixon, one of only four major junior players on the Atlantic roster. "He was just so much bigger and stronger and he had amazing skill. Our guys had never been in against a player like that. It was an eye-opener."

Ovechkin's game might have been aesthetically pleasing but it was marred by players on both sides acting out. Two hundred minutes in penalties were doled out, including majors for spearing and elbowing. Match penalties made a couple of players unavailable for Russia's final game in the opening round and others were banged up.

Predictably, Team Pacific, the strongest Canadian squad, shut out the weary Russians 5–0 and sent them home without a medal. Not that it mattered much to the scouts and agents in attendance. Ovechkin scored 11 goals in four games to lead the tournament—the second leading scorer, Nathan Horton, had five goals in six games.

Dallas Stars scout Jimmy Johnston called Ovechkin's performance "one of the two most dominating" he had seen in more than a dozen under-17 tournaments. He said the only player who could be mentioned in the same breath as Ovechkin was Ilya Kovalchuk, who led Russia to the gold medal at the under-17s in 2000.

"Kovalchuk had great skating ability, probably better than Ovechkin at that point," Johnston says. "Both had enough skill that pretty much at will they could take over a game. What separated Ovechkin, though, was the physical component. He beat up anyone who skated in his way. Kovalchuk was a 'cool' player, controlled, where Ovechkin had fire. He rolled over guys in a way that you just don't see European players do very often. In that way he was closer to the Canadian and American kids—he was a pure power forward. The other thing, though, is that he had a good sense of the game— not in a creative way, a play-making way. But it looked like he knew where to go and exactly when to get there. There was nothing over-anxious . . . nothing forced. He didn't pick his spots—he didn't have to—but still you could see that he had hockey sense."

NHL scouts are loath to make snap decisions or read too much into a couple of games or one tournament. They pride themselves on their skepticism. Johnston was comfortable making an exception after the under-17s. With a late September birthday, Ovechkin wasn't going to be eligible until the 2004 NHL entry draft. Johnston thought Ovechkin was the closest thing to a sure bet in scouting. "I'd have had him first pick in 2003 if he were eligible, maybe even No. 1 in 2002 as a 16-year-old," Johnston says. "It was just a week and the Russians only won two of their four games but Ovechkin made a pretty strong case that he was the best prospect not in the NHL."

That was the unanimous opinion among the NHL scouts who saw Ovechkin at the under-17s in January. It was going to become league-wide consensus by the spring. By then they would get his name right.

● ● ●

The world under-18 tournament, a spring fixture on the IIHF schedule, is always the most intensely scouted of tournaments because it serves as a showcase for elite prospects eligible for the NHL entry draft two months later. So it was in April 2002. Dozens of NHL scouts and several general managers booked tickets to Piestany, a spa town in Slovakia that was hosting the tournament. They wanted to get a last hard look at 1984 birthdays. They also wanted to get a glimpse of the Russian kid who wasn't going to be draft-eligible for another two years. Some of the scouts and a few executives who had been to Russia knew about him—they knew that this kid, just in his middle teens, was already dressing for Moscow Dynamo in the Russian elite league, but it mostly seemed like a novelty act. With Dynamo he only would get a few shifts in games against professionals, no opportunity and no fair measure of his talent.

Those who knew the teams best rated the Russians as the tournament's most talented outfit. That said, the insiders considered Ovechkin's team a co-favorite with the United States and the Czech Republic, because the Americans' and Czechs' team play was much better than that of the Russians. History had been turned inside out. The old Soviet teams were the Big Red Machine and its hallmark was unselfish play—if Soviet players had been criticized for anything, it was not for hogging the puck but rather for over-passing it. The Russian players at the 2002 under-18s, well aware of the NHL scouts in the stands, were nothing like those who had worn CCCP on their red and white sweaters. Their agents were in their ears, telling them how their performances at the under-18s would factor into their chances to make millions in the NHL. Many approached the tournament as individual showcases. As talented as Ovechkin and his teammates were, those following the tournament with a professional interest thought that selfishness would hurt the Russians' chances.

The Russians did live up to their billing in an 8–4 victory over Canada in the first game of the tournament. "They easily had the best talent there," a scouting director with a Canadian-based NHL team says. "Ovechkin was very good but the first player who got my attention was Nikolai Zherdev. It was just his skating. Ovechkin looked like a very good skater—it would be one of his strengths as an NHL player. Zherdev, though, could fly. His speed would put him in the top one or two percent of guys in the NHL. There wasn't anyone in the tournament that could stay with him. He would get the puck and pass everyone on the ice."

Many scouts had the same first impression, but, as Russia rolled through the tournament undefeated and only challenged a couple of times, they noticed that Zherdev carried the puck right by opponents and teammates without a glance. The criticism of Ovechkin at the under-17s was that he "could have used his linemates more," but Zherdev didn't even seem to notice them—neither team could get the puck off him. By the end of the tournament, Ovechkin's talent thoroughly overshadowed Zherdev's—scouts considered the Russians' youngest player to be the soundest, least-selfish prospect in their lineup. Ovechkin again led the tournament in scoring with 14 goals and four assists in eight games. His Russian teammate and future Washington Capitals sidekick, Alexander Semin, was second in tournament scoring with eight goals and seven assists.

It was a glorious stretch for Ovechkin. (On the IIHF score sheets, he was now *Alexandre Ovetchkine*.) It all came apart, however, in the final game of the tournament. Russia only needed a tie against the United States to come away with the championship. Though coming off a shutout loss to the Czechs, the Americans could win the gold if they managed to beat Russia—or if the Russians managed to beat themselves. That's what happened. The final score: United States 3 Russia 1. As time wound down in the game, Russian players seemed to take turns trying to win the game with coast-to-coast rushes, bypassing open teammates. Led by future U.S. Olympians Zach Parise and Ryan Suter, the Americans played a tight defensive game and looked to quickly counter Russian forwards who chased the puck too deep and to exploit Russian defensemen who pinched too often, seeking their own bit of glory.

Even with the silver medal, the Russian team underachieved, but those scouting for the NHL viewed Ovechkin as blameless in the loss. He was the player of the tournament. NHL teams had to wait; the agents couldn't. They had been in the crowds in Selkirk and Stonewall. They were in Piestany. Now, they were going to follow Ovechkin back to Moscow.

* * *

To understand the business vortex that was about to engulf Ovechkin leading up to his draft in June 2004, you had to go back to Fort Lauderdale, Florida, and the 2001 NHL entry draft.

Ilya Kovalchuk sat in a booth in a bistro at a five-star hotel and gazed out at reporters with notebooks or tape recorders in hand. The 2001 entry draft was just two days off, and the 18-year-old Kovalchuk was considered the best junior talent that the league had seen for several seasons, maybe since Mario Lemieux 17 years earlier. He was already a dominant player in the Russian elite league, scoring 35 goals in 47 games against veteran professionals, including some former NHLers. The Atlanta Thrashers, a team owned by media mogul Ted Turner, owned the first overall pick and were certain to select Kovalchuk, a native of Tver, Russia. The dark-haired prodigy wore a Moscow Spartak sweater and a look of bemusement about the sports-media circus that unfolded around him. He smiled when the reporters asked him questions and hung on his every word, no matter how fractured his English.

Yes, he wanted to come to North America. Yes, he thought he was ready to play in the NHL. No, he didn't know much about Atlanta. No, he wasn't going to showboat in the NHL the way he had in international junior tournaments.

Some questions were a little more challenging and made him pause.

Who's your agent? What about the Porsche he was driving around Moscow?

Alexander Mogilny had walked away from the Soviet team with just the clothes on his back. Kovalchuk was going out the front door already accustomed to the perks of professional life. So, too, were his countrymen, Alexander Svitov and Stanislav Chistov, who would be selected third and fifth overall by Tampa Bay and Anaheim respectively. These three were the first real products of the new Russian hockey establishment.

The top Russian prospects selected in NHL drafts in the mid-'90s had started out in the old Soviet system and attended state-sponsored sports schools. Even after they made NHL millions, those memories lingered and the players were a part of a transitional time. Alexei Yashin, the No. 2 overall pick in the 1992 NHL entry draft by the Ottawa Senators, was an instructive example. Yashin held his hands apart about a foot when he explained his situation in a 1998 interview. "If Russia is over here and Canada is here, I am in the middle of nowhere. When I come to my parents' home [in Ottawa], we speak Russian. But when I go to Russia each summer to visit, I feel like a tourist now [because] I have been gone for five years now and it's not the Russia that I remember." Yashin would go on to sign a $90-million contract with the New York Islanders, but he still kept his Soviet sports school ID card in his trophy case.

On the other hand, Kovalchuk had no real memories of the old Soviet sports schools. In his earliest memories the Soviet Union was already fracturing. Even as an adolescent, the NHL was his realistic goal. Kovalchuk was also in the middle of something, though. He wasn't in a no-man's-land between East and West. No, he was in the middle of a contest to represent him, a contest between agents who had their elbows up and paid little attention to the rule book—if they acknowledged that there was a rule book at all.

In Fort Lauderdale, Kovalchuk paused when a reporter asked about his agent. He was uncomfortable with the question because a few weeks before he had fired Scott Greenspun of Impact Sports Management, a tiny boutique sports agency based in New York City. Kovalchuk had dumped Greenspun for Jay Grossman, becoming another in a parade of top Russian teenage stars who had stiffed their agents to hook up with Grossman's SFX Hockey agency in New York. SFX described itself immodestly but not inaccurately as "the world's largest promoter, producer and presenter of live entertainment events." Millions of dollars had been at stake, but Greenspun tried to shrug off the loss with a world-weary fatalism. "We had an agreement with him going back a year before," Greenspun said.

"His leaving us was a disappointment but not a surprise. We saw it coming."

Greenspun had reason to see it coming because he saw it play out with the other two top Russian prospects, Svitov and Chistov. They had both signed with and then fired two agents before landing with Grossman. It didn't just bother Grossman's stiffed rivals, and it wasn't just these three who were jumping agents. Kovalchuk, Svitov, and Chistov were not the only Russians who moved from one agent to another before playing a game in the NHL, just the cases with the highest profile. It was a concern of NHL teams that would tie their fortunes to the young Russian players. They were worried that business off the ice, agents trying to woo them with cash-filled envelopes and luxury cars, would distract them from the game on the ice. They were worried about the commitment of young prospects who looked to renegotiate on a whim, who were easily influenced by the last voices in their ears. Inevitably, agents and NHL executives described the new Russia as "the Wild West."

● ● ●

All the major agencies representing NHL talent were in Piestany for the 2002 world under-18s. This was the norm. Agents have to make it out to major international age-group tournaments, the under-17s, under-18s, and under-20s. Attendance at these events is their research and development, finding as-yet-unrepresented talent. It's also a matter of security, heading off any rivals who might have designs on young clients. Virtually all of the Canadian players had signed representation contracts with agents, as was the case with the best of the Swedish and Finnish teenagers. Most of the American players had "family advisors," informal handshake deals with agents that allowed the teenagers to remain eligible for U.S. college hockey. The best uncommitted talents were to be found in Eastern Europe—and even those who had committed to agents could be considered in play. The consensus among agents with an

East European player, was that you never "owned" him as a client
. . . you just had the lead on him and protecting that lead was a
challenging task.

After hearing about Ovechkin's performances in Selkirk and
Stonewall all the big agencies put the teenager on their lists, his
name underlined and exclamation-marked. Still, three months later
in Piestany, no one owned Ovechkin. No one had a lead on him.
The chase was on.

Grossman was in Piestany along with an associate, Vadim
Azrilyant. Grossman could trade on his successes with Kovalchuk.
Another selling point for Grossman was his success in securing
Svitov's and Chistov's releases from the Russian elite league's team
in Omsk and from military commitments that threatened to keep
them off the ice for a year or more.

No one was conceding Ovechkin to Grossman, however. The
smaller fish in the business were scared off by Greenspun's tale
of woe. Such is the lot of the minnows in hockey representation;
inevitably they are either swallowed by the sharks or their clients
are. The major players on hand in Piestany were led by the
International Management Group (IMG) and Newport Sports.
IMG's hockey division had represented Wayne Gretzky and other
elite players, keeping its client list relatively short but star-studded.
By contrast, Newport's approach was to capture as many NHL
players as possible, and in 2002 the Mississauga-based agency
represented fully one-sixth of all NHLers.

The agents in Piestany didn't have much luck getting beyond
handshakes and maybe the passing of a business card. The security
detail with the Russian team was tight, though extra time with a
prospect was available for a negotiable price. Still, no deal was
going to be sealed without the approval of the teenager's parents.
No one was going to take a lead with Ovechkin until he got back
to Moscow.

•   •   •

After the under-18s the Ovechkin family met with an agent with deep connections in Russia. The agent has requested anonymity but believes that his experiences were similar to others who were courting the prospect.

"We went out to dinner, sushi," the agent said. "It was clear from the start that the mother was in charge. She chain-smoked through the meeting and asked all the questions. The kid sat and smiled and just had a good time. Very easy going. Very polite. You could see a lot of him in his father, who was relaxed, too. Just happy to get out for a dinner, have a couple of drinks, meet someone new. He wasn't about dollars and cents and neither was the son. Alex's brother just sat there, mute, didn't say a word. The mother, though, that was another story. [Agents] spend most of their time explaining the business to families when they meet but in this case it was [Ovechkin's mother] explaining to us exactly what she expected and what she demanded. She let me know that they were talking to other agents. I left the meeting with a good feeling about Alex. He's hard not to like. But I didn't have a good feeling that we would end up representing him."

The agent who picked up the check that night had only this one brush with Tatiana Ovechkina. She didn't tell him he had dropped from contention. She just didn't return his calls. His lesson would be one learned by agents around the league and by anyone who was going to have dealings with Alexander Ovechkin. If you had business to do with No. 8, you had business to do with the woman who had the number first.

When Alexander Ovechkin arrived in North America, the newspaper stories and television features about him would inevitably mention that his mother was a prominent player on Soviet basketball teams that won Olympic gold in 1976 and 1980. Less frequently cited in these stories would be Tatiana Ovechkina's roles as the coach of the Moscow Dynamo women's basketball team and an executive in the sports organization. Ovechkina wasn't just an ex-athlete living vicariously through her players and her son. She was deeply involved in the day-to-day business of the Moscow branch of Dynamo, a former Soviet sports organization that dates back to 1923 and reached across the U.S.S.R. CSKA (known as Red Army) was historically tied to the military, and Dynamo's strongest associations were with the state's political police, including the KGB. Tatiana Ovechkina couldn't have won influence in Dynamo's administration on the basis of former glories on the basketball court. Plenty of famous sports heroes had passed through Dynamo's doors, many far better known that she was, yet she had risen through the ranks above almost all of them. Although Ovechkina's basketball teams had won national titles and sent players to Russia's Olympic squads, they were eclipsed in profile by the men's soccer and hockey teams. Ovechkina's clout in the Dynamo organization was a testament to her ambition and political skill. She had game on the court and off.

• • •

In late 2002, Don Meehan and Newport took the lead in the chase for Alexander Ovechkin. Meehan believed he had a not-quite-secret weapon in these negotiations: Anna Goruven, a Ukrainian émigré who was the only woman certified as an agent by the National Hockey League Players' Association.

Newport's partners and associates each staked out specific territories. Meehan looked after the all-stars, the biggest contracts. Others tracked the Canadian junior leagues, NCAA, or European regions. Goruven's turf was Russia.

Goruven's ability to speak directly to the Ovechkins in Russian seemed to put her in a good position as a point person on the negotiations. The Newport group also had to believe that having a woman at the table in these talks with Meehan and his associates would have some appeal to Tatiana Ovechkina. And Goruven's connections in the Russian hockey community were strong—she had met Vladislav Tretiak when she was serving as a translator at the 1988 Olympics and thereafter looked after the North American business interests of the legendary goaltender. Being able to invoke

Tretiak's name had given Goruven the inside track on recruiting Russian players to the Newport stable, including San Jose goaltender Evgeni Nabokov, Toronto forward Nikolai Antropov, and Anaheim defenseman Oleg Tverdovsky. No agent was ever more fierce in defending clients' needs than Goruven—for the young Russian players she was like a den mother, not just negotiating contracts but helping them make the transition from East to West, translating leases and other paperwork, doing everything short of bringing over hot meals. Agents will sometimes talk about "babysitting" their clients, but it was almost the literal truth with Goruven. For instance, Goruven was in the room for the birth of Antropov's daughter. For this type of attention many of her clients weren't simply loyal to her—"devoted" would be a better description.

Meehan, Goruven, and Newport associate Craig Oster made several trips to Moscow starting in the fall of 2002. The agency's finder in Moscow, Sergei Isakov, had set up a series of meetings with potential clients. Ovechkin wasn't their only target. They had appointments with Red Army's Nikolai Zherdev and others. Still, they considered Ovechkin the prize. For Goruven the stakes were even higher than the commission on a single contract. A few of her clients had struggled in recent years. Neither Antropov nor Tverdovsky had set the NHL on fire—though they had been high draft picks, they hadn't come close to all-star status. Another client, Alexander Volchkov, was an even greater disappointment. An electrifying junior with the Barrie Colts of the Ontario league, Volchkov was drafted fourth overall by the Washington Capitals but completely washed out as a pro. Volchkov was out of hockey (i.e., not bringing any money into the agency's coffers) by the time the Newport team went to Moscow in pursuit of Ovechkin. Meehan, Goruven, and the rest believed that Ovechkin was going to be among the NHL's highest-paid players in the near future. They also believed they could bask and profit in Ovechkin's glow; his successes and association with Newport could help make the agency the first choice of the next generation of Russian teenage stars.

Isakov had told the Newport contingent that the competition for Zherdev was intense and that he was likely a long shot to sign on with the agency. The meeting lived down to Isakov's expectations. The meeting with Zherdev and his advisors from Red Army lived down to Isakov's expectations. It was like a stare-down with a Moscow airport customs officer. Those on the other side of the table seemed to be awaiting an envelope stuffed with cash, the offer of a car, or any other enticements that had been floated by other agents vying for his services. The Newport team soon realized that they were wasting time with Zherdev.

Isakov was more optimistic about Ovechkin. Others in the hunt for the prospect believed that Newport had the inside track. "Isakov was Bilyaletdinov's guy and they had a pretty good working relationship," a rival agent said. Zinetula Bilyaletdinov had been a defenseman for Dynamo in the Soviet league back in the late '70s and '80s. In 1993, he had been brought in by the Winnipeg Jets' general manager Mike Smith to serve as an assistant coach with the NHL club and lasted four seasons in the organization. Dynamo with the 17-year-old Ovechkin in the lineup hired Bilyaletdinov as coach for the 2002–03 season. Isakov was going to be able to work the coach and Goruven the mother. At least that's what the Newport team thought.

The Newport team's experience at the meeting with the Ovechkins played out like the scene the rival agent described. Meehan and his team met the Ovechkins at an exclusive sushi restaurant in Moscow. The Ovechkin men enjoyed their meal while Tatiana picked at her food disapprovingly and chain-smoked. Goruven tried to break the ice by offering Ovechkina a gift: a vase from a high-end Toronto interiors store. Ovechkina responded with an unimpressed shrug and a sneer, like Goruven hadn't peeled off a dollar-store price tag.

Meehan's genial manner seemed to be appreciated by the Ovechkin men but ignored by the matriarch. The agent showered praise on the teenager's talents but warned that there were dangers out there for young prospects—one bad contract, one misstep in money management, one "i" not dotted or "t" not crossed and the young prospect would lose money that he might never have another chance to earn. It was boilerplate stuff for an agent, establishing the need for representation.

Tatiana Ovechkina was impatient. She wanted to cut to the chase and did. She aired her grievances with the Dynamo team, with the Russian national program. She complained that Dynamo hadn't treated a leg injury Alexander had suffered. She wasn't happy with the dental treatment that the team had lined up after her son took a puck in the mouth—that injury even made chewing sushi painful.

Meehan issued one assurance after another. "We'll fly him to Toronto for an MRI and any work he needs with his injury . . . We'll get him in to see a dentist or a dental surgeon . . . We've had lots of experience with Russian clients . . ." It was a constant, almost furious stroking, like a canoeist paddling up the white water with Niagara Falls at his back. Meehan expressed a concern about the well-being of the phenom as if he were the agent's own son, as if he were Goruven's own son.

By the end of the evening it wasn't quite signed, sealed, and delivered. But Newport had the lead.

• • •

Less than a year after he had played in front of a couple of hundred fans and scouts in tiny Stonewall Arena, Alexander Ovechkin stood in front of dozens of reporters under the stands of the Metro Atlantic Centre in Halifax, Nova Scotia. Less than a year after the official scorer printed *Alexandre Overchrine* on the game sheet, the reporters went to lengths to get the spelling and pronunciation right. The media and fans of hockey across Canada didn't know Ovechkin but they knew of him. He was the talk of the 2003 world junior tournament before it had started, although on the eve of the semifinal game against the Finns, most fans hadn't yet seen him play. Russia had played its opening-round games in Sydney, Nova Scotia, a four-hour drive away, and the games hadn't been televised. The Russian juniors, the defending champions, had run through the opening round undefeated and mostly unchallenged, and the 17-year-old Ovechkin was leading the tournament in scoring despite most players being more than two years older than him. This wasn't a shock to the scouts—they knew that Ovechkin had been moved onto a top line under Bilyaletdinov with Dynamo, that he was performing in the Russian elite league at a higher level than even Kovalchuk had. All the NHL scouts had made the trip to Sydney to see the United States take a run at the Russians, but Ovechkin led his team to an easy 4–1 win with a hat trick that was even more spectacular than anything he had done at the under-17s and under-18s.

Ovechkin's Russian teammates stayed away from the Canadian media—or, at least, team officials kept them away. But having signed Ovechkin to a representation agreement with Newport, Meehan and Goruven set up an impromptu press conference; the media wanted to find out the phenom's story. It didn't start out promisingly. He brushed off a question about his team's game. "Everybody comes here to win," he said, with Goruven translating for him. "The rest is a mystery."

He was just slightly more expansive when asked about his personal goals and his prospects for the 2004 draft. "This tournament is taking place in a very special country which is the birthplace of the game of hockey so it's very important for me," he said. "My personal goal is not so much to show what I'm capable of doing, but to win the gold medal. I don't care if it's No. 1, No. 2, or No. 10 in the draft."

Had he seen Canada play? "We watched Canada's games on TV when we were in Sydney," he said. "They are a very good team with a lot of enthusiasm when they go on the ice. But I think if we make the final, we can handle them, too. We'll see who's the better team."

It seemed like nothing more than a photo op with rote answers. But then Ovechkin opened up. Many young Russian players were wary of the North American press but Ovechkin seemed to engage it. He talked about his mother's basketball career, about playing with Dynamo, about the San Jose Sharks being his favorite NHL team because of the logo, about Mario Lemieux being his favorite NHL player, about Alexander Maltsev being his favorite Russian player (though he played well before Ovechkin was born, Maltsev had taken an interest in him during his days in the Dynamo youth program). Throughout, he smiled a gap-toothed smile.

Then a reporter asked if he had any siblings. Goruven stepped in immediately. She told reporters that his older brother Sergei had died in a car accident. She didn't elaborate, didn't say when or where. She preempted any follow-up, saying the family wouldn't talk about the circumstances of Sergei's death. Goruven never asked Ovechkin or his parents about their willingness to discuss Sergei's death—it was a point that they had already made clear. That didn't stop Ovechkin from talking about the influence Sergei had on him. He told the reporters about how he had picked up a basketball for the first time at age three and how his mother wanted him to play the same game that she had. He told them that Sergei had stepped in and against their mother's wishes enrolled him in a hockey program. "Every game I play I think of him," Ovechkin said. "He put me back on the ice."

Asked if he knew any other English, he looked across the room. "Don Meehan," he said.

It produced a big laugh from the reporters, the agent, and the client. It seemed that, in Meehan, he had a protector, a surrogate for Sergei.

• • •

The Finns hadn't been able to slow Ovechkin and the Russians in the semifinals, setting up a gold medal confrontation with the host nation, a country hungry for its first world junior title in six years. Ten thousand ticketholders were wedged into the arena in

Halifax and three million hockey fans across Canada were tuned into the world junior final. The Canadian roster featured 20 players who would go on to play in the NHL and the best among them was Marc-Andre Fleury, a spidery goaltender who played for Cape Breton in the Quebec league. Off his showing in the world junior tournament, Fleury would end up as the first overall pick in the 2003 NHL entry draft. There wasn't a real star among the Canadian skaters, no one who emerged later as a franchise player as a pro. They were earnest, workman-like, and diligent—any other polite adjective to flatter character and overlook skills could apply.

The Canadian juniors carried a 2–1 lead into the third period on the strength of Fleury's goaltending, home-ice advantage, and, seemingly, the power of prayer. Men vs boys, but the boys' most inspired effort was good enough for 40 minutes. As their teams had in so many international tournaments, the Russians played only well enough to beat average teams in the early stages and held some of their game back in reserve for the time of greatest need, catching opponents by surprise. So it was this night. The third period of the game looked nothing like the first two periods, and though the final score ended up Russia 3 Canada 2, it was one of the most one-sided one-goal games that you might ever see. Ovechkin didn't figure in the scoring. In fact he skated mostly on the third line, which was a telling bit of evidence about the strength of the Russian team. Zherdev didn't even get off the bench during the game. He was a passenger as the 13th forward. "It seemed like a dozen of their guys could step right into the NHL," Canadian defenseman Brendan Bell said. "They were just so strong and skated so well. We were looking for Ovechkin and you could see he had a lot of talent, especially for a 17-year-old. But it was the other guys who killed us."

The best was Igor Grigorenko, a second-round draft choice of the Detroit Red Wings. Grigorenko did the most damage, scoring the tying goal five minutes into the third period and setting up linemate Yuri Trubachev for the winning goal a few shifts later. The game was effectively over. In the third period Canada didn't create a scoring chance. The Canadians only briefly had possession of the puck inside the Russian blue line. So one-sided was the play in the period that the Russians started trash-talking, mocking the Canadians. The Russians didn't even bother to wait until stoppages in play—they dropped f-bombs and laughed while they had the puck on their sticks.

On the television screen it might have looked like any other victory celebration and medal presentation, but down at ice level it was something else entirely. When the teams lined up on their blue lines, the Russians kept up with the trash talk. Some of it was directed at fans in the front rows, the rest at their opponents, whose heads were hung and eyes were red. It kept up while they set up for their team photo at center ice.

"We didn't like [the taunting] and the crowd didn't like it," Canadian forward Joffrey Lupul said. "It was kind of unnecessary. During a game, maybe there's some taunting that goes on, but after the tournament's over I think you should just stand there, be quiet and show some class."

It looked too familiar to another forward, Scottie Upshall, who had played on the Canadian team that lost to Russia at the world juniors the previous winter. "I guess that's the way they're brought up," Upshall said. "I actually thought they handled themselves as a team better this year than at the last [world juniors]."

A couple of hours after the game the disappointed Canadian fans left the nearby bars, their sorrow half-drowned, and started to make their way home. On the street they came across a small mob in the middle of George Street, next to the arena. The fans might have mistaken them for sailors on leave. It was the Russians, draining 40-ouncers of vodka, smoking unfiltered cigarettes, stripped down to the skin though it was well below freezing, falling over one another in complete stupors. Ovechkin was in the center of the mob. Most thought, like Brendan Bell did, that the bulk of celebrating Russian teenagers would be back in North America to pursue NHL careers, some as early as the following fall. Only five of them would sign NHL contracts. Five months later, the player of the game in the final, Grigorenko, broke his leg in a car accident, developed a life-threatening embolism in his lung, and never again looked like the same player. Remarkably, only Ovechkin was going to stick in the NHL.

• • •

The gold medal from the junior tournament seemed to boost Ovechkin's confidence when he went back to Moscow Dynamo. Coach Bilyaletdinov gave him more ice time and he scored six goals in 17 games to end the season—not awe-inspiring numbers compared to goal totals in the NHL, but the Russian elite hockey league featured scoring just about as low as the national soccer league. Sergei Isakov checked in with the Ovechkins daily, didn't miss a game. Meehan made a return visit to Moscow in the early spring. Others from Newport made it to the 2003 world under-18s in Russia in April where Ovechkin, still eligible, was again the leading goal scorer (nine in six games) and was named top forward. Anna Goruven, however, had to stay home.

A few weeks after the world juniors, in Halifax, Goruven was diagnosed with stomach cancer. Doctors told her that they thought they had caught it in time. She was to undergo aggressive treatment, radiation and chemotherapy. This time her clients were calling to see what they could do for her. Nikolai Antropov offered to drive over and help her around the house. Evgeni Nabokov paid her way to a Caribbean resort after her final round of chemo. She did her best to keep in touch with Ovechkin by phone. Though they had only met in Moscow a few months before and spent some time together in Halifax, he seemed shaken by the news.

Newport offered Goruven indefinite leave. She missed only a few days. She was as tough as Tatiana Ovechkina. Goruven made it her goal to attend the 2003 NHL draft at the Gaylord Center in Nashville. She sat with Meehan and the Newport team in the stands and they watched Zherdev, the prospect that had eluded them, walk up on the stage, selected fourth overall by the Columbus Blue Jackets. With the rest of the Newport team she stood up and applauded and hugged their teenage clients when they were drafted and the television cameras focused in on them. It was Goruven's will to keep working. It was also business as usual, just a message to send to any vultures who might be circling her clients with news of her illness. She didn't want to let them get the idea that Ovechkin might be in play. She wanted to remind them that Newport had the lead.

The Newport team and the cameras were long gone from the Gaylord Center when the Florida Panthers announced the 265th pick of the draft. If Ovechkin had been in attendance, he would have had a chance to walk out of the stands and onto the floor of the arena, because the Panthers, in a surprise move, used their pick in the ninth and final round of the draft to select him. Executives and scouts at the tables of other teams stirred and for one awful moment wondered if the Panthers had information that they didn't. It turned out that the Panthers didn't. Prospects eligible for the draft must be 18 years old as of September 15 of the draft year. Ovechkin was not going to turn 18 until September 17, those two days making him and the NHL wait a full year. Panthers general manager Rick Dudley made the case that Ovechkin would be 5,972 days old—18 years old—on September 15, 2003, if you took into account leap years. Word of Dudley's premise for the challenge made the rounds of the arena floor and it produced laughs, not worry. NHL officials told Dudley that the player wasn't eligible and to make another pick. Dudley later characterized it as a "no-risk, high-reward" move, but it turned out to be a bizarre footnote to the draft. It also captured the injustice of Ovechkin's situation.

September 15 and September 17. A matter of just two days. Ovechkin was certain to be selected with the first pick of the 2004 NHL entry draft. Still, those two days delayed the start of his NHL career by two years.

chapter 4

Washington

"How Could Something Which on Paper Looked So Right Be So Wrong?"

THOUGH DUDLEY'S PLAY for Ovechkin at the 2003 draft seemed far-fetched, it was positively commonsensical next to the original idea of establishing an NHL franchise in Washington. The capital had sports traditions, but none whatsoever for hockey. It was a football town first. The Redskins had dominated the market for decades. It was a basketball town second. Abe Pollin moved his Baltimore Bullets to the Capital Center, the arena he built in Land-over, Maryland, in the '70s. And it was a baseball town third. The few fans who used to come out to see the Senators remained loyal even though the team bolted the capital for Texas in 1972. Hockey, however, just didn't register.

Still, the NHL was in an expansion mode in the early '70s. Washington wasn't anyone's idea of a model hockey market, but it had to look good next to the other cities that were finalists for a new team: Baltimore, Cleveland, Phoenix, San Juan, and Mexico City.

Pollin, who made his money in the construction business, paid a $6-million expansion fee to join the NHL. He had no idea what he was getting into. At that point he had never seen a hockey game in his life. His push for an NHL team had nothing to do with love of the game—it was strictly business; he needed another tenant for the Landover arena.

It appeared that the NHL was rolling out the welcome mat for the Capitals when they awarded the team the first pick in the 1974 draft. The hockey man trusted with that pick was Capitals GM Milt Schmidt. Pollin had hired Schmidt on the recommendation of Boston Celtics general manager Red Auerbach. The basketball legend knew him from their days together at Boston Garden where Schmidt had been a high-scoring center with the Bruins and later the franchise's genial ambassador. Schmidt used the first pick in the 1974 draft to select Greg Joly, a rangy Regina Pats defenseman who had been named the most valuable player in the Memorial Cup, the Canadian national junior championships, that spring. As it turned out, the Caps didn't select the best player in the draft. They didn't even select the best player on Joly's junior team.

For the new Washington franchise, draft day was a disaster—few teams had ever made so little of a great opportunity to build a team. The Capitals selected 25 players in their first draft, and they played a total of 884 games. Ten players selected by other teams in that draft each played more games than all of the Caps' selections put together. It wasn't the best draft pool of all time, but it wasn't the worst. Twenty-one players from the 1974 draft went on to be all-stars, 15 would win the Stanley Cup. The Kansas City Scouts, an expansion team alongside the Caps, had the second pick in the draft and landed Wilf Paiement, a winger who went on to score 40 goals in a season and earn a reputation as one of the league's toughest players. The New York Islanders landed two Hall of Famers: at No. 4 in the first round, Clark Gillies, Joly's teammate on the Regina Pats, and in the second round, Bryan Trottier.

The NHL hasn't lacked lousy teams over the years, but the Capitals are widely regarded as the worst ever. They finished their first season 8–67–5, far and away the worst record in the league.

Their eight wins are the fewest ever for an NHL team playing at least 70 games, and their .131 winning percentage is still the worst in NHL history. The Capitals set records for most road losses (39 out of 40), most consecutive road losses (37), and most consecutive losses (17). They allowed a record 446 goals that season and scored just 181. At their team banquet, the Capitals presented their overworked goaltender, Ron Low, with a bulletproof vest.

The coach, Jim Anderson, best summed up the frustration and humiliation of the Capitals' first season. "I'd rather find out my wife was cheating on me than keep losing like this," Anderson said. "At least I could tell my wife to cut it out."

"We're a good team," the Capitals' leading scorer Tommy Williams said. "We're just in the wrong league."

Schmidt decided to put Joly in the lineup even though none of his teammates thought that he was ready for the NHL. They were right. Joly played in 44 games that year and was a horrific minus 68. His teammate Bill Mikkelson outdid him, registering a record minus-82 rating, a mark that still stands. Joly is philosophical about his experiences with the first Washington team. "There was no parity in the NHL at that time, and we didn't have a lot of quality players," Joly said. "[Hall of Fame coach] Toe Blake couldn't have won with our team. There was a lot of pressure on me being the first pick in the draft and I got hurt [he missed 35 games with a knee injury], but in all fairness I didn't play as well as I could, either. But I did learn a heck of a lot, and we did have some fun."

Though they were able to laugh at themselves, they were the laughingstock of sports for a winter. The humiliation began with their first game when the team debuted with a fashion statement: white hockey pants. Unfortunately the seats of those pants grew dirty every time players sat on the bench or brushed up against the boards, thus giving them the appearance of oversized soiled diapers. Worse, when players began to sweat, the hockey pants became see-through.

The most-often-retold tale was the team's celebration of its first—and, that season, only—road victory, a 5–3 win over the almost as hapless Seals in Oakland near the end of the season. After that win, the Capitals took turns hoisting a garbage can in the dressing room like it was the Stanley Cup.

Teammates thought any fun came at the expense of Joly's development. "I felt sorry for Greg," said Bob Gryp, a forward in the original Capitals lineup. "If he had played on a good team and been allowed to break in slowly, he probably would have become a very good player, maybe even an all-star."

Less than three years after he was the first overall pick of the 1974 draft, the Capitals traded Joly to the Detroit Red Wings. Across a professional career that lasted into the late '80s, he played more games in the minors than he did in the NHL.

● ● ●

Bobby Carpenter's name became known outside of hockey circles when *Sports Illustrated*'s February 23 issue hit newsstands back in 1981. The NHL rarely made the cover of *Sports Illustrated* and, with the exception of the Miracle on Ice team at the 1980 Olympics, hockey outside the NHL didn't make the cut at all. That made the cover of the *SI* issue memorable: a 17-year-old Carpenter, curly hair flopping, pulling to a sharp stop and sending snow spraying at an ice-level camera. The display copy told his story: "The Can't Miss Kid: He's 17 and hails from Peabody, Mass. NHL scouts say that he's the best U.S. prospect they've seen. Ever." U.S. high school athletes occasionally made the cover of the magazine, but they had always been basketball, football, or baseball phenoms, not hockey ones.

Carpenter had no idea how that photograph and the *Sports Illustrated* story that accompanied it would follow him the rest of his life. "In December I didn't even know if I was going to be drafted," Carpenter said. "I was just a high-school kid who liked to play hockey. Then I had a real good world junior tournament and it got momentum from there."

As high school underclassman, Carpenter had torn up state tournaments. By his senior year, dozens of NHL scouts were showing up at his games. And in the *Sports Illustrated* story, Carpenter came off as the All-American boy, a likeable, self-effacing kid, a dutiful son of a police lieutenant, a good student who loved the game and wasn't caught up in stardom at all.

Abe Pollin had never seen a hockey game before buying an NHL franchise, and in the same way he anointed Carpenter as his franchise savior without ever having seen him play. From his years with the Bullets, Pollin understood the power of the cover of *SI*, effectively the sports establishment's seal of approval. "We're not drafting a kid from some small town in Canada ahead of an American kid who's on the cover of *SI*," Pollin told Caps' GM Max McNab. McNab's task was to figure out a way to land the object of Pollin's desire, not easy given that the Capitals owned the No. 5 pick overall in the 1981 draft.

McNab had it gamed out. No. 1: Winnipeg was going to pick Canadian junior star Dale Hawerchuk first overall. Nos. 2 and 3: Carpenter's father had told the Los Angeles Kings and Colorado Rockies that his son would be going to college if either drafted him, and it seemed likely that the Kings would draft Doug Smith. No. 4: The Hartford Whalers seemed like the best fit for Carpenter. "We wanted to go somewhere that was going to allow me to stay close to my family," Carpenter said.

The Carpenters let McNab know their thinking months before the draft, and the general manager let the matter drop, careful not to tip off his interest in the Can't Miss Kid before the draft at the Forum in Montreal. McNab made it seem like he was conceding the pick to Hartford. It caught everyone by surprise when McNab managed to flip his No. 5 pick for Colorado's No. 3 by throwing in later draft choices. It certainly caught Bob Carpenter Sr. by surprise—he was sitting at Hartford's table on the Forum floor when he heard that the Capitals had used the third pick to select his son.

"Everything I was thinking was turned upside down," Carpenter said. "I knew then this was a business I was getting into. Things change in a hurry."

Hartford, caught unawares, scrambled and ended up taking a player Pollin had disparaged to McNab, an 18-year-old from northern Ontario who'd go on to become the franchise's greatest player and a Hockey Hall of Famer, Ron Francis.

At first the Carpenters balked at sending their son to Washington. Carpenter had signed a letter of intent to go to Providence College and already had been in touch with the roommate he'd be moving in with in the school's residence. That summer he played in pick-up games with college players and he thought that college would better suit him than a jump to the pros. "Some days I'd get six or seven points in the game and I'd think, okay, I'm ready to go pro," Carpenter said. "Then the next day I'd get no points and I was getting physically beaten up by these guys who are four or five years older than me and I'd say uh-oh, what am I getting myself into?"

The contract talks lasted all summer, and Carpenter had gone as far as enrolling at the school. But as the start of school drew near, the Capitals signed Carpenter to a four-year $500,000 contract. The Capitals sold the Carpenters on the idea of avoiding putting too much pressure on the teenager. That idea lasted until the ink on the contract dried.

"The day after I signed they said that they wanted me to come down to Washington for a promotional campaign, a Save the Caps rally," Carpenter said. "I had been a 17-year-old kid playing high school hockey and nine months later I was supposed to save the franchise."

The Capitals, who had failed to post a winning record since entering the NHL, looked like they couldn't be saved. They lost 13 of their first 14 games in Carpenter's rookie season, and coach Gary Green was fired. But even though Pollin thought Carpenter was going to be a savior, McNab and the Capitals' management understood that there was going to be a learning curve, that the *SI* article was reaching when it compared Carpenter's hands to Wayne Gretzky's. His teammates didn't resent the contract he signed and the attention he commanded. "Veterans on the Capitals treated me like gold," Carpenter said. "They looked out for me."

Carpenter's rookie year was remarkable for a player with no minor-pro, major junior, or college experience: he finished fourth on the team in scoring and racked up 32 goals in 80 regular-season games. That set a standard that he would match through his first three NHL seasons, even though he clashed with Bryan Murray, the coach the Capitals brought in to replace Gary Green. Carpenter had been a streaky player—for 20 games he looked like an all-star but for the next 20 he'd be a liability. Murray had no patience during the bad stretches and regularly benched Carpenter.

Carpenter's fourth season was a magical one. He scored 53 goals that year, becoming the first U.S.-born player to pass the 50-goal mark. The SI cover had gone from millstone to prophecy. He timed his breakthrough perfectly to cash in. His contract was up. He was a free agent—the prospect of an American-born star had made him attractive to Pollin, the reality of it was going to create a market for him outside of Washington. Neither Carpenter nor the Capitals knew his days as the franchise player were over.

When training camps started that fall, Carpenter was still unsigned, and the New York Rangers and Boston Bruins were rumored to be in the running to sign him. The Capitals did end up re-signing Carpenter, and his four-year $1.2-million contract almost tripled his salary. When he signed, Carpenter said that Washington had been his first choice all along and offered up platitudes about loyalty. The Capitals' brass forced smiles.

The Capitals' management thought Carpenter arrived at camp out of shape—he hadn't skated in the summer like he had in previous years. He had married, started taking college courses, and, to their mind, lost his competitive fire with his new contract. He went from being the young player that the veterans had protected to a star who was temperamental and abrasive. The idea of Carpenter as a franchise savior was losing traction. And, in fairness, in hockey terms Carpenter was an old 22-year-old—he had never missed a game in his first four seasons and had played through injuries that would have sidelined most players. He had started wearing a knee brace. The grind caught up to him in his fifth year with the Caps: he had his lowest-scoring season to that point, just 27 goals. He would never score that many goals in a season again.

Twenty-two games into his sixth year with the Capitals, David Poile, successor to Max McNab as the general manager, ran out of patience. He sent Carpenter home after an incident at a practice—an assistant coach overheard Carpenter say to a teammate that he had "to get out of this organization." The Capitals had hired Bob Carpenter Sr. as a scout but Poile pulled him off the road—there were no more special favors for the soon-to-be-former Capitals star. Murray went public with his gripes with Carpenter. He said that there had been "two sets of rules" for too long. "I had 56 meetings with him last year and 15 more this season," Murray said. "We did for him things we didn't do for others. That disturbed some players."

Carpenter sat out a month of games before Poile traded him to New York. Carpenter had gone from the Can't Miss Kid to the Kid the Capitals Wouldn't Miss.

● ● ●

Ted Leonsis had one up on Abe Pollin: when Leonsis decided he wanted Jaromir Jagr as the Capitals' franchise player he had seen him on the ice and not just on a magazine cover. Jagr had one up on Bobby Carpenter: when he first donned a Capitals sweater he was arguably the best hockey player in the world, not just the best player in the Massachusetts high school leagues.

When Leonsis purchased control of the Capitals from their founder in 1997, Jagr already owned two Stanley Cup rings and scoring titles with the Pittsburgh Penguins. He had proven star quality: an ability to make breathtaking plays rivaled by only Wayne Gretzky and Jagr's Pittsburgh teammate Mario Lemieux. He was well-liked among contemporaries, a charming man-child with a Brillo pad mullet who made everyone smile when he walked into a room. He didn't have a star attitude—he was more mischievous than egocentric, he liked a good joke rather than an ego stroke.

The way Leonsis tells it now it sounds like love at first sight. "After watching Jaromir Jagr practice in 2000 I said, 'I want one of those,'" Leonsis said. That's a rewriting of history. Jagr would have been hard for Leonsis to miss: Pittsburgh had twice won playoff series against Washington on Jagr goals, and he had five winning goals in 42 playoff games against the Capitals.

In a *Washington Times* interview in 1999, Jagr's was the only name Leonsis came up with when asked about the ideal free agent that the Capitals should sign—even though Jagr wasn't a free agent at the time. "Jaromir Jagr . . . young, fills the seats, makes people around him better," Leonsis said. "If league rules would have allowed it, he would have been a guy to build around. And if he's there, then other people want to play. But there are a lot of free agents that aren't worth their salt, and many times it's not their fault. But I think a lot of free agents aren't worth the money they're paid. They're only worth the money if they get you home."

In another interview, Leonsis again flirted with tampering when *Times* reporter Dave Fay dropped Jagr's name. "I'm sure there is going to come a day when so-and-so is available," Leonsis said. "And one of the great things is these are private companies; it's not like we have to go to the stockholders and ask for permission."

After the 2001, season Leonsis pushed his management team to acquire Jagr from Pittsburgh. Team president Dick Patrick and general manager George McPhee tried to convince Leonsis that this wasn't the way to go. McPhee, while with Vancouver, had seen the Canucks give up a package to land Alexander Mogilny, who played well but didn't make the team much better. For his part, Patrick was a little suspicious that his cousin, Pittsburgh GM Craig Patrick, was looking to dump the Czech superstar. Leonsis, however, was not to be swayed. He believed Jagr would attract fans and make his hockey business profitable.

Usually, teams don't have players in Jagr's class on the block—then 29, he had led the league in scoring with 52 goals and 69 assists in the previous season. Pittsburgh, however, was a motivated trader. By the summer of 2001 the Penguins were in desperate financial straits, and Jagr's contract called for him to be paid $9.9-million and $10.8-million for the seasons left on his contract. Lemieux, the team's owner, had come out of retirement, and Jagr wearing the captain's "C" made for an awkward situation in the dressing room.

The Penguins didn't have any leverage in the talks with the Capitals—few teams were prepared to pick up Jagr's contract. The New York Rangers were the obvious candidates and Los Angeles and St. Louis were less likely ones. McPhee was able to get Jagr for three forgettable prospects, Kris Beech, Michal Sivak, and Ross Lupaschuk, and $4.9 million in cash.

"This puts us on the national scene, because we now have a really, really great hockey team," Leonsis said. "I hope this knocks the chip off people's shoulders in Washington and they come out and buy tickets. Now's the time to prove this is a hockey town, that it loves sports, and we're as good a team as any others."

Leonsis's enthusiasm came at the time when he claimed a loss of $20-million for the 2000–01 season despite a seven percent increase in attendance, an average of more than 15,000 fans per game. It was hard to fathom how the addition of a $10-million salary to a money-losing proposition improved the franchise's outlook, but Leonsis defended the business sense of the trade.

"I do think these things are smart business moves," Leonsis said. "We'll sell more tickets and we'll sell more [corporate] sponsorships. But we did this primarily because we want to win. This is a great player and they don't come around that often."

In fact, a lot of what Leonsis said sounded like his later enthusiasm for Ovechkin.

"I would expect that if we do a good job, Jaromir can pay for himself," Leonsis said. "This was a good business move. This guy is a brand. Brands win. Jagr is a global brand."

The acquisition got the Capitals and Leonsis great press. Jagr seemed to be the draw the team was looking for: 300 season tickets sold in three hours after the announcement of the trade. Leonsis announced that he'd be raising ticket prices at least 10 percent, more than covering Jagr's salary by his math.

Leonsis believed in the Jagr effect so much that he doubled down before Jagr had even played a game, starting negotiations on a new contract although his existing deal still had two seasons to run. To Leonsis, the acquisition of Jagr was the starting point, but the team needed to sell fans on the idea that he'd be a Washington Capital for life. When the Capitals announced the signing of Jagr to a $77-million seven-year contract with a team option for an eighth year, the largest contract in league history, McPhee's peers knew it wasn't his deal but Leonsis's.

After he locked up with Washington, Jagr was asked about his role in the Capitals' five-year plan to win a Cup. "Maybe three now," he said.

It turned out to be a disastrous trade and an even more disastrous contract. In less than three years he'd be gone from Washington, but Leonsis was going to keep on paying.

●   ●   ●

Even in the first twenty games of the 2001–02 season, something had clearly gone wrong. It's hard to imagine how, but the Capitals, who lost no significant players from the previous season, were worse with the addition of Jagr. But then again, he wasn't the Jagr that fans and teams had grown used to seeing. He fell from 52 to 31 goals. He was dropped from the first unit power play. He missed a dozen games with injuries to a wrist and a knee—previously it seemed he'd been indestructible. His physical woes, though, were less troubling than his body language in games. He seemed moody and disinterested. Off the ice, those around the Capitals organization worried about his emotional well-being. Behind the scenes he seemed distracted and detached. He needed teammates to drive him to the rink every day. His mother was living with him in Washington and trying to take care of him. Soon it became clear that his life outside the arena was in turmoil.

By the time Jagr arrived in Washington, he brought with him almost a half-million dollars in online gambling debts—*Sports Illustrated* reported that the owner of a gambling website confirmed these debts after Jagr defaulted on a payment schedule. "It was stupid," Jagr told *SI*. When the first reports appeared, others came forward with accounts of Jagr gambling six- and seven-figures in casinos. Even a million-dollar debt wouldn't have been so difficult for the player to dig his way out of, if not for another money woe, this one much larger: an IRS tax lien against him for $3.27 million. Jagr filed a lawsuit against his accountant claiming that he'd lost $6-million by late filings.

None of it could be resolved fast enough for the Capitals. The team missed the playoffs in Jagr's first year despite having the league's sixth biggest payroll at $56 million. According to *Forbes* magazine, no North American professional sports franchise lost as much that season as the Capitals did: $25 million.

The franchise was in unmitigated dysfunction. Leonsis gave his coach, Ron Wilson, a vote of confidence, declaring that "there won't be any changes," but a month later McPhee fired Wilson and brought in Bruce Cassidy, a coach without NHL experience, to handle a room with not a few potential coach-killers.

In most circumstances, an owner once burned by Jagr would be twice shy, but it was at Jagr's insistence that the team signed the most expensive free agent in team history, his former Pittsburgh teammate Robert Lang. The deal was scheduled to pay Lang $25 million over five years—just two seasons before, he had been playing for $1 million for the Penguins. Though Leonsis had ordered

McPhee to trim $8 million from the payroll, the owner signed off on the Lang contract because he thought it would help protect his $77-million investment in Jagr.

With Lang, Jagr's second season with the Capitals was marginally better than the first. They finished 10 games over .500, but Jagr's scoring slump continued, with just a small bump up to 36 goals. When the playoffs rolled around, Jagr wasn't the difference-maker that Leonsis had described as his ideal free agent. Tampa Bay eliminated Washington in the first round of the playoffs, and Jagr failed to score in the last four games of the series.

Jaromir Jagr, it turned out, was not a global brand. Beset by office problems, he was a once great player who was aging, still very good but not as good as he used to be. He had no illusions about his game. Asked if he was measuring up to the standards he set in Pittsburgh, Jagr was embarrassed. "It's not even close," he said.

Leonsis's enthusiasms aren't easily extinguished but they were by December of Jagr's third season in Washington. The Capitals stood 29th out of 30 NHL teams. McPhee was able to trade Jagr to the New York Rangers for journeyman Anson Carter, but there was a significant string attached: the Capitals were stuck paying $20 million of the $44 million left on Jagr's deal.

"I couldn't understand it," Leonsis said. "How could something which on paper looked so right be so wrong? Most of everything I thought coming in proved to not be right. There's so much counter-intuitive in this business."

But just a few months after Jagr's last game—and while Leonsis was still writing checks for Jagr—McPhee and his staff were telling the owner that they had designs on another franchise player. And they sold him on the idea.

chapter 5

Helsinki, Moscow, Pittsburgh, Washington, Toronto

"Is Pittsburgh Beside the Ocean?"

THE SCOUTING OF OVECHKIN over the 2003 season was almost, but not quite, perfunctory. Ovechkin had separated himself from all other eligible players but one, another Russian teenager, Evgeni Malkin of Metallurg Magnitogorsk. Ovechkin was almost, but not quite, the unanimous first choice among scouts. For the dissenters, it was a matter of position. Though all would concede Ovechkin was the most dynamic player who had come along in more than a decade, he was a natural left-winger. Play was supposed to end on his stick. He was a finisher. As a center, Malkin would be more involved in the play. Play was supposed to go through him and on to others. He was both a finisher and a creator.

"It came down to your priorities," Calgary Flames scout Tod Button said. "If you wanted to sell tickets there wasn't much question that you wanted Ovechkin. But some people thought that going with Malkin would give a team a chance to win sooner. With either one it wasn't a question of upside. The feeling was that Ovechkin was more ready to step into the NHL than Malkin, who was long and lanky and needed to fill out, but they had all kinds of game. You had to like both of them for different things. Sorting it out was a question that most teams didn't have to consider, though. You were going to have to finish way out of the playoffs to worry about it."

Button's characterization of the two prospects' games was borne out by their play at the 2004 world juniors in Helsinki. Ovechkin scored the goals: five in six games to lead the Russians. Malkin created the chances: four assists in six games with less ice time than Ovechkin. Ovechkin was pounding the net with eight or even 10 shots a game, while Malkin's best showing came in a 5–3 win over Sweden, picking up three assists. However, the Russian roster was much thinner than that of the squad that rolled over Canada in Halifax the previous winter. The defending champions also hit hot goaltenders in Helsinki—Jaroslav Halak made 31 saves to key Slovakia to a 2–2 tie with Russia, and Al Montoya stoned them in America's 4–1 win in the final opening-round game. The United States wound up winning the tournament with a one-goal victory over Canada in the final. The Russians' desultory tournament came to an end with a 3–2 win in a rematch with Slovakia in the fifth-place game.

The forgettable tournament did nothing to damage Ovechkin's status among NHL scouts. It would have been just a footnote but for tragedy off the ice. Anna Goruven wasn't feeling well on New Year's Eve, the day of the Russia–United States game. She decided to stay in her room rather than go to the arena, thinking she had just come down with a virus. She was rushed to a Helsinki hospital overnight and died there hours later. An autopsy was inconclusive about the cause of death. "You had to believe that she pushed herself so hard and had been through so much that her body just gave out," Meehan said.

Meehan told Mikhail and Tatiana Ovechkin the news, and they decided that they would wait until after Russia's final game on January 4 to tell their son. Each day they found a way to explain her absence after practices and games to Alex—she had to go back to her room to call her daughter, she had the flu and didn't want to give it to anyone. When Ovechkin emerged from the dressing room after the fifth-place game, his parents were waiting for him and told him the news. Meehan was standing behind them. "I don't know what was said but Alexander broke down," Meehan says. "He was inconsolable."

First it had been his brother Sergei, then his coach Vyacheslav Kirillov, and now Anna Goruven.

* * *

Though Newport had a written commitment from the Ovechkins, other agents still had designs on the prodigy. By mid-winter, NHL teams were starting to have designs on him, too. When Ovechkin went back to Moscow, he didn't know that he was going to be the prize in a comical competition, the turtle race, the "chase" to the back of the pack.

Every spring the pursuit of the Stanley Cup produces images that are burned in the memories of hockey fans: Bobby Orr airborne with Noel Picard's stick in his skates, Ray Bourque raising the Cup over his head. Those most lasting images evoke the idea of excellence and just reward. NHL turtle races turn that notion inside out. The very worst teams have the best opportunity to receive the ultimate prize, a first-overall draft pick, a player who offers hope. Despite occasional busts like Greg Joly, bad teams are more likely to land franchise players with the first picks in a draft than anywhere else, and so a dead-last finish has become the non-contenders' unholy grail.

The original draft turtle race was the best: "Operation Sealslump." Months in advance of the 1971 NHL draft, the Montreal Canadiens' canny general manger, Sam Pollock, had targeted Guy Lafleur, a forward with the Quebec Remparts juniors. Pollock believed, rightly as it turned out, that Lafleur was the player to build a Stanley Cup championship team around. The Canadiens, though, were among the league's elite and had no shot of landing him in the draft with their own picks, so Pollock set about acquiring other teams' selections to give him a fighting chance. It was a series of hustles that would have given a convicted con man bragging rights on the cell block. Pollock dealt journeymen Ernie Hicke and Chris Oddleifson to the awful Oakland Seals for another journeyman, cash, and their first-round pick in 1971. Pollock hedged his bets by engineering similar deal with Minnesota to secure the North Stars' first pick. The plot thickened when it seemed that the Seals might "lose" their turtle race to Los Angeles and finish ahead of the Kings (who had been suckered by the Boston Bruins into trading away their own first-rounder). So Pollock did the Kings a favor by sending them a useful veteran, Ralph Backstrom, for pennies on the dollar, and Backstrom's help kept the Seals in the league basement. "Operation Sealslump" was a resounding success and had only a few less moving parts than a multi-billion-dollar merger.

Pollock's theft of Lafleur was a cautionary tale for NHL general managers who, for more than three decades after, have mostly avoided cashing out future first overall picks for immediate help. More often, the turtle races involve bad teams who own their own picks and sandbag their season to acquire a player in the mould of Lafleur.

For instance, the Pittsburgh Penguins rolled out a patchwork lineup and played over-matched minor-league goaltender Vincent Tremblay in a successful effort to get the first pick of the 1984 draft and, with it, Mario Lemieux. A decade later the Ottawa Senators were convincingly accused of releasing established NHLers and tanking games in their inaugural season to get the first overall pick—their owner, Bruce Firestone, was fined $100,000 by the league after media reports circulated that he had basically owned up to the deception. The Senators succeeded in getting the No. 1 pick at the cost of their dignity and $100K, but ultimately failed by using the selection to acquire Alexandre Daigle, an under-achieving enigma who sucked $15 million out of the organization.

Because of these infamous turtle races, the NHL instituted a lottery that gave the worst team in the league something less than a guarantee of No. 1 at the draft. The NHL lottery is set up so that only the five worst teams in the league have a shot at drawing the first overall pick, and the lottery is weighted so the last-place team has almost an even-money chance of landing that first selection.

By January 2004, the field in the turtle race had sorted itself out. Once again the Penguins were in the race, a legitimately bad outfit from the top down. The coach, Ed Olcyzk, had no experience behind the bench and was working as the broadcast color analyst for the Pens when he was hired. The lineup was a mix of journeymen at the end of the line and several previous draft misfires (Milan Kraft, Rico Fata, and Richard Jackman). Lemieux played 10 games at the start of the season and then didn't dress the rest of the way due to back problems. The Penguins dealt their leading scorer, Martin Straka, to Los Angeles and filled the roster with minor-leaguers.

Lemieux, who both played for and owned the Penguins, and his general manager Craig Patrick fully appreciated the value of a franchise player. They had concerns, however. It was the Russian thing. Lemieux and Patrick knew all about the Senators' travails with Alexei Yashin, who was seemingly never happy with Ottawa's management and did everything short of trying to renegotiate his contract between periods. The Senators foisted Yashin on the New York Islanders who, despite questions about his commitment, signed him to a ludicrous 10-year $90-million deal. Lemieux and Patrick knew all about the crash and burn of the Russians in the first round of the 2000 draft—six first-rounders who played little over 300 career NHL games combined. They also knew about Alexander Svitov and Stanislav Chistov, who were held back in Russia for a season when their NHL clubs' negotiations with their Russian teams broke down. When the two arrived and signed contracts, their games hardly resembled what they had showed as 18-year-olds.

Lemieux and Patrick didn't want Yashin Redux. They didn't want history repeating itself with Russian teenagers who took something like early retirement after they signed their first contracts. Lemieux and Patrick wanted to know all about Ovechkin. They needed the intel. So they sent Mark Kelley to have sushi with the Ovechkins.

• • •

Kelley had been the Penguins' Boston-based scout for a few seasons, but he knew the ins and outs of Russian hockey from first-hand experience. He didn't have to crawl under the barbed wire like Nick Polano. He went in the front door when then-Pittsburgh owner Howard Baldwin bought an interest in the CSKA franchise in the Russian elite league a few years earlier. Kelley served as Baldwin's point man in Moscow. Baldwin's plan to run a North-American-style team in the Russian capital was a misbegotten idea, and he bailed out when military holdovers from Red Army days staged an executive putsch. Still, Kelley learned enough from his stay in Russia to work Pittsburgh's Ovechkin file as a scout-slash-gumshoe.

Pittsburgh was in last place in the standings in February 2004 when Craig Patrick asked Kelley to go back to Moscow for several weeks. Patrick wanted a thorough work up on Ovechkin. Kelley had to file game reports, but there wasn't much work to do on Ovechkin at the arena. For two years he had performed at a level unmatched by a generation's worth of prospects. Patrick wanted Kelley to focus on Ovechkin away from the arena. The general manager wanted a sense of the character of the player who could be Pittsburgh's next Lemieux.

Kelley went to the games but, as he expected, he saw nothing that could dissuade him from his opinion that Ovechkin was the clear No. 1 in the draft. Kelley pumped a few hockey people in Moscow for anything that might present a problem for the NHL team that drafted the teenager. Nothing. He met up with Tatiana and Mikhail. Through a translator he explained his position with the team most likely to draft their son. He offered to take them out to dinner. They seemed to hit it off. What Patrick intended as a fact-finding mission for the Penguins was just as much a fact-finding exercise for the Ovechkins.

"We met three times . . . went out for sushi with a translator each time," Kelley says. "I thought I came away with a pretty good read of the kid. He seemed really genuine when I asked him about playing in the NHL. Right up front he said he wanted to and was ready to play right away. He seemed curious about the league. He asked about Mario. He asked about other players . . . about what teams did in practice. He wanted to know what he could do to make himself a better player—another good sign, that he was looking at what he could do and not what the team could do for him."

Kelley came away with the same impression of Mikhail Ovechkin as Meehan and his associates had: an easy-going, soft-spoken guy. No red flag there. The scout's experience with Tatiana was unlike the Newport team's. She didn't voice any complaints about her son's situation with Dynamo. Like her son, Ovechkina asked questions.

"She wanted to know if Pittsburgh was beside the ocean because she always had wanted to live by the sea," Kelley says. "She asked if Pittsburgh had a NBA team because basketball was her favorite sport and she wanted to be able to go to games. There really wasn't a lot of hockey stuff that she asked about—at least nothing that looked like a red flag. They were hockey parents like you see anywhere else—they had some concerns about their son's future but it wasn't like they were dictating terms."

Kelley's report from Moscow to Pittsburgh: all good on the Eastern front.

● ● ●

Like Meehan and Newport, the Penguins had the lead on Ovechkin, but their lead was precarious. Others were "competing" for the last-pick overall. The Penguins had set a very low bar, and the

Washington Capitals did their very best (or worst) to skate under it.

On paper, the Capitals looked like a playoff contender. Their first two lines looked as good as any NHL team's. Jaromir Jagr had Stanley Cup rings, league scoring titles, and a place reserved for him in the Hockey Hall of Fame. Peter Bondra was the franchise's all-time leading goal scorer and was a bona fide, if under-rated, sniper. Center Robert Lang and defenseman Sergei Gonchar were talents who could win places on any Stanley Cup contender. Goaltender Oleg Kolzig was a former all-star and had carried the team to a place in the Stanley Cup final in 1998.

But the Capitals had an awful start to the season, winning just eight of their first 25 games. That cost Bruce Cassidy his job as head coach. General manager George McPhee replaced him with Glen Hanlon, but the Capitals made no significant improvement into January.

Everyone in the dressing room and the front office realized that the season was a waste. McPhee had to convince Leonsis that tearing the team down was the right course of action. In fact, it had been an idea that Patrick had floated a year before, but the owner and the general manager didn't bite. A couple of months into the 2003–04 season, McPhee saw the light. He made the calculations grounded in reality. A: The team was heading in the wrong direction. B: The Capitals' best assets were aging players. C: Rebuilding the roster could start with one of the two top picks in the draft, Ovechkin or Malkin, preferably Ovechkin. The drop-off in draft-eligible talent thereafter was steep. D: Memories in sports are short. If the Capitals were bad for a season it would be forgiven and forgotten. This would be even more likely if, as many expected, the NHL and the NHL Players' Association couldn't come to a collective agreement over the summer and the league locked out the players. The prospect of an NHL lockout the next season liberated McPhee to enter into the turtle race.

Leonsis is the ultimate glass-half-full executive, a perpetual optimist. In any other circumstance he wouldn't have been open to throwing in the towel and looking to the far-off future. But Leonsis's optimism had been tested that season. The Capitals owned the league's second-worst record and their season-ticket base was down to 4,500. Leonsis was losing millions. There were media rumbles about contraction forcing the NHL to drop at least two teams, Washington being a leading candidate. The low point, though, was reached on the concourse of the Verizon Center. During a game, a fan taunted him, waving a sign that read "Caps Hockey, AOL Stock—See A Pattern?" Leonsis had steered America Online to billion-dollar revenues and bought the team and a 44 percent share in the NBA's Washington Wizards in 1999 with a slice of his proceeds. AOL investors had, however, seen a deterioration in their investment since Leonsis had jumped into the business of professional sports. After the game, Leonsis confronted the sign-waving fan, Jason Hammer, out on the concourse, and a scuffle ensued. Hammer said he was grabbed by the neck and thrown to the ground. Leonsis denied that, but later apologized and was suspended for one week by the NHL, paying a $100,000 fine levied by the league. "It defines a little bit of me," he said. "It's a stain."

Leonsis accepted McPhee and Patrick's strategy. There was no fixing the team this season. It had to be torn down and it wasn't going to be pretty.

Some teams in the Capital position brazenly dumped games in pursuit of the first-overall draft pick. The Capitals didn't, per se. There's a difference between throwing games and throwing in the towel on a season, and the Capitals did the latter. It's just a matter of transparency.

McPhee shipping Jagr to the Rangers was only the biggest move of the teardown, which included sending Lang to Detroit, Bondra to Ottawa, and Gonchar to Boston. If physical misery could be considered a good break, then the Caps caught one with injuries to Kolzig and forward Dainius Zubrus. The Capitals' most talented rookie, Alexander Semin, bolted the team late in the season and went back to Russia. The Capitals barely pursued Semin, Ovechkin's former teammate on the Russian junior squad. Management let him go, avoiding the risk that the Capitals' lose-at-all-costs gambit might wreck his relationship with the team and sour him forever on playing in North America.

The Capitals went from a playoff contender to the premise for a TV sitcom. The Bad News Caps. Over the course of that season, the Tampa Bay Lightning used 27 players in their lineup en route to the Stanley Cup. By contrast, 52 players, most of them unrecognizable names, worked at least one game for the Capitals. It seemed like every marginal minor-leaguer from A (Mel Angelstad) to Z (Dwayne Zinger) found their way into the Washington lineup that year. McPhee made the team the station at the end of the line for players not likely to return to the NHL after an extended lockout—Jason Doig, Jean-Luc Grand-Pierre, John Gruden, and Andrej Podkonicky were players whose less than distinguished NHL careers wound down with the Capitals that season. McPhee called up minor-leaguers whose entire NHL careers would consist of their tenures with the Caps in this absurd season—Garret Stroshein, Owen Fussey, Darcy Verot, Roman Tvrdon, and Matthew Yeats played a few weeks with Washington but never again in the league. But the best representative of the awful Capitals in the spring of '04 was Mel "The Mangler" Angelstad, a 32-year-old who had sometimes played and mostly fought for 20 minor-league teams over his 12-year career.

A sequel to *Slap Shot* could do worse than appropriating the story of Angelstad's hockey life. Angelstad was a 20-year-old defenseman with the Flin Flon Bombers of the Manitoba Junior Hockey League, a full step below major junior, when he was invited to the Ottawa Senators' training camp in 1992. Even before he was through the first practice Angelstad realized he was overmatched—if he had a future in the game, he was going to have to fight. He dropped the gloves 12 times with teammates over the course of 10 days before being sent down to the minors. Over the years he went to nine more NHL training camps and was cut nine more times. By the spring of 2004, Angelstad had played hundreds of minor-league games and fought hundreds of times. His face had been reconstructed and he was suffering daily headaches. His fingers had been bent out of shape by fractures and dislocations.

Angelstad was playing for the Capitals' American Hockey League affiliate in Portland, Maine, when he heard about the plans George McPhee had for getting the first overall pick. "I didn't know anything about him [Ovechkin], just that he was a Russian kid," Angelstad says. His Portland teammates were being called up to Washington, one or two a week, and he had heard that he had a shot too. But the Pirates' coach told McPhee that Angelstad had a shoulder injury and that he would put in an injury claim if he was going to be called up, leaving the Capitals on the hook for an NHL salary during the lockout. Knowing that hundreds of thousands of dollars could be at stake, McPhee instead called up the young tough guy who had been Angelstad's protégé in Portland, Garret Stroshein, all 6-foot-7 and 250 pounds of him

McPhee went up to Portland looking for more call-ups late in the season and caught a game between the Pirates and Providence. One of the Providence players took a run at one of the Capitals' prospects and Angelstad stepped in to defend him. After watching Angelstad leave the Providence player in a heap on the ice, McPhee said to an associate: "His shoulder looks fine to me."

McPhee sought out Angelstad after the game and told him the situation—he needed a body in the Capitals' lineup but he couldn't afford an injury claim.

"I promise I won't file an injury claim . . . even if I break my femur in three places," Angelstad said.

"We'll call you up but you're not going to fight," McPhee said. "That's not what you're there for."

A couple of nights later Mel Angelstad became the first, and so far only, player to wear No. 69 in an NHL game.

"Funny thing is, I was playing three or four minutes a night with Portland but with the Caps they had me on the third line," Angelstad says. "I was playing 14 or 15 minutes a night with Washington. I was with the Caps for two games. First one was at home against the Rangers and I was interviewed on air for the ESPN broadcast of the game. Then we went to Pittsburgh for the last game of the season. We lost but I stayed in the best hotel I had ever been in."

But Washington's worst, however, wasn't bad enough.

Before their victory over the Capitals in Game No. 82, the Penguins had clinched last place in the NHL standings. Pittsburgh's record was 23 wins, 47 losses, and 8 ties for 58 points in 82 games. Chicago and Washington ended up with 59 points but, by virtue of tie-break rules, the Blackhawks edged out the Caps for second-last place.

In a two-deep draft, the Caps were in the worst place possible, sitting third from the bottom. The lottery was the wild card.

• • •

The way the ping-pong balls are loaded into the bingo tumbler, the lottery made the Penguins the big favorite in the field of five also-rans. Pittsburgh's chances of having the No. 1 pick were 48.1 percent, just about even-money. The chances of the four other teams dropped rapidly after that. Chicago had an 18.8 percent chance, going off at about five-to-one. Washington had a 14.2 percent chance, a seven-to-one proposition. Carolina and Phoenix were even longer shots to land first prize. Other teams that didn't make the playoffs had balls in the tumbler and chances to win the lottery, but could only move up five slots—in a case like that, Pittsburgh would still hold on to the top pick.

The NHL lottery doesn't chill tanking as effectively as the NBA's lottery, which gives any non-playoff team a chance to have the first overall pick. That was most dramatically demonstrated when the Orlando Magic barely missed the playoffs, had only one ball in the tumbler, and, with a 1.5 percent chance, landed the top pick in the 1993 NBA draft. Still, going into the 2004 NHL entry-draft lottery, history had been cruel to the last-overall clubs. The Boston Bruins finished at the bottom of the league standings for the 1996–97 season and won the lottery, using the No. 1 pick to select Joe Thornton, but long shots won the lottery the next six years. Going into the 2004 lottery, teams in the third slot—the seven-to-one bets—had come away with two of the previous three No. 1 draft picks.

It happened again. A Washington ping-pong ball came out of the tumbler.

The Capitals couldn't believe their luck. For the members of Washington's scouting staff it was one of those moments when they remembered where they were when they got the news. McPhee was in his office when the call came from league officials in New York. Capitals scouting director Ross Mahoney was at home in Regina when McPhee called him. Scout Dale Derkatch was in his car driving to the supermarket when Mahoney called him. Within a few minutes, e-mails and texts were sent and calls were made to everyone in the organization. Those who listened to voice-mail messages thought that they were being set up for pranks.

Everyone in the organization smiled when they picked up newspapers the next day and read what McPhee had told reporters on a conference call. "Maybe we're getting rewarded for the task we did, restructuring and building for the future," McPhee said.

The news stories reported that McPhee hadn't ruled out trading the top pick, but the No. 1 pick wasn't going to be in play. The Caps' scouts had filed dozens of game reports on Ovechkin. They had done some background checks on him—stuff gleaned from those who knew of him, stuff overheard in the arena. Still, no one from the Capitals' staff had met up with Ovechkin prior to the lottery. That would have to wait until the NHL combine in June, where the NHL Central Scouting Service oversees medical examinations and physical testing on the top 100 draft-eligible prospects and the teams bring in the teenagers for interviews.

• • •

Chris Edwards, a scout with Central, was waiting to pick up Ovechkin at Toronto's Pearson International Airport and drive him to a hotel a few days before the combine. "He didn't really speak any English but still he seemed like a pretty positive, upbeat kid," Edwards said. "Polite. 'Please and thank you.' Smiling non-stop. I've had other kids come from Europe and ask for spending money right off the top. Their meals and their rooms and everything at the hotel are already paid for but they still ask for it and a lot of the time we end up giving it to them. Ovechkin didn't though. He just seemed happy to be there and happy to get a ride to the hotel."

Those who've worked the combine have watched business being conducted around the hotel. It was another place where agents staked out their turf and protected their property. Those who didn't make it out risked letting their clients forget about their commitments and meet up with other agents who would try to win them over. Sometimes those teenagers who were hitting up Edwards and his Central Scouting colleagues for fifty bucks would later that week be rooting through envelopes that contained $5,000 in cash. Because of scenes like that, all the agents on Newport's staff, including Don Meehan, were in the lobby doing surveillance and making small talk with their clients and NHL executives.

A hotel out by the airport was taken over by the combine. Every room in the place was taken up by prospects or agents or teams that were setting up for their prospect interviews. An upstairs conference room was converted to a makeshift medical lab where doctors examined the players. The full basement was converted into a gym where the players were put through a battery of physical tests—everything from the basics (bench press, standing vertical and long jumps) to aerobic and anaerobic tests to see how many liters of oxygen players could take in and how long they could sustain lactic-acid buildup. Organizations differ on the value of the testing. Some put value into the results as a measure of the players' physical readiness and conditioning, but others say it doesn't make much of a difference one way or another. Bottom line either way: no one moves up in the draft on the basis of combine testing performance. A poor performance might raise a red flag, but still, it's what's on the ice that counts.

Many teenagers who arrive at the combine are bundles of nerves, worried that making bad first impressions might hurt their draft standing, costing them hundreds of thousands of dollars or maybe even their careers. Those who coolly finish chances with one-timers from the slot with the season on the line will have white knuckles and damp palms when they open doors and meet the general managers who might draft them.

Ovechkin wasn't nervous in the least. He knew exactly what his status was and that nothing he did or said here was going to hurt it. Others wore business suits when not in their workout gear for testing. Ovechkin wore fire-engine-red jeans, matching wrestling shoes, a stretchy T-shirt that looked like it had been painted on, and suspenders that he didn't pull over his shoulders. If there was a dress code at the combine, he figured the prospective No. 1 was either exempt from it or got to write his own.

Before the testing began, scouts did double-takes when he walked by. Even in his street clothes he looked bigger than when he was measured and weighed by Central in mid-season. "He looked like a man next to a bunch of boys when he came out for testing," Edwards said. "He was a powerhouse, thick through the chest and shoulders. If you didn't know who the first pick was, you'd pick him out of a lineup. Physically and just the way he handled himself."

Physically, Ovechkin lapped the field. He was well above average in every component of testing but nowhere did he stand out so much as in the VO2 Max—the endurance test. Slogging away on a stationary bicycle, breathing into a plastic tube, he lasted longer (almost 15 minutes, set at the highest resistance level, while most struggled to last 10), generated more output (680 watts compared to an average of 552) and recovered more quickly than the other top

100 prospects. At 18, he already had the heart, lungs, and sinew of an elite adult athlete—not just a 30-year-old journeyman's fitness, but a player who'd rank in the top one or two percent of his game.

Meehan and company set up a mini press conference for Ovechkin with one of Central Scouting's translators helping out. Most of what he said was straightforward and predictable.

When asked if there was a chance that he might stay in Russia and continue to play for Dynamo if the money were right, he made his position clear. "[The NHL] is the best hockey there is and I think I'm ready to play there, wherever I'm drafted," he said. "I talked to Alexei Yashin and Oleg Tverdovsky and they told me that I should go [to the NHL] right now. I think that there won't be any problem with the adjustment from the European game to the [smaller] NHL rink. I had a chance to play in North America at the world juniors last year and the ice surface wasn't a problem for me then. We won the tournament. I think that my game is good for either game. It has always been my dream to play in North America and in the NHL."

When asked about the possibility of a lockout putting his dream on hold, Ovechkin told the reporters that he would return to Dynamo. "There are still things that I can work on with Dynamo," he said. "I'd rather be playing there than not playing at all. I always want to be playing hockey. It's what I love. Hockey, hockey, hockey."

Ovechkin wasn't so straightforward and predictable with a couple of exit questions.

Asked about the rumored $3 million transfer fee Moscow Dynamo would demand to release him to the NHL, Ovechkin just shook his head. "Don't know," he said in English.

And asked how he was affected by the death of Anna Goruven, he said that the matter was off limits and that he wouldn't take any more questions from reporters.

Ovechkin would be asked other questions at the combine behind closed doors. At least a half dozen teams put in for interviews with him—not Pittsburgh and not Chicago, but others that thought they had a hope of trading into the top slot. Only one interview with a team mattered.

"It was funny how it went," said Dale Derkatch, who was scouting for Washington at the time. "There are always translators available at the combine but Alex insisted that he didn't want one and that he didn't need one. When he came in he shook everybody's hand, smiled and then he sat down. 'I'm Alexander,' he said and he smiled again. We asked him a couple of questions and he smiled. He wasn't sure what the questions were so he just talked in broken English— said something that had nothing to do with the questions we were asking him. When he knew he made a mistake he just laughed, a lot of looking at each other and shrugging. The funny thing is, there was nothing he could have said that would have meant more than just the way he was—he was too proud to ask for a translator, he wanted to come to the league and he wanted to get along. That's all we needed to know."

With the awful season behind them, with a lockout looming, with a league limping along, the Capitals had the player they wanted: this crooked-nosed kid who looked like he cut his own hair, who couldn't put a full sentence together in English.

chapter 6

Washington

"It Was On From the First Time He Stepped on the Ice"

BY SUPER BOWL SUNDAY of 2010, a little over five-and-a-half years since the Capitals drafted him, Alexander Ovechkin had justified Ted Leonsis's faith in him many times over. Without him, there wouldn't have been an NBC production truck parked out on snow-covered 6th Street that day. Without him, no one would have been tuned in, watching him, as casual as could be, leaning on his right elbow on the boards and talking to Pierre McGuire, NBC's rink-side analyst. Or, at least, he listened to the hyperventilating McGuire doing his best impression of Joan Rivers on the red carpet. He stopped just short of noting what Ovechkin was wearing. In the publicity run-up to the Super Bowl Sunday hockey game, McGuire had called Ovechkin "the best player in the world" and said that "you have to go all the way back to Rocket Richard to find a player like him." This might well be true but it wouldn't have registered with a lot of young fans or, especially, new ones. Nothing Ovechkin said was memorable. Ovechkin seemed somewhat embarrassed about being the object of McGuire's man-crush. In truth, since taking on the captaincy of the capitals a month earlier, Ovechkin was more often opting for the safe quote rather than the outrageous—the braggadocio of the *Men's Journal* interview had given way to the banal one-game-at-a-time platitudes.

The bigger story was playing out on the ice, away from the spotlight, outside the frame of the monitors and television screens. It was the stuff that the producers of the broadcast and the fans could not have seen. Pittsburgh Penguins center Sidney Crosby was bent over at the waist, torso parallel to the ice, his skates spread wide. First he glided in slow circles. Then he came to rest at the face-off circle. Not looking over at Ovechkin and McGuire, he tapped the point of his stick blade where he wanted the puck dropped. *Now.* Nothing subtle about it. Just Crosby's way of saying that Ovechkin was keeping everyone waiting, that no one is bigger than the game. Maybe Crosby would have been obliged to do the same as Ovechkin in different circumstances. But as a player as old school as a wooden stick and, one keenly aware of a century's worth of hockey etiquette, he would have made sure that he didn't seem to enjoy the attention so much. *Rocket Richard didn't do the red carpet.*

Crosby had to be irritated by the fact that he and the Stanley Cup champion Pittsburgh Penguins had risked their lives just to make it to Washington. A two-foot-deep blanket of snow, the worst snowstorm in the city's history, had made the streets of the U.S. capital impassable. Much of the eastern seaboard was also shut down. Caps head coach Bruce Boudreau and others with long commutes home had to decamp at hotels near the arena after a win over Atlanta at the Verizon Center on Friday night, and the Capitals cancelled their practice on Saturday afternoon. Still, GM George McPhee was reasonably confident that his players were going to be able to get to the arena Sunday morning—even though Ovechkin's Mercedes SL65 AMG didn't handle snow that well. The Penguins, though, were another matter. They had lost to the Canadiens in Montreal on Saturday afternoon and scheduled a charter flight to Washington immediately after the game, but the airports were shuttered in and around the District of Columbia. Fear of a cancellation on the highest day of the national sports calendar led to panic-filled phone calls from the league execs to officials on both teams. The progress of the Penguins to Washington was tracked from the league's Sixth Avenue offices like NASA's Mission Control tracking a shuttle landing. It took a plane from Montreal to Newark, the nearest airport not to be buried in the storm, and then a bus moving at a slow crawl through whiteout conditions down Interstate 95 to get the Penguins to their hotel at 4 a.m., just eight hours before game time. That would be business as usual in the juniors or the minors but not in the NHL, where players grow used to first-class-cabin treatment. The visiting team had to be in a foul mood.

One NBC camera was trained on Ovechkin at the opening face-off, another on Crosby. Several times in a shift of 40 seconds the images going back to the truck overlapped. In all but the final sequence, they were just ships passing. But when the puck was dumped into the Pittsburgh end of the rink at the end of the shift, Crosby skated back to support the blueliners chasing it down. In front of the Penguins' goaltender, Marc-Andre Fleury, Crosby was about to cross over and circle back up the ice when Ovechkin threw a shoulder into him—just below the base of his neck, right about where the B in his name is sewn into his sweater. A speed wobble. *It's on.*

• • •

The NHL has tried to capitalize on the rivalry between its two brightest stars, playing it for laughs in television promotions for the league. One commercial had the league's top young talents, clad in their team sweaters, fooling around in a hotel like a bunch of schoolkids; the payoff gag portrayed Ovechkin pulling a prank on Crosby. The commercial opened with Ovechkin putting in a massive order with room service—not caviar, blini, and champagne, but practically everything else on the menu—and then giving Crosby's name. At the end of the spot, bellhops arrived at Crosby's door with a long line of trays and hot plates. Realizing he has been pranked, Crosby clenched his fists, looked away from the camera, and said "Ovechkin" through gritted teeth, giving it a sort of "Curses, foiled again" reading.

The commercial hints at what hockey fans can intuitively glean from action on the ice—it's personal when a guy knocks off an opponent's helmet, facewashes him, taunts him, and then flaps his arms like a chicken, like Ovechkin did to Crosby in the spring of 2009. The hard feelings between some antagonists make it hard for others to sit in the same room with them. The hate between Sidney Crosby and Alexander Ovechkin is so visceral that it would make thousands in the same arena uncomfortable if it weren't so thrilling.

Jamie Heward, a teammate of Ovechkin in his rookie NHL season, suggests that it started from a simple grievance, a rivalry that evokes *The Brady Bunch* and Jan's envy of Marsha. "Alex came into the league with a lot of attention and a lot of hype but he also knew that if he was mentioned Crosby was. And really it was Crosby who was getting more public attention—a Canadian kid who'd been in the headlines at the draft that summer [2005] with the lottery. That somehow Crosby was seen as the savior of the Penguins and maybe even the league. [Ovechkin] was overshadowed. The focus was on Crosby *Sidney, Sidney, Sidney*. People didn't know what [Alex] had done in Russia. He wanted them to know that he was a player. Most guys won't think that way. They're happy to accept that sort of thing and wait for it to play out over time, that at the end of the day or at the end of the season, they'll get their due. Not Alex. No way. He wouldn't wait for the next game or even the next shift. It was on from the first time he stepped on the ice."

Andrew Gordon was one of the few who knew both players— he played with Crosby as a boy and a teenager in Halifax, and as a winger alongside Ovechkin in in training camp as a Capitals farmhand from 2007 onwards. "They're opposites in personality," Gordon says "Alex is out-going. Sidney's quiet." Interestingly, Gordon saw in Crosby an intense competitiveness that was even evident on hockey trips as 12-year-olds when they'd have elevator races in hotels, an echo of how Ovechkin would play frenetic games of the Demons with his childhood friends in the elevators of their Moscow apartment building. "Their games don't have a lot in common, but underneath they have a desire to be the best—not something they talk about, but it's there," said Gordon." They never take a game off or a shift off."

The animosity that grew between the two young NHL stars had to be bigger than a difference in styles or personalities. It's a hate too big to issue from a single incident. It had taken years to properly fester.

It goes back before they arrived in the NHL, before they played against each other, to a time when Ovechkin had no idea who Crosby was. It started as the 2003 world junior tourney in Crosby's hometown of Halifax. Crosby looked like just another 15-year-old autograph seeker lurking around the Metro Centre during the tournament. In fact, Hockey Canada had already identified him as the best Canadian player born in 1987 and invited him behind the scenes with the home team. He saw and heard the Russians heap abuse and profanities upon the beaten Canadians in the gold medal game. Ostensibly, he worked as a stickboy during games, but really the experience was a field trip, a chance to gain some insight about a tournament he was destined to play in someday. It was a priming him for a big moment.

That moment came two years later at the world junior tournament in Grand Forks, North Dakota. By that point, the Washington Capitals had drafted Ovechkin and Crosby was being heralded as the best North American prospect in a generation. Ovechkin was available to play for Russia because of the NHL lockout, and the Canadians were even more fortified by the labor dispute. In fact, Team Canada's captain, Patrice Bergeron, had played the entire previous season for the Boston Bruins. Perhaps as many as a half dozen other Canadians would have been in NHL lineups that winter if the league had been open for business. Ovechkin was expected to lead the Russians, while Crosby was moved over from center to wing and played a part in a collective effort.

The Canadian team routed all comers en route to the final against Russia. Still, the Russians had owned Canada in this tournament since 1997—and Ovechkin was a bigger talent than any that the Canadians had faced in Grand Forks prior to the gold-medal game.

The hate between Crosby and Ovechkin really began with their first meeting—physical meeting that is—midway through the first period. They weren't ships passing in the night then—more like trains colliding at the crossing. Canadian coach Brent Sutter matched the line of Bergeron between Crosby and Corey Perry against Ovechkin's line, with the punishing defence tandem of Dion Phaneuf and Shea Weber backing them up. Crosby was only 17, had to wear a full faceshield under IIHF rules and had been moved to the wing from his usual center position in deference to his older, more experienced teammates. He wore No. 9 on his red Team Canada jersey, not the No. 87 he would make famous. With Russia down 2–0 partway through the first period, Ovechkin carried the puck down the left wing and pulled up just outside the Canadian blueline rather than take on Weber directly, taking a sharp turn to his right. It wasn't that Ovechkin was being too cute—that type of curl-up with puck possession is routine in European hockey, and would become one of Ovechkin's trademark moves in the NHL. This time, however, he underestimated the danger on the NHL-sized rink at the Ralph Englestad Arena on the campus of the University of North Dakota and the speed that back-checking forwards could close with. He also had his head turned, looking for teammates to catch up and didn't pick up Crosby skating hard into the frame. He only felt him. In the crosshairs. Though giving away four inches and 30 pounds at a minimum, Crosby drove his hip and shoulder into Ovechkin's torso, separating him from the puck. Ovechkin was staggered by the blow, and while he didn't fall, he was clearly hurt as he winced and shook his head. Crosby had been winded himself but didn't want Ovechkin to know, so he got up the ice like it was just another day at the office. Ovechkin played a few more shifts and continued to absorb punishment, including a pair of hard checks to his chest from Bergeron, plus shots from Perry and Mike Richards. It felt like when he was a kid and every time the elevator door opened The Demon would ambush him. He couldn't play. By the second period he was watching from the bench. By the time of the post-game press conference, he had his right arm in a sling, protecting a separated shoulder. If the hit wasn't pre-meditated, exactly, it was an opportunity that Crosby had been looking for, and he took it with relish. "Yeah, I knew it was him [Ovechkin]," Crosby said. "And really it was a situation that we knew to look for. From watching him and from the scouting reports we knew that Ovechkin liked to pull up at the blue line and skate towards the middle."

Ovechkin went back to Moscow where he'd heal and eventually rejoin Dynamo and wait out the rest of the NHL lockout. Crosby went back to Rimouski, a small town in Quebec where he was playing for the local major junior team, and still managed to steal Ovechkin's thunder. Though he hadn't even been drafted yet, Reebok signed the 17-year-old Crosby to an endorsement deal that paid him a bigger sum than many NHL all-stars who had deals with the sportswear manufacturer.

Ovechkin had gone to his NHL draft with the media drumbeat that accompanies most No. 1 picks, but the fanfare for Crosby drowned out anything that had gone before. With teams having been on the sidelines for a season and with the business side of the NHL radically changed by a new collective agreement, Crosby was the object of a one-time super-lottery, with all 30 teams having a chance to win the right to select him with the first overall pick. It seemed like any general manager in the NHL would have traded a vital organ for the right to sign Crosby. Having lost out to Washington in the lottery the year before, Pittsburgh beat much bigger odds to win the top selection in the 2005 draft.

• • •

Fortune has smiled on the NFL, major league baseball, and the NBA in recent years, but it seemed like the NHL could never get a break. The Stanley Cup has landed in Raleigh, North Carolina, and St. Petersburg, Florida, but managed mostly to miss the major media markets. The Rangers, New York's favorite team, have managed only one championship in 70 years. Likewise, the state of California, host to several teams since 1967, has been home to only one Stanley Cup winner, a franchise that was named for a forgettable Disney kids' movie. Deals between the NHL and U.S. national television networks inevitably went sideways and were short-term arrangements. And when the NHL followed the NBA's lead and sent players to the Olympics in Nagano in 1998, the move yielded no popular bounce, not when the Czechs beat the Russians in the gold-medal game, a contest that was easy to miss as it played out in the wee hours of the morning back in North America.

Labor problems, meanwhile, were hardly unique to hockey. NFL stars went out on strike and owners fielded teams of replacement players in the late 1980s. Major league baseball lost a World Series due to a players' strike back in '94. Still, if any league was going to lose a whole season, it was going to be the hard-luck NHL. By 2004, the NHL was a basket case; at least half its teams were money-losing propositions. Commissioner Gary Bettman's Sunbelt initiative, expansion into non-traditional hockey markets, was at best a very limited success. The league's hopes of landing a major U.S. network television deal were just so many unanswered prayers.

George McPhee and Dick Patrick had both been around the league a long time, too. They bet on there being a lockout in the fall of 2004, and possibly a lost season, and they were on the money. McPhee, Patrick, and Ted Leonsis might not have wagered on the NHL coming away with a collective agreement that closed the huge gap between first- and second-division clubs, the large and small markets, and the teams that could snap up free agents at will and teams that struggled to avoid drowning in red ink. The owner and his chief executives hoped for that deal but couldn't have known that they'd get it. They did: in the summer of '05, after a cancelled season, the league and the players struck a collective agreement that allowed for revenue sharing, a salary cap, limits on player salaries, and other measures that would heal some, if not all, failing small- and new-market franchises and make the most successful major-market teams more profitable than ever. The Capitals executives came away with what they thought they needed to succeed—under the revenue-sharing plan, Leonsis received as much as $14 million a season from his partners to help fund his operations—but it turned out the league needed something more.

It wasn't just that the books had gone bad. No, the game itself was broken.

During the lockout, leaders in hockey—some of them players, others coaches, managers, and even owners—realized that the challenge of winning fans back wasn't going to be met with the same style of game that had been played for the previous decade. One of the reasons they struggled to sell the NHL game was that scoring had plunged from the run-and-gun '80s. The NHL had become a defense-first league. Some called it the Dead Puck Era. There were many other culprits in dragging the game down, including but not limited to coaches content with a 1–1 tie if it helped keep their jobs another day and referees who would only pull out their whistles when infractions reached the level of borderline felonies. In its best markets, the NHL had always charged a top dollar, but, given the turn of the game, the fans were getting less and less entertainment value for their hard-earned buck.

When management and the union were at a complete impasse in the labor negotiations, parties from both sides met away from the lawyers to talk about improving the game. When the NHL re-opened for business it implemented major rules changes that ended up being critical to getting the game back on track with fans. Strict enforcement of rules against obstructing players without the puck opened up the game. Players were able to carry more speed up the ice. Taking out the red line for offside created a climate for longer passes. Skilled players didn't have to break tackles to make plays. Aesthetically, the game of hockey was much better after the lockout than before.

And it was much better for Alexander Ovechkin and Sidney Crosby—they were going to have more room to operate and be able to utilize their skill and speed more than if they had landed in the NHL five years before. "Ovechkin and Crosby would have been great players in any era because they would have found a way to be the best," said Brendan Shanahan, a three-time Stanley Cup winner, who had taken the lead in these talks on the players' side. "They grew up playing under the old rules and still managed to be the best. If the rules hadn't changed they would still have become superstars but in a different form. They would have had to do it differently. The way they got to do it was more entertaining—otherwise it would have been a bit more *slushy*."

● ● ●

The timing for generating an NHL rivalry between Ovechkin and Crosby was perfect—Ovechkin was almost 23 months older, but they entered the league at the same time, October 2005. They both joined franchises that were rebuilding but wouldn't be handicapped by troubled finances. They began their careers at a time when the rules of the game helped speed up action and open up ice to skilled players. Their races for statistical thresholds, for honors, for trophies, and ultimately for championships would start that season after the lockout.

Comparisons were made to the two towering talents of the previous generation, Wayne Gretzky and Mario Lemieux, but clearly the arrivals of Ovechkin and Crosby were a different matter. Gretzky and Lemieux didn't arrive on the scene at the same time—Gretzky signed with the WHA in 1977 and landed in the NHL in 1979, while Lemieux played his first NHL game in 1984. By the time Lemieux joined a dreadful Pittsburgh team, Gretzky's Edmonton Oilers were a star-studded powerhouse. Through their primes, Gretzky played in the Western Conference and Lemieux in the East, limiting the number of match-ups. They never met in the playoffs. Lemieux's career was interrupted by injuries and threatened by Hodgkin's lymphoma. And, the truth is, they were abundantly talented but only rarely met head-to-head on the ice— in their final meeting, when Gretzky and the New York Rangers went to Pittsburgh in 1996, the two were on the ice together for a total of four seconds during a line change. Their most famous moment came when they skated together in the 1987 Canada Cup, the often-replayed pass from Gretzky to Lemieux for the winning goal, but it's hard to find a photo capturing them in action against each other. In their first meeting at the world juniors, on the other hand, Ovechkin and Crosby produced one more head-to-head vignette than the predecessors did in their entire Hall-of-Fame careers.

Basketball might provide a closer parallel with the arrival of Larry Bird and Magic Johnson in the NBA in 1979. Like Ovechkin and Crosby, Bird and Johnson had one meeting before turning pro that established the rivalry: the NCAA championship game between Bird's Indiana State team and Johnson's Michigan State squad. Like Ovechkin and Crosby, their life stories provided a contrast—for the hockey prodigies, it was a matter of nationalities; for the basketball stars, race. Ovechkin and Crosby came into the NHL at its popular nadir, after a season lost to the lockout, much like Bird and Johnson joining the NBA when television ratings had bottomed out with games being shown late at night on tape-delay, and drugs had damaged its image.

The NHL had reason to hope that Ovechkin and Crosby were even better positioned for a lasting, league-lifting rivalry than Bird and Johnson had been. Bird and Johnson were on opposite sides of the court 37 times in their careers: one game in college, 17 games in the regular season, and 19 more in the NBA finals. Bird's later career was limited by back injuries and Johnson's was shortened by HIV. Their last meeting in the playoffs came in 1987, when Bird was 31 and Johnson 28. Thereafter they met at most twice a season until Johnson's retirement in 1991. On average, a Hockey Hall of Famer's career runs longer than his basketball counterpart's Gretzky played to age 40, while Lemieux, after hiatuses for injury and treatment for Hodgkin's, led Canada to an Olympic gold medal in 2002 at age 36, and also retired at 40. Given Ovechkin's and Crosby's dedication to training, there is every reason to think that they are going to be around into their 40s, as long as they stay healthy and their competitive fires burn.

• • •

His name wasn't recognized by hockey fans as often as Crosby's at the start of their rookie seasons in the fall of 2005, but by the spring Ovechkin was getting the top billing. In most years, Crosby's performance, 39 goals and 63 assists for sixth place in the NHL scoring race, would have won him the Calder Trophy as the league's top first-year player. As it turned out, he wasn't even close to Ovechkin, who finished third in scoring with 52 goals and 54 assists. Ovechkin was named the First All-Star team's left-winger, while Crosby wasn't voted onto either the First or Second teams. Ovechkin also impressed as a member of the Russian team at the 2006 Olympics in Torino, scoring the goal that knocked Canada out of the medal round. Crosby's boy-scout persona was at odds with an abrasive style on the ice, including a habit of baiting officials, and with a dissension-ridden Penguins' dressing room where he found himself on the outs with some of the veterans. It was a bad-karma season for Crosby: in a decision that generated no controversy, Canadian general manager Wayne Gretzky opted not to select Crosby for the Olympic team; Lemieux was forced to retire because of an irregular heartbeat; and the Penguins won only 22 games. Maybe the best measure of Ovechkin's trumping of his rival came when he received an ovation from the crowd in Vancouver when he went up on stage with Leonsis and McPhee to announce the Capitals' 2006 first-round draft pick, Nicklas Backstrom. The Capitals didn't even play Vancouver that season, but he had captured the hearts and minds of hockey fans everywhere with his sense of fun and his spontaneity—he was the anti-Crosby.

Crosby captured the second leg of this race. He won the Hart Trophy as the NHL's most valuable player and the scoring title with 36 goals and 84 assists in the 2006–07 regular season. Though Ovechkin was, like Crosby, voted to the First All-Star team, he didn't finish among the league's top 10 scorers. Head to head, Pittsburgh swept the Capitals that season, with Crosby scoring two goals and three assists, while Ovechkin registered just one assist in the four games. But most of all, Crosby was the driving force behind a vastly improved Penguins team that registered 25 more wins than the previous season. Ovechkin's Capitals once again finished out of the playoffs. After their post-season run stalled in the first round versus Ottawa, the Penguins named Crosby team captain; two months shy of his 20th birthday he became the youngest captain in league history. It was just a "C" stitched on a sweater but it signified teammates' respect and, because Crosby had it, Ovechkin had to covet it. This wasn't all that Ovechkin coveted.

• • •

By the end of his second season in the NHL, Crosby was still far and away hockey's biggest moneymaker off the ice. That didn't sit well with Ovechkin. Don Meehan's Newport Sports agency had helped set up and negotiate signing shows and they fetched handsome sums of money for little more than attendance. Crosby didn't do anything like that and still, with his endorsements and licensed collectibles, he made two or three bucks for every dollar Ovechkin earned away from the rink. Ovechkin and his parents were impatient with this situation and not satisfied that Newport Sports was doing everything possible to get him into the market. And the way the market had heated up for NHL player salaries, they also knew that the stakes with his next contract were going to be very high: his four-year entry-level contract called for a little under $1 million in a base salary and paid out another $3 million in bonuses and incentives, but the Ovechkins were looking at more than doubling this number as soon as they could negotiate an extension. With this looming, the Ovechkins sent word to Meehan that his services would no longer be needed. They abruptly terminated Ovechkin's player-representation contract with Newport.

It was certainly something Ovechkin was entitled to do. Players break up with agents frequently—getting out of a standard representation agreement is not much more difficult than peeling off a sweater at the end of a game.

Still, this seemed a cold-blooded business decision. The decision put no value on Meehan's work negotiating his entry-level contract after the lockout—the Capitals had a very brief window to sign Ovechkin before the 2005–06 season and if they had failed to get a deal done within a 48-hour period, Ovechkin was going to have to spend the entire winter in Moscow. The decision put no value whatsoever on the TLC Newport had offered Ovechkin in his rookie season with the Capitals. Anna Goruven's daughter, Susanna, had moved to Washington back in the fall of 2005 to help Ovechkin get around town and serve as his translator—it was exactly the kind of thing that Anna Goruven had done for her clients and they had all loyally stood by her. It seemed it was going to be the same with Ovechkin and Susanna. He had made a point of thanking her when he accepted the Calder Trophy at the NHL awards night in 2005. "Susanna does a great job, support me all season," he told the audience. "She'll be with me sometimes [to] help me buy car, food. She cooks me food, cleans my house, so thanks very much, Susie." But by the end of his second season, with his parents in Washington and Susanna Goruven's help no longer needed on a daily basis, all she had done for him was behind him, and Ovechkin and his family weren't looking in the rearview mirror.

The details of the loss of Ovechkin as a client aren't anything Meehan has ever wanted to discuss. Likewise, he made the decision not to talk about the money involved. He had lost clients before, Jaromir Jagr being one who left on the eve of an industry-shaping contract. He learned a long time ago that there was nothing to be gained by reopening cases that had already been decided. If he were to carve a former client, it would only make him seem bitter and mean-spirited, and that would be a liability in a business that depends on building relationships. It would be like trashing your ex when you were on a first date with someone else. Meehan and Ovechkin crossed paths several times in the season after the break-up—an inevitability because Meehan has to park himself in hallways outside dressing rooms after games, waiting to meet Newport clients like Ovechkin's Capitals teammate Mike Green. There was never a scene, never words, but it was still uncomfortable, Ovechkin not acknowledging Meehan or, when he did, not being able to look his former agent in the eye. Despite missing out on several millions of dollars in commissions on the deal that Ovechkin later signed in January 2008, the few words Meehan said about Ovechkin were not critical. "I like the young man," he said.

Ovechkin's dismissal of Meehan and Newport was a sharp contrast to Crosby's story once again. By the time Sidney Crosby was 15, his parents had signed him to a representation agreement with J.P. Barry and Pat Brisson of what was then IMG's hockey division (which later reverted to the Creative Artists Agency, CAA). The relationship with Barry and Brisson started the year before and there was never any sort of tug-of-war or game-playing with agents in the run-up to his signing. Crosby's father, Troy, and Brisson had both played for Verdun in the Quebec Major Junior League in the early '80s. That connection, as well as IMG's history of representing Gretzky and some of the other biggest names in the sport, cinched the deal. Those in the business circle around Crosby have remained in place throughout—Frameworth Sports Marketing, for instance, has handled all of Crosby's signed merchandise and collectibles since he was in the junior league. His relationship with Tim Hortons was tied to his uncle, Rob Forbes, vice president of the company's marketing division. "The Crosby family had a plan and they stayed with it," hockey marketing executive Brad Robins said. In Ovechkin's first two seasons, there hadn't been one plan—there had been new ones all the time, because of a shifting circle of friends and advisors, mostly Russian-speaking, not affiliated with Newport. Ovechkin had been easily swayed by the last person he spoke with. Meehan, Goruven, and others at Newport had often been drowned out by the hangers-on and by the end of his second season they were cut out completely.

• • •

The push and pull between Ovechkin and Crosby continued to play out in their third seasons, the 2007–08 campaign, and Ovechkin won back the hearts and minds of hockey fans. In the games between Pittsburgh and Washington, Crosby had the advantage again, with the Penguins winning the three games he played in, and the Caps' single victory coming when Crosby was out of the lineup with an injury. The bigger battle played out across the regular season, with Ovechkin claiming the league lead in goals (65) and points (112) and winning the Hart Trophy for the first time. Ovechkin was again named the First All-Star team's left-winger, beside centre Evgeni Malkin—Crosby was passed over for one of his teammates. If Crosby felt slighted, he was able to take comfort in the fact that his team racked up 102 points during the regular season and advanced to the Stanley Cup final, extending the Detroit Red Wings to six tense games before bowing.

By their fourth NHL seasons, the characters of Ovechkin and Crosby were well defined—those who followed the game regarded Ovechkin as flashier and Crosby as sounder in the game's fundamentals. On that basis, many thought Crosby's team would have a chance to win a championship before Ovechkin's. However, it didn't seem that way in the early going, with the Penguins' poor start costing coach Michel Therrien his job. It looked like the Capitals were poised to overtake the Penguins as the young powerhouse in the conference, winning three of four games over Pittsburgh, with Ovechkin registering four goals in those games to Crosby's one. Pittsburgh's lone win came in a shoot-out in their final match-up of the regular season. And it looked like Ovechkin was strengthening his case for status as the game's best player—a second straight Hart Trophy and another First All-Star berth. He also won the Lester B. Pearson Trophy, MVP as voted by the league's players. He dedicated the award to his beloved grandfather, Nikolay Kabayev, who had died the previous fall. Ovechkin had missed two games to travel to Moscow to see his gravely ill grandfather. Meanwhile, it seemed like Crosby might also have been passed by a teammate: Malkin won the scoring title, finishing three points ahead of Ovechkin and landing First All-Star honors at center. The regular season, though, was just a prelude for a breathtaking showdown in the 2009 playoffs.

The series went seven games and, though it only played out in the second round, it eclipsed everything else in the postseason. The Capitals beat the Penguins 3–2 in the opening game at the Verizon Center, but that was only a tune-up for a classic in the next go-round. It was still a contest of teams and there were others on the ice at the same time, but the puck seemed to follow Ovechkin and Crosby around the ice. In Game 2, the two exchanged hat tricks, Ovechkin scoring his second and third goals in the last seven minutes to secure a 4–3 victory. David Steckel scored the Capitals' second goal of the game but it almost felt like he was intruding, like a stagehand wandering out from behind the curtain during a two-actor play. With less than five minutes remaining, Ovechkin scored what turned out to be the winning goal, gathering a pass from Viktor Kozlov at center ice, skating down the wing, and unleashing a slap shot past defenseman Sergei Gonchar and goaltender Marc-Andre Fleury. Each of the two stars' goals was a small, self-contained miracle of talent and played out not just to the wonderment of the crowd but also to that of the other players. "The best thing about Alex is that he takes the level so high, and then there's another night that he takes it higher," Capitals forward Brooks Laich said after the game. "I was on the bench for all of his goals and I just look up and it's unbelievable. He's our leader and he's the difference in the game."

It seemed an impossible level of tension and suspense to maintain, but somehow the two teams managed to pull it off for four more games. The Penguins were on the brink of falling a game away from elimination at home in Game 3, needing an overtime goal from defenseman Kristopher Letang to keep their hopes alive. Games 5 and 6 went to overtime as well, with the road teams winning both times, Malkin scoring in the Verizon Center and Steckel in Pittsburgh's Mellon Arena. Only in Game 7 did the magic vanish.

The NHL.com account summarized it well: "The hype for the first installment of Sidney Crosby vs Alexander Ovechkin in the playoffs? Unprecedented. The goods? Delivered. The end? Um, can we get a do-over?" Crosby set the tone, scoring the opening goal and adding another and an assist in a suspense-free 6–2 rout. Ovechkin scored a goal but failed to impose himself on the contest like Crosby did. All around Ovechkin, his teammates stepped back rather than up. Semyon Varlamov, the rookie goaltender from Russia, had been sensational in the Capitals' playoff wins but looked vulnerable in Game 7.

The Penguins went on to beat Carolina in the conference final and out-last Detroit in another seven-game series to win the Stanley Cup. Crosby became the youngest captain to raise the Cup, and Malkin won the Conn Smythe Trophy, but those involved inevitably returned to the Washington series as the defining moment. "This was Magic and Bird from back in the day. It was just a great series for the league . . . and the game of hockey," Pittsburgh winger Bill Guerin said of the Penguins-Capitals games. "I don't know if I've ever been in a series with as many up-and-downs as this one." It was the rivalry that played out in the first six games of that series and in the first four seasons of their careers that the NHL hoped to bring to NBC audiences on that Super Bowl Sunday, in February 2010, at the Winter Olympics just days after that, and in the playoff run in the spring.

* * *

Ovechkin wasn't on the ice when Crosby hopped over the boards seven minutes into the even but uneventful Super Bowl Sunday game. It turned out to be a shift that would have a less self-assured coach than Bruce Boudreau second-guessing his philosophy of not matching lines—not Ovechkin's linemates up front, but rather the Capitals' defensemen who would be on the ice when Crosby was.

Tom Poti and Tyler Sloan weren't Washington's best defensive pairing. Or the second best. The 32-year-old Poti was a journeyman NHLer, a player who had never made, and will never make, an All-Star team but who had made a very comfortable living for 12 years. Of the league's 700 players, he would slot south of the equator. That would still leave him well ahead of Sloan, however. The 28-year-old from Calgary had more experience in the East Coast League than in the NHL. In fact, he had played his first NHL game the previous season. He was scarcely better than many guys he had toiled beside on the Dayton Bombers and the Las Vegas Wranglers.

From their first shift against the Penguins, Poti and Sloan had looked vulnerable. Under modest pressure on the forecheck with teams at even strength, Poti had turned the puck over and given up a scoring chance. This time it was Sloan's turn to cough up the puck. From beside the Capitals net, Sloan tried a long, searching stretch pass. *Look at his eyes. Telegraphed.* It might have been Eric

Fehr he was trying to hit or maybe Brendan Morrison. There was no telling because it had gone only halfway before it hit the blade of Crosby's skate on the left wing, two steps inside the blue line. Almost reflexively, Crosby kicked the puck up to his stick and skated in with nothing but ice between him and Washington goalie Jose Theodore. Poti and Sloan scrambled to get back into the play but Crosby was moving too fast. Theodore tried to press the issue and challenge Crosby, but Crosby skated hard to his right, taking the puck across the front of the net and then lofted a backhand over the flailing goaltender. Pittsburgh 1 Washington 0, and something close to a hush fell over the Verizon Center. Those in the lower bowl could hear Ovechkin jawing at Brooks Orpik at the Pittsburgh bench. *Don't celebrate yet.*

The goal energized Crosby's teammates who had looked like they left their legs on the bus. Two shifts after the goal, with Pittsburgh again pressing around the Washington goal, Brooks Laich tried to hold up Jordan Staal and was whistled for an interference penalty. Crosby came back into the game with Malkin and Guerin on the Pittsburgh power play, one of the league's most potent and all the more threatening with one of Washington's best penalty-killers, Laich, in the box. For a full minute the Penguins controlled the puck in the Capitals' end and then Gonchar, Pittsburgh's most creative power-play point man, found Malkin stationed on the right side of the ice. For a moment the Washington defensemen, Mike Green and Jeff Schultz were locked in, frozen where they stood, as stationary as Xs on a chalkboard. In one motion Malkin snapped a touch pass to Crosby directly on the other side of the ice. *Lots of time, he'll blink first.* Theodore was at Crosby's mercy and desperately guessed that Crosby was going to backhand it to the short-side. Again, Crosby waited out Theodore, this time drawing the puck over to his forehand and firing a wrist shot to the glove side. Pittsburgh 2 Washington 0, and the Verizon Center fell as silent as the snow-covered streets of Washington. Crosby was demure in celebration, no stick-on-fire, nothing to incite the crowd or his

nemesis. *Act like you've done it before. Respect the game.* The early in-
dications were that a team that has to kill hours on a bus might have
an advantage over players who had to dig out their driveways.

It looked like the league's hope for a broadcast showcase was
going to wind up Crosby's star turn. Only two of Pittsburgh's 22
losses had come in games when the Penguins had a two-goal lead.
But the Capitals' firepower was such that comebacks from two-
goal deficits, while not everyday stuff, were within the realm of
possibility. In fact they had managed to come back from two goals
down against the Rangers at Madison Square Garden the previous
Thursday. After that game, a wild, run-and-gun affair, Boudreau's
former junior-hockey teammate John Tonelli had gone down to
the Washington dressing room and the coach said: "How's that for
fuckin' trap hockey?"

· · ·

That snowy Sunday, the Capitals had sleepwalked through the
game's first ten minutes, generating only four shots on goal, none
of them producing a quality scoring chance. They looked not at
all like the league's hottest team. A couple of shifts after Crosby's
second goal, Ovechkin tried to fire up his team just as he had in
Manhattan. Crosby's winger Chris Kunitz was sent off with a minor for interference, and the Penguins' captain stayed out on the
penalty kill. Ovechkin was back at the point. The Capitals weren't
able to generate much pressure off the face-off, and Crosby took
possession of the puck, carrying it across the Washington blue line.
Green was squarely in front of him, so Crosby pulled up and kept
possession, looking to kill as much time as possible with his team
shorthanded. Ovechkin lurked in the center of the ice—he had no
defensive responsibilities because none of Crosby's teammates had
joined the rush. What Ovechkin saw was an opportunity to take a
clean shot at his nemesis. It looked like Crosby couldn't have seen

him coming—*and this one will be just like Grand Forks for you*—but just before sucking up a big hit, he dumped the puck into a corner and spun away, at the last possible instant. It was like Crosby's Spider-sense was tingling.

A couple of minutes later, after Kunitz's penalty expired, the Penguins set about Ovechkin with their own bad intentions. Crosby was on the ice but he didn't dirty his gloves with Ovechkin, leaving the task to Craig Adams, not a designated enforcer, just a journeyman claimed off waivers from Chicago the previous March. Adams's role with the team was a purely complementary one, and he knew that in circumstances like this he had to serve as a messenger. Ovechkin was facing the boards at a standstill when Adams took a run at him: a shove in the back above his number, a patently dangerous play. *Do unto others and all that.* Ovechkin barely had time to get his hands up to break his fall. By the time he staggered to his feet, head down, bent over at the waist, he could hear the crowd roaring.

His linemate Mike Knuble had jumped Adams from behind and they were trading punches at center ice: proxy versus proxy for the combat between Nos. 8 and 87. At Knuble's four previous stops in the league he had ridden shotgun for four Hart Trophy winners, Hall of Fame talents all: first with Steve Yzerman in Detroit, then with Wayne Gretzky in New York, Joe Thornton in Boston, and Peter Forsberg in Philadelphia. Never a fighter, and even less so at age 37, Knuble saw Adams's cheap shot on the Capitals' meal ticket as a threat to the team's Stanley Cup chances. *There are just times you have to go.* Knuble was given a minor for instigating, a major for fighting, and a 10-minute misconduct. So it was that one-third of the Capitals' first line—by Knuble's own admission, the lesser third—was banished for almost half the time remaining in regulation. For the first two minutes, Ovechkin sat beside Knuble in the penalty box and served the veteran's minor.

Ovechkin and his teammates did rally over the balance of the first period, peppering Marc-Andre Fleury with 10 shots, but the Pittsburgh goalie could challenge them with the confidence of a two-goal lead. Ovechkin and Crosby were back on the ice in the last minute of the period, and the Caps were buzzing the Penguins' goal until Crosby seized a careless turnover by Semin and cleared the zone. The first round of a three-round fight belonged to Crosby, decisively so. The outcome: NBC's analyst Mike Milbury, formerly a tough guy with the Boston Bruins and a New York Islanders general manager, told viewers that Crosby had once again established that he was "Ovechkin's daddy." His broadcast partner McGuire momentarily looked like a love-struck teen who had just been told that his cheerleading crush was going to the big dance with the school's football hero.

• • •

The two marquee attractions were back on the ice for the start of the second period, with Crosby beating Backstrom on the face-off. One mark of Crosby's attention to detail and focus on self-improvement: in his first four NHL seasons he had been regarded as weak on face-offs but, through dint of practice after his first Stanley Cup, he turned himself into one of the league's best. Over the course of 35 seconds, Ovechkin took a couple of runs at Crosby, missing him the first time in the corner, planting him later down the ice, away from the puck. *I don't need Knuble or anyone else to look after my business.* When Crosby scrambled back upright, he gave the ref a dirty look but said nothing.

On an offside call, Pittsburgh coach Dan Bylsma made a quick change, bringing Crosby and his linemates to the bench and sending out Malkin and linemates Pascal Dupuis and Ruslan Fedotenko. In the usual run of things, Boudreau doesn't try to match lines and he'd leave Ovechkin out for a minute, a minute and a half, or more. This time, however, the coach sent out the line of, left to right, Fleischmann, Laich, and Semin. An industrious if not particularly gifted forward, Laich drew an interference penalty on Gonchar just a couple of deep breaths after the face-off. Ovechkin's respite was brief. Boudreau sent him and the rest of the frontline talents over the boards.

The Capitals' power play was the league's best at the time, yet it didn't manage a shot on net over the next two minutes. The players, Ovechkin no less than the others, looked unfocused and out of sorts. *When is this going to happen for us?* This was Washington's third game in four days, and Boudreau had bemoaned the lack of practice time for his team in the previous couple of weeks. The coach thought that the session he had planned for the Saturday prior to this game was going to be important to getting his team back in sync but had to cancel it because the players couldn't make it through the snow to the rink. Boudreau thought his players needed the practice to tidy up play in their own end of the rink. But in the second period against Pittsburgh, the issue seemed to be hockey's best power play, Ovechkin and Green, the league's top-scoring defenseman, back at the points, with Backstrom, Knuble, and Semin up front. The unit usually looked like an offensive laser-show, but on Super Bowl Sunday they were five flashlights with dying batteries.

The first eight minutes of the second period were tense but not terrifically artistic. Ovechkin steamrolled Adams on one shift. *Payback*. Semin stayed in character, too. More selfish than opportunistic, Semin stayed out too long on a shift and, winded, took a hooking penalty trying to hold up Letang. The Penguins' power play managed only one shot and no serious scoring chances. The game seemed to flatline emotionally, like it was just another game on the NHL schedule, one-eighty-second of a season's work, and not an installment of the sport's best rivalry, a prelude to a showdown at the Olympic Games just a couple of weeks off.

The Capitals found an unlikely source to spark their offence. At 6-fooft-6, defenseman Jeff Schultz lumbers about the ice, a big body whose arms and long stick suffocate chances. He hadn't made an NHL All-Star team and won't, doesn't get anything for style points but, when effective, makes skilled forwards as bereft of grace as he is. At almost the game's midway mark, Schultz controlled the puck in the Caps' end and, under no forechecking pressure from the

Penguins' fourth line, spied Ovechkin at center ice—a break-out chance. Schultz and his defense partner Brian Pothier were more likely to be out when the Caps were protecting a lead than when they were playing catch-up. Still, Schultz knew O's tendencies—his ability to beat defenders shows up on highlight reels, but his ability to lull defenders to sleep makes opposing coaches grimace when they break down game video. *I don't know how they lose him. He's too big too hide. Everybody knows when he's on the ice.*

They call it dangling or floating but that suggests motion, and at this point Ovechkin was at a dead stop, seemingly taking a momentary break from the action. In any game, he's as often in park as he is in fifth gear. When Schultz gathered the puck, Ovechkin was like a statue at center ice. When Schultz looked up ice, Ovechkin made a break, no more than two explosive strides into the gap between Pittsburgh defensemen Mark Eaton and Gonchar. *An opening.* Schultz led Ovechkin with the pass—it looked a little too hot, like Ovechkin wasn't going to be able to get a stick on it, like it was going to go for icing. But Ovechkin did get his stick on it, not quite controlling it on the first touch but slowing it enough that he could race towards it—a clean breakaway. He bore down and snapped off a shot that beat Marc-Andre Fleury and broke the NBC camera in the Pittsburgh net. The crowd erupted. The game was back to a coin flip.

•   •   •

Ovechkin's goal seemed to engage him, but it didn't turn the game around. Pittsburgh kept coming. Less than three minutes later, Penguins center Jordan Staal tipped a point shot past Theodore to restore Pittsburgh's two-goal lead. If anything, Ovechkin's goal seemed to stoke the visitors' competitive fire. A melee ensued after Staal's goal when Orpik got his stick up into the face of Pothier and Ovechkin tackled Letang, sitting on top of him and squeezing the life out of him with a bear hug. *They stand up for me, I have to stand up for them.* Matt Cooke, Pittsburgh's designated shit disturber, made a token effort to budge Ovechkin. Even Backstrom, usually a peaceful sort, wrestled with Tyler Kennedy.

That meant Staal's goal came with a bonus for the Penguins. The refs sent Ovechkin and Letang off with coincidental penalties, and Backstrom and Kennedy were handed 10-minute misconducts. The teams would be four-on-four, and Washington wasn't going to have its two most talented forwards available. In fact, the Caps' first line was in the box together, with Knuble still off for his part in the first-period fight. *We're supposed to be out there.* It was going to be an advantage for the Penguins, giving their best players open ice. Crosby and Guerin were on the ice versus Fleischman and Laich on the face-off, and the Caps held them off for a shift. On the next one, though, Malkin and Staal faced Brendan Morrison and Semin—and when Poti turned over the puck, Staal scored on his second consecutive shift to give the Pens a 4–1 lead.

At this point those in the NBC production truck had to be thinking up story lines. The Pens still looked like the Caps' daddies. It wasn't quite Crosby's Canada triumphing over Ovechkin's Russia at the world juniors—national allegiances were moot with Malkin setting up Staal's second goal. Still, it was more Crosby's day than Ovechkin's with just seven minutes left in the second period. Along press row, reporters were getting a jump start on writing stories that reflected a Pitt win. *Cup champions make statement before Olympic break.* The independent fanboy bloggers invited in by the new-media friendly Leonsis were mournful.

With less than three minutes left in the second period, Fehr took a pass from Morrison, peeled around defenseman Jay McKee and put a non-threatening backhand on the Pittsburgh net. Fleury turned the shot aside, but Fehr pounced on the rebound and jammed it by the Penguins' goaltender. Fehr, anything but flashy on skates, isn't a player who inspires intense fan interest, never mind idolatry. If you had sorted through a thousand Capitals sweaters in the crowd that afternoon, not one of them would have had his No. 16 or his name, yet it was his goal that players and coaches on both sides would point to as the game's turning point. *It's not supposed to be Fehr who scores these goals.*

The Caps went into the intermission down by two goals, but it could have been worse. Right after Fehr's goal, Semin took another penalty in the offensive zone, and on the penalty kill, Tom Poti was hit with a minor for interference—a five-on-three penalty kill for 90 seconds. Again, it wasn't the Washington all-stars who were called on but the plumbers: Boyd Gordon, Steckel, and Schultz, three anonymous journeymen, Boudreau's guys, players he worked with in the AHL. *The pipes burst, you call the plumbers not the artists.* The Caps were able to hold off the Penguins. First it was Steckel blocking two shots from the point. Then, as the seconds wound down in the period, it was Theodore making a play as big as Fehr's goal.

Crosby had the game on his glove and then his stick. He was standing unchecked 10 feet to his right of the crease, waiting for the puck. Theodore's attention was on the other side of the ice. The puck came across the ice, almost chest high, and Crosby, in a fraction of a second, knocked it out of midair with his glove and right onto his stick for a one-timer. It looked like a sure goal, a hat trick to mirror his effort against the Caps in Game 2 of the playoff series the previous spring.

It was like a flashback to earlier years, before the lockout, before Ovechkin and Crosby burst onto the scene, when Theodore was for a time the best goaltender in the game, an undersized netminder in a league full of oversized spiders. Theodore, who won the Hart and Vezina Trophies with the Montreal Canadiens in 2002, stole goals and games almost nightly back then. This time, he slid from one side of the net to the other, stoning Crosby whose head dropped and whose face twisted into an eye-rolling grimace. *Shoulda been.*

When Theodore came off the ice at the end of the period moments later, Ovechkin waited for the goaltender by the gate at the bench to let him know that the team was going to pick him up. *These are the games we're winning. It's going to come.*

• • •

The Capitals' penalty killers were back on the ice at the start of the third period, and they were able to keep Crosby, Malkin, and the rest of the Penguins at bay. By the time Washington was back at full strength and he rolled over the boards, it had been more than three minutes of game time since Ovechkin had been on the ice. Ovechkin had watched his teammates weather a few bad shifts—the Penguins could have run up the score. Still, he had to sense that Pittsburgh's play was getting a little loose. The Capitals were winning every battle for the puck along the boards. Passes that the Penguins' defensemen had pushed up the ice to Crosby and the others in the first two periods were starting to miss the mark. *It's coming.* Maybe Crosby and the rest were feeling the fatigue from the trip to Washington. Or maybe, just as likely, the pace of the Capitals' run-and-gun game was starting to take its toll.

The way the game often goes, a team wins a shift before it scores goals, but when the goals come they'll come in a rush. What takes minutes in the buildup is finished in a blink of an eye. That was how the third period went. At the five-minute mark, Ovechkin was finally reunited with the other two-thirds of the Capitals' first line, back out with Backstrom and Knuble for the first time since the first period. And on their third shift together, Ovechkin scored his second goal of the game, a backhand in traffic in front of Fleury, more opportunistic than transcendent. Brooks Orpik had blocked a shot from the point but Ovechkin pounced on it and slid the puck into the net. Ovechkin had the Capitals back within a goal at 4–3, although it felt like they had been soundly outplayed.

Ovechkin's next goal happened so fast that it made Doc Emrick, NBC's play-by-play man, stutter—one of those times when words can't quite capture a puck moving 90-miles-an-hour traveling a distance of 30 feet. Backstrom won a face-off in the Pittsburgh end and sharply pulled the puck back to Ovechkin, who teed it up for a one-timer that blew past Kunitz and Fleury in a blink.

Ovechkin jumped up into the glass back-first and was mobbed by his teammates while Crosby, head down, skated through a slalom course of hats on the ice. He had his two goals, but Ovechkin now had three and the game was tied, 4–4.

Moments like this are rare in an NHL season. Four months into the 2009–10 campaign there had been nothing like the run of the game leading up to Ovechkin's hat trick, this confluence of skill, energy, and sense of moment. For Theodore's robbery of Crosby, the game's two top stars would have had hat tricks head to head. Through the last 10 shifts of regulation time, the game was just as frantic, action going end to end, but it wasn't going to be decided until overtime.

• • •

The Capitals' dressing room later descended into happy chaos. Laughter. Television cameras. Ovechkin stood in front of reporters and was going to great lengths to say the right things. No inflammatory quotes. No trash talk. No jokes. It seemed the game had bleached out the color and turned down the volume. He smiled but wasn't about to ratchet up emotions in the Penguins' dressing room. He wasn't about to rile Crosby. "It's always nice to win when you are a little bit frustrated in the first period," Ovechkin said. "The game didn't go well for us right away."

Knuble was describing to the media what happened on the winning goal that he scored as overtime wound down. Or trying to describe it. Washington was gifted a power play late in the overtime period—Semin drew a dubious high-sticking penalty on Orpik—and Ovechkin had fired another scorching one-timer, like on his third goal. Knuble was standing on the edge of the Pittsburgh crease, trying to distract Fleury. "I never saw it," he said. "I thought they had blown the horn for his [Ovechkin's] shot. But [the puck] was under Fleury. I didn't see anything. I just got my stick on it and poked it through. Then I heard everybody yelling and I didn't really know what happened."

Ovechkin's shot had in fact hit the post—it just happened so fast that fans and even some players on the ice, including Knuble just a couple of feet away, thought it was in the net. A fourth Ovechkin goal would have been a fitting ending to the game, but still it was the Capitals' day against their rivals and Ovechkin's against his own.

It was a lost weekend for Crosby and his teammates and none took it harder than Orpik. He had no grudge with Ovechkin—he targeted his words at Semin, who had been a little too theatrical on the high-sticking call. "He sells it all the time," Orpik said. "The kid's a baby. I have zero respect for the kid."

If the NHL could have ordered up a showcase game, one to air on Super Bowl Sunday, it would have looked exactly like this one, a 5–4 triumph for the snowed-in team. The ratings weren't great—in fact, the NBC broadcast of the game, not surprisingly, was the least-watched program on the high holiday of network sports broadcasting. Boudreau was holding court and momentarily able to set aside some of the holes in his team's game—complaining about the details after a win like this would have been like complaining about cold cocktail wieners at the party of the year. An ebullient Leonsis walked around the room shaking the hands of employees and asking passersby if they have copies of his business self-help book, *The Business of Happiness.* He was a walking ad for the tome at this point. It was the last home game before the Olympic break and, yeah, it would have been great if more people had been able to make it through the snow to the game. Still, he had to believe that the playoff dates would more than cover any shortfall in revenues this day. He had to feel like the franchise, his pride and joy, was destined for special things. McPhee smiled, but he wasn't about to give in to enthusiasm that would overtake almost anybody else. He made it seem like just another win on just another Sunday. He made it seem like his chief concern was how he was going to get home through the snow.

It had been a glorious run of games—14 straight winds for the Caps—and this one topped it all. The Capitals had stepped up against the team that they believed they'd have to beat to get to the Stanley Cup. What's more, their best player, Ovechkin, had stepped up and outplayed Pittsburgh's top players. The best line belonged to Pothier: "Ovie's like the Incredible Hulk . . . the madder he gets the stronger he gets."

By the time Milbury was making his way out of the press section and to the elevator after the game, one of the bloggers accredited by Leonsis heckled him. "Who's Ovechkin's daddy?" the blogger said. The blogger continued to bait Milbury and used a cell phone to record video of the commentator's reaction, including profanities. Then the blogger, who weighed in the neighborhood of 300 pounds, tried to elbow Milbury as they boarded the elevator, leading to a fairly one-sided shoving match. Advantage Mad Mike. Despite the blogger's enthusiasm, the "daddy" issue wasn't a done deal just yet. Bigger things were in the offing. And it wasn't ever going to be something that would be settled in one game.

• • •

That Super Bowl Sunday contest between Pittsburgh and Washington in advance of the Vancouver Olympics was the 25th game matching Ovechkin vs Crosby in their careers. Ovechkin's team had won 9, Crosby's 16. The individual numbers were much closer: Ovechkin with 23 goals and 19 assists, Crosby with 19 and 24 respectively. In fact, the two could well have played even more often if the stars had lined up right—Canada and Russia didn't meet at the 2004 world juniors when Crosby was the tournament's youngest player. Nor did they meet when they played for their countries at the 2006 World Championships. Crosby missed a game against the Capitals with an injury in January 2008. And prior to the 2010 season, their teams had met just once in the NHL playoffs. If they were to remain relatively healthy, if they were to stay with competitive teams in the same conference, if they were to play in the Olympics and other international tournaments down the line, it would be reasonable to expect them to play each other 50 times at the bare minimum and, if the gods of professional sport smiled on the NHL, it might turn out to total 100 times or more. With no apologies needed to Bird and Johnson, theirs could be a rivalry without precedent in the modern history of sport. This Sunday in February had proved it one more time.

chapter 7

Madison Avenue, Washington, the Champs-Élysées

"You Basically just Signed the Babe Ruth of Hockey"

THE MONDAY AFTER the Super Bowl was a banner day in the New York offices of International Management Group. To be expected. One of the agency's clients, Drew Brees, had led the New Orleans Saints to an upset victory over the Indianapolis Colts. Few things are better to take to market than a Super-Bowl-winning quarterback. Then again, IMG had the biggest game of the year well covered. They also represented the quarterback on the other side of the line, Indianapolis's Peyton Manning, who, by the reckoning of sports-marketing experts, was already the hottest property among all athletes in the pro-sports leagues. Just as Manning could walk up to the line and call out audibles before his next throw, he could walk down Madison Avenue and call out the names of advertising outfits that wanted him pitching for them. And on that February morning in 2010, Drew Brees took his place alongside Manning.

While most people at the IMG offices were buzzing about the Super Bowl, David Abrutyn was thinking about the other game that played out that Sunday, the Capitals' win over the Penguins. Abrutyn and a team of marketing planners had invested a lot of time, expertise, and marketing clout in getting Alexander Ovechkin's name out there. They envisioned him endorsing a sports drink or a restaurant chain, but that was for down the line. In the first few months of their relationship with Ovechkin, they hadn't moved far beyond spitballing. They'd talk in terms of Ovechkin's "mythology" and "iconography." Super Bowl Sunday was the stuff that Ovechkin myths are made of. His performance befitted someone who was more than a star or hero, someone more like an icon.

Icons are nothing new, indeed they go back to the dawn of sport's modern era. There was a difference between the public image of Babe Ruth and the real-life George Herman Ruth. Images were the old media's narrative quiltwork, stories that would play to the public, that would sell papers or get listeners or, later, viewers. No one ever sat down and cooked up a Babe Ruth to sell to the public—a smart-alecky, hot-dog-eating, good-hearted guy who promises and delivers home runs for kids on their death beds. It came together by happy accident, the old media's almost involuntary forging of legends. The same played out for later Yankees heroes like Joe DiMaggio and Mickey Mantle, for Joe Louis and Sugar Ray Robinson, and for athletes in the whole range of pro sports.

The commoditization of athletes was the byproduct of Mark McCormack's push to realize the commercial potential of golfer Arnold Palmer in the '60s. So was IMG, the company he founded. Using a golfer to endorse products wasn't an original idea. Even though Bobby Jones was an amateur on the course, he was a professional off it, renting out his name and image back in the '20s and '30s. Golfers for all ensuing generations followed suit. But McCormack had another idea: building Arnold Palmer as a *brand*. McCormack had the perfect prototype: heroic, likeable, respectable, principled, and, most of all, authentic. He knew that Palmer's popularity was grounded not just in winning but in personality, in playing with style. McCormack also had an astute strategy—looking not for the highest bidder but rather the products that fit his image. "I made clear to Mark McCormack from the beginning that I didn't feel comfortable pitching a product or service I wouldn't use or didn't think was very good. That just seemed dishonest to me and I was pretty sure the public would see right through it," Palmer said.

McCormack taking Palmer to market was a seminal event in the branding of athletes and, in a larger sense, in the branding of celebrities. Hundreds of athletes across all manner of sports have followed Palmer to McCormack's door at IMG and profited from their branding and selling. Although Palmer now struggles to hit ceremonial tee shots, and most people aren't old enough to remember him winning majors, he remains an enduring brand. Others have stepped up and are poised to be Palmer-like figures for the next generation. Circa 2010, the lead brands on IMG's list are the Colts' Peyton Manning and tennis's Roger Federer. Still, the agency's bench is deep. It seems like they have half the big names, past and present, on the golf tours and the tennis circuits. The list of international soccer stars is long. Danica Patrick is the hottest name on IMG's grid of auto racers. And Olympic stars abound.

• • •

Though he had a hole in one in his first-ever round of golf at a team tournament, it's not clear how much Alexander Ovechkin knows about golf history. Still, David Abrutyn did say that IMG's long history with Palmer and his rival Jack Nicklaus factored into Ovechkin's decision to sign on with IMG in November 2009. No doubt IMG's work with Tiger Woods had a bigger influence on Ovechkin. A few years ago, Tiger Woods became the first athlete in history to earn one billion dollars in winnings and endorsements across the course of his career. The majority of money was made from his work off the course—it started with a huge deal with Nike and spread all around the Fortune 500.

When Ovechkin was negotiating with IMG, Tiger Woods was No. 11 on the Davie Brown Index (DBI), a listing of the celebrities who are most appealing for endorsements. This isn't just a list of athletes, but also celebrities drawn from every walk of famous life. The DBI is compiled by Omnicom Group Inc. from an online polling pool of more than 3.5 million respondents, and features 2,300 actors and entertainers, recording artists, politicians, athletes, and even cartoon characters. Woods had been in and out of the top 10 for most of the decade, ranking alongside Bill Cosby, Will Smith, Tom Hanks, Morgan Freeman, Robin Williams, and Oprah. The only athlete who gave him a run for his money was Lance Armstrong. "Tiger made a country-club sport cool and accessible to the broad public," says Matt Delzell, a director with Davie Brown. "Palmer and Nicklaus might have been on a list like this back in the '60s and '70s. There wouldn't have been an [active] golfer in the top 100 before Tiger."

Delzell said that the top 50 names "rarely change . . . they just switch places, moving around in their group." Yet not long after Ovechkin signed with IMG, Woods's serial infidelities with a gallery of ditzes and floozies were playing out in the tabloids and his stock fell to earth like a 9-iron to the green. His image as the cool Zen master, dutiful son, and private family man was shattered as was his marriage. He went from international brand to Jay Leno's nightly punch line in a matter of days. On the DBI he had plunged to No. 2,250, which is on par with comedian Pauly Shore and actress Pamela Anderson. His was an unprecedented fall from grace. What made it all the more remarkable is the fact that the DBI is weighted more heavily for awareness than for popularity. "You can't judge someone's influence or trustworthiness or likeability if you don't know who he is," Delzell said. "You can only start to judge that when you know who they are. Any situation, positive or negative, that gets them more exposure, tends to raise scores. Chris Brown, Rhianna, were well known but not by all demographics—when they start appearing on *Entertainment Tonight* or on *People* magazine covers they become recognizable to suburban soccer-moms or other less-aware demographics. Their scores went up, just because of awareness, despite bad publicity. Even negative publicity, scandal, can increase scores just by awareness—it's the old line about there being no bad publicity. But from our point of view—branding—there certainly is bad publicity. Bad PR is bad PR." In Woods's case, his awareness numbers would have been unchanged. His plunge was fuelled entirely by his image taking a battering—the collective resentment of the big lie.

One of the fundamental rules of branding is authenticity, what people within the public-relations and advertising industries call "brand truth." It was always true in corporate sponsorships, as demonstrated with the successes of Arnold Palmer. It is, if anything, even more crucial today with the advent of social media, 24-hour news, and an overheated blogosphere. Tiger Woods was able to soar on the DBI and other indices because, over the years, he was able to get out his carefully crafted image to the public. The risks of inauthenticity were demonstrated with the instant flatlining of his brand after the revelation of his serial infidelities. The only thing that the public likes less than a bad guy is being lied to, being played for fools by those who market a reprobate as an aspirational figure.

Delzell said that he thought Tiger Woods's fall was going to change the rules for branding and corporate sponsorships for celebrities going forward. "He has spoiled it," Delzell said. "We've used the term the Tiger effect in the past—what he was able to do for ratings on the last day of a tournament, what he was able to bring to sponsors of a tournament he played in, what he was able to do for the brands associated with him. As much positive as he did before, he's done as much damage after to celebrity endorsements in general. There's just a different approach, a lot more image-conduct clauses in a contract, a lot more research and background prior to signing somebody, more insurance clauses in a contract—he has made companies step back and think twice about associating themselves with a single celebrity endorser. If there was one person who you thought you could trust and then he plummets . . . who can you trust as a celebrity endorser?"

• • •

When Ovechkin signed on with IMG in November 2009, he was in the range of the 1900s on the DBI. There were only three figures from the game of hockey on the list. Wayne Gretzky was No. 467 and Sidney Crosby was 1,869. According to Delzell, this was mostly a function of "awareness." The sampling pool is most aware of and responds more strongly to actors, entertainers, musicians, and other public figures than it does to athletes, and those in the higher-profile sports—in football, baseball, and basketball—are simply known more widely than those in hockey, which is regarded as a niche sport. That Gretzky was so high on the list was just a long-term carryover from the spate of publicity he received in the '80s, including a *Sports Illustrated* Sportsman of the Year award—his name was known to almost 80 percent of the DBI's respondents. However, Crosby's ranking ahead of Ovechkin wasn't a function of a greater familiarity—Ovechkin was actually three percentage points ahead of Crosby in the awareness numbers—but rather a product of a more positive perception of Crosby. "Crosby scores well in the attributes other than awareness—in all the others he scores higher than the [celebrity] average," Delzell said. "Those that know him think pretty highly of him. We'd rather see that than someone who's well known but has low attribute scores. Ovechkin's attributes are lower than our average. The people we poll don't view him as trustworthy."

Yet IMG trumpeted the signing of Ovechkin. "IMG Worldwide, the premier global sports, media and entertainment company, announced today that it has signed hockey superstar Alex Ovechkin, for exclusive worldwide management, sponsorship, licensing and marketing representation," an agency press release announced, calling him "one of the most talented and exciting players in the game today." The press release went on to list his many awards and trophies and his status as an "Official Ambassador" to the 2014 Winter Olympics in Sochi, Russia.

In the press release, Ovechkin is quoted as saying that it was "an honor to join the list of some of the world's iconic athletes that IMG represents." It's hard to imagine that a guy who had to bribe a grade-school teacher with flowers for a passing mark would go around dropping "iconic" in his musings, so it's likely that IMG's first piece of business with him was scripting his statement—it wouldn't have been the first time that the image-makers had put words in an athlete's mouth, just one of the most painfully implausible ones. The truth is, the decision to sign on with IMG was made not by Ovechkin alone but by his team: his mother, his father, and Stephen Screnci, an attorney who advises the family. "Getting him out there in the mainstream and having him transcend hockey to the mainstream is why we thought IMG was best suited for him," Screnci told the *Washington Business Journal.*

IMG's enthusiasm for the signing of Ovechkin is hard to square with the DBI—he looked a long way from the mainstream—but it made sense to David Abrutyn. "This is really about Alex as an individual that has the ability to transcend his sport and be successful in the commercial arena," he told the *Washington Post.* "We've got a very long and distinct track record of working with global icons. The way that he plays, with sort of the energy and passion and excitement, when brand marketers are looking to align themselves with athletes or talent to cut through the very crowded marketing arena, those are things from an image standpoint that will translate very clearly. Alex's passion and excitement are going to be difference-makers for him and difference-makers for those companies that we align him with."

Abrutyn suggested that Ovechkin's personality—goofy, exuberant, fun-loving—made him the most desirable of hockey stars to bring into the fold. "Personality is a great asset that he brings to the equation from a brand-building standpoint," he said. "You're touching on something that not only hockey fans but other people recognize as something unique about Alex—that natural personality."

Unstated but understood was authenticity, the idea that the Alexander Ovechkin that we see is the real Alexander Ovechkin, that there are no complications, no issues when it comes to the construction of the "mythology" and "iconography" of IMG's latest client. Unstated but understood was the idea that the agency was placing bets on Ovechkin. A parlay: first, Ovechkin would have success on the ice, at the Olympics or in the Stanley Cup, preferably both, and then that success would make him a saleable celebrity.

• • •

The NHL has struggled to score its own wins in the forum of public opinion. For more than a generation—or two—the league has struggled to get its own brand out. The most successful initiative was at once a nod to the game's history and a marketing buzz-maker: the Winter Classic, an annual outdoor game. The league launched the event on January 1, 2007, with 71,000 people huddling for warmth in Rich Stadium, home of the NFL's Buffalo Bills, to watch the Sabres host Sidney Crosby and the Pittsburgh Penguins. In its four installments, the league had established a defined footprint on New Year's Day, previously the exclusive property of U.S. college football.

Though an earlier outdoor game with the Montreal Canadiens and the Oilers in Edmonton's Commonwealth Stadium had been a big one-off hit in Canada, no one anticipated the Winter Classic's breakthrough success in the United States, not even the executive who dreamed it up, John Collins, the NHL's chief operating officer. It's easy to connect the dots between his background and his brainchild. Collins came to the NHL after 15 years as an executive in the National Football League, both with the league marketing operations and with the Cleveland Browns. Not surprisingly, he sees Ovechkin in football terms. "Alex reminds me of Brett Favre," Collins said. "He's got that boyish, infectious enthusiasm."

When he first met Ovechkin on an NHL media tour, Collins saw marketing potential, even if others only saw a fashion disaster. "He was wearing black leather pants and a blue Cookie Monster T-shirt," laughed Collins. "He looked like a rock star. He acts like a rock star. He *is* a rock star. You can see the wattage coming off of him. It could light up Times Square."

Ovechkin presented a marketing guru like Collins an opportunity to draw new fans to the game, to get them to see the light and forget the league's troubles. After losing the entire 2004–05 season to a labor impasse with the players' association, the NHL was desperate to heal its image. Instead, it seemed every news cycle featured tales of woe. Teams in the Sunbelt losing buckets of money and, in the case of Phoenix, heading to bankruptcy court. Owners who cleared the NHL's background checks later being charged with financial frauds by the feds. NHL executives trumpeted triumphs, like the resurgent franchises in Boston, Chicago, and Washington and increases in corporate sponsorships, but still the league needed heroes. John Collins needed heroes.

The NHL's brass has talked about implementing a strategy borrowed from the NBA: the promotion of star players, the league's biggest names, as a means of promoting the league. Ovechkin and Crosby were made for that strategy. "We need to put our muscle behind a select few players and help them crack through the clutter," NHL executive vice president of marketing Brian Jennings said. "We need a surgical, precise approach."

By 2010, Ovechkin and Crosby were in their fifth seasons and other young stars were in position in major markets, yet the strategy hasn't exactly taken flight. Why has it stalled? Unfamiliarity: The league had never before pursued this type of marketing strategy. Culture: The game's unwritten rule was that no one, not even Wayne Gretzky, was bigger than his team or than the sport. So instead of showmen and characters, Collins was working largely with a cast of soft-spoken, impeccably polite, and, frankly, slightly dull twentysomethings. Resistance: Some, Crosby in particular, were willing to help out when called on, just as long as they weren't called too often and distracted from their day jobs.

Star promotion is still an initiative that the NHL pushes pretty gently. Jennings said that "using our stars in a heroic way" is a priority. It seemed that way when, back in 2008, the league brought in Young & Rubicam, one of the world's leading advertising agencies, to work on a campaign that featured Crosby and a few other young stars, with Ovechkin conspicuous by his absence. In Crosby's spot, Y&R superimposed Crosby on a still shot of his Pittsburgh teammates on the bench after they lost the Stanley Cup to Detroit that spring and had him speaking to fans, an eerie effect, as if he lived within the picture. Crosby said: "Getting this close and not winning the Cup. But, I know it will make our team stronger. I never want to be in this photograph again." It was a winning campaign but out of the NHL's comfort zone. It seems to regard its traditions as more bankable than emerging stars. Even while the Olympic tournament was playing out, Y&R was at work at the creative end of the NHL's next campaign—not surprisingly, one that celebrated great historical moments in the game, showing the likes of Bobby Orr, Wayne Gretzky, and Mario Lemieux in video-rewinds of their greatest plays. To marketing executives and mere onlookers, it would have been hard to tell if the league was mining its past or simply stuck in it. It was spectacular stuff, but, still, it was nostalgia.

The NHL has proven better with things than people, thus Collins and others in the New York offices have been focused on building large events, like the Winter Classic and the NHL awards, moving the ceremony to Las Vegas. They've bought into the idea that event-based marketing is a surer way to reach a mass audience in the short run. Even though the league understood the game, it was still working on a game plan for its young stars, Ovechkin, Crosby, and the rest.

There seemed to have been one move that could bring together the league's biggest event and its biggest star: getting Alexander

Ovechkin to the 2010 Winter Classic. Crosby had played in the first Winter Classic and it was a rousing success in North America. Getting Ovechkin into the New Year's Day game might make it break through in Russia and the rest of Europe. It made so much sense that the Capitals went so far as to book hotel rooms in Boston for December 31, immediately after the league announced that the Bruins were going to host the event at Fenway Park. When it was later announced that it would be Philadelphia, not Washington, playing in Boston, the Capitals were dumbfounded.

It was a missed opportunity to push the league's star through the clutter. Another missed opportunity, one that puzzles more than McPhee and the Capitals. "Alex has the biggest upside in the sport for now," said hockey marketing expert Brad Robins. "The question is, where is the game going?"

That was a question Ted Leonsis also asked, a couple of years after Ovechkin came to Washington.

• • •

By the spring of 2007, Capitals fans at the Verizon Center were cheering Leonsis during the pre-game ceremonies. His team was playing to capacity crowds, over 18,000 on average. After burning tens of millions in losses in his first seasons as owner, Leonsis was boldly talking about finally making money.

On the business side, a number of factors were in play, including a cap on team payrolls and a revenue-sharing plan. On the ice, a group of prospects were emerging as real players. Still, a lion's share of credit had to go to No. 8. In just two years he had become the biggest name in the Washington sports market. Leonsis kept clear eyes about the situation—he believed an important piece of business had to be addressed to sustain the Capitals' turnaround: a contract that secured Ovechkin's services for the long run.

Leonsis was trying to hold on to customers used to seeing the team come close but never win, and used to seeing talented players come to town and then leave. "People wanted to love the team but they were accustomed to a situation in which as soon as an Alex-Ovechkin-like player could leave, he would leave," said Leonsis. "They felt it wasn't a hockey market, not a hockey town, free agents don't want to play here. I think they trusted me. But we were a have-not."

This was the same reasoning that Leonsis applied in unnecessarily and ill-advisedly extending Jagr's contract, but he could better justify this one based on Ovechkin's performance on the ice and his impact on the business end. If the hungry-for-love owner didn't want to hear taunts again, if his franchise was going to keep its cachet, it was going to take the big deal. As it would turn out, to keep Alexander Ovechkin, Ted Leonsis was going to have to spend more money than he spent to buy the Capitals in the first place about $88 million. It was going to be the price of doing business, the price of staying relevant and, yes, the price of love. It was going to be the biggest deal that George McPhee ever negotiated.

• • •

The first piece of negotiation was a destination; that is, where they should get down to business. In the summer of 2007, McPhee was in Washington and Ovechkin was at his dacha in Russia. Geographically, they decided to split the difference and meet in France. This was the single instance of the two sides meeting halfway.

Neither the executive nor the franchise player had ever been to Paris. Instead of setting up in a conference room with contingents of advisors, the two strolled down the Champs-Élysées, took in the sights, and dined at fine restaurants, accompanied only by the Capitals' Russian scout, Gleb Chistyakov, a linguistic chaperone in case language became a problem. "The nice thing was," recalled McPhee, "that we could walk around and nobody knew him." Those sitting outside cafes had no idea the three walking down the street were talking about huge numbers, eight- and nine-figure dollar values. They just looked like mismatched tourists.

McPhee didn't just have experience in contract negotiations. He thought his knowledge of Ovechkin was going to be an asset in the talks. It went beyond seeing him around the arena like he had other players. Ovechkin had been a house guest of McPhee and his family when he first came to Washington at age 18, and he had gone out on bicycles with McPhee and his son.

In Paris, McPhee first had to get a read on Ovechkin's vision of his future: his comfort with the city of Washington and his belief in the Capitals' chances to become a championship team. In terms Leonsis would have understood, McPhee had to determine if Ovechkin was happy and if he was, what it would take to keep him happy. In Paris, McPhee had to figure out if Ovechkin could love his team enough to make a deeper commitment.

Ovechkin made his prime objective clear, and it was decidedly unromantic. "He wanted to be one of the highest paid guys [in the league]," said McPhee.

And so the dance began on the streets of Paris.

McPhee had originally targeted a five- or six-year deal in the neighborhood of $6 million per season, but the market for NHL talent was heating up, going from simmer to boil. Jarome Iginla and Joe Thornton, NHL all-stars, had been signed to long-term deals at around $7 million per year by Calgary and Boston respectively. Edmonton had extended an offer sheet to restricted free agent Tomas Vanek, seven years for $50 million. The Buffalo Sabres felt that they couldn't afford to let their 40-goal scorer walk away and grudgingly matched Edmonton's offer.

The new standard, however, was set by Pittsburgh's Sidney Crosby. Just before McPhee and Ovechkin arrived in Paris, the Penguins announced a new contract for Crosby: five years for $43.5 million, an average annual salary of $8.7 million, to match the No. 87 that Crosby wore and his birthdate (8/7/87). Two years younger than Ovechkin, Crosby had nonetheless shot past Iginla and Thornton. This raising and reraising of the bar meant $6 million or even $7 million wasn't going to cut it with Ovechkin.

Even before the deals for Iginla, Thornton, Crosby, and the rest, McPhee knew this wasn't going to be a conventional negotiation. It wasn't just that he had buttonholed Ovechkin on his own. In fact, Ovechkin did not have an agent certified by the NHLPA. He couldn't relay the progress of the talks to an experienced deal-maker capable of sorting through the numbers and strategizing. Ovechkin had been a client of Don Meehan, one of the biggest agents in the sport, when he first signed on with the Capitals in 2005, but by the summer of 2007 that relationship had gone sideways and ended. Ovechkin's only advisor, his de facto agent, was his mother, Tatiana Ovechkina. His father, Mikhail, assumed a far lesser role. For the duration of the contract talks, in Paris and for months going forward, it was clear that she set the rules. Before Ovechkin wanted to be one of the highest paid players in the league, his mother wanted him to be the highest paid. On her scorecard, the person with the most money wins. And there was no chance he would take less than Crosby. No chance.

McPhee and Ovechkin left Paris without a deal but with an understanding that they would pick up their talks later. Given the scale of the deal and the emotions in play, others were going to have to be in the room.

●　●　●

McPhee and Ovechkin stayed in touch over the rest of the summer by phone. Personal calls gave way to conference calls, with McPhee backed up by Ted Leonsis and team president Dick Patrick, and Ovechkin by his parents with Chistyakov doing the translating. By the time training camp rolled around, all the parties were meeting in a war room in the Capitals' offices. By this point, George Landa joined in, a family advisor who spoke Russian and was the president of ProAthlete Inc., a Boca Raton–based company. "I'd say it was mostly Alex and his mother," said Patrick. "His dad doesn't speak English too well. There were position papers talked about before we got into any negotiations, where we were coming from, where they were coming from, Sidney Crosby's contract came up right away just for a pride standpoint from their point of view. They were very determined. Very clear in what they felt things should be and what was important to them."

The Ovechkins didn't have to compromise if they didn't want to but to get a deal done, Leonsis and Patrick knew that the Capitals management team would have to—compromising not in dollar terms but rather in business principles. They were both "league" men. Leonsis had been a hawk among owners during the lockout, an outspoken critic of a system that allowed salaries to run up to unsustainable levels. His message: it didn't take a spendthrift to be happy. Patrick's league values were practically written into the coding of his DNA. His grandfather was Hall of Famer Lester Patrick, the coach of the New York Rangers team that won the Stanley Cup in 1940. Leonsis and Patrick thought that NHL Commissioner Gary Bettman had delivered a collective agreement that had brought labor costs under control. They knew that it would look like out-of-control salary escalation when the numbers being discussed went from eight figures to nine. That came when they tabled an offer of 12 years for $100-million.

Bettman couldn't impose his will on an owner's business, but all the league's governors knew he frowned on long-term deals. "Just generally, he thinks you could be making a mistake to enter into these contracts with an uncertain future and other CBA negotiations coming up," Patrick said. "You're taking away flexibility and you never know what's around the corner. He just thinks as a business practice, regardless of the player and the team, any team would be better off limiting the length of their contracts. And it's a valid point."

Leonsis and Patrick thought the $100-million offer was going to get the deal done. It didn't. On an annual basis it would have worked out to less than Crosby's salary—the kiss of death.

Weeks passed and talks continued. Finally, on January 10, 2008, the two sides agreed to a monstrous 13-year $124-million contract. The deal called for $9 million a season for the first six years and $10 million per season for the final seven. The average salary was $9.538 million, significantly more than Crosby's deal. Without an agent in on the contract, with just the son and mother tag-teaming the Capitals, every penny would go to Ovechkin.

It had started with talk about the love of the game and ended up as a matter of commerce. The terms seemed to leave some room for McPhee to build a team, but that was never expressed as a priority on the other side of the table—in contrast, that had been a consideration when Crosby did his deal with the Penguins. McPhee knew that this deal had significant risks—if he had come back from Paris with news that he had offered Ovechkin $124 million, Leonsis and Patrick might have either fainted or fired him. Still the general manager was reassured when the conservative Patrick had signed off on it. Leonsis was going to announce the signing at a meeting of season-ticket holders that night, a victory lap, a chance to get past the incident with the angry fan on the concourse. This was seemingly the ultimate piece of *The Business of Happiness.*

"His mother and I went into the corner of the room, she put her hands on my shoulders and looked me in the eyes and asked, 'George, is this a good contract?'" McPhee said. "I told her, 'It's a great contract.' But I remember wondering whether we were doing the right thing for our league. Things changed. The contract turned the market on." It also had the effect of turbocharging Ovechkin— often athletes grow complacent after signing a massive contract, but McPhee said Ovechkin started "playing even better after the deal was done."

Some agents with top NHL clients didn't regard Ovechkin's deal—an airtight, non-negotiable agreement under league rules—

The Canadian Press/Jacques Boissinot

At 17, Alexander Ovechkin was the leading scorer on the Russian team that won the 2003 world junior tournament in Halifax. He was also among the leaders in trash-talking and taunting the Canadians in the gold-medal game. Barely twelve months earlier he burst on the international scene with a dominating performance at the under-17 Challenge in Manitoba.

The Canadian Press/Karl Deblaker

Tatiana Ovechkina hugs her "Sasha" after his name is announced as the first overall pick in the 2004 NHL entry draft in Raleigh, N.C. She and her husband Mikhail (left) spared no expense when it came to developing his hockey talent. To this day the Ovechkins have stayed involved in the day-to-day affairs of their son. Tatiana looks after the business, while Mikhail, like he did in Moscow, sits in and scrutinizes every practice.

The Canadian Press /Paul Connors

In a game in Phoenix halfway through his rookie season, Ovechkin scores "The Goal," indisputably the most spectacular scoring play in NHL history. "At the time I didn't realize what had happened," said Brian Boucher, the victimized goaltender on the play. "I didn't know he was on his back. It was more I couldn't believe that the angle that he was at that it went in. I guess I'm proud to be a part of it. He's a world-class player. My son certainly gets a kick out of looking at it on YouTube."

The Canadian Press /Gerald Herbert

Ovechkin's scoring and the Capitals' play took off when Bruce Boudreau (in all red) came in as the team's interim coach. Boudreau had spent most of his career as a player, and all of his career as a coach, in hockey's minor leagues. Here, Boudreau talks with defenseman Brian Pothier, who saw his best chance at a Stanley Cup go up in smoke when the Capitals shipped him to the worst team in the league at the 2010 trading deadline.

The Canadian Press /Nick Wass

Ted Leonsis had gambled and squandered tens of millions of dollars on Jaromir Jagr as the Capitals' franchise player. Still the Capitals' owner believed Ovechkin was the key to making the perpetually money-losing team into a profitable enterprise. Here, in January 2008, Leonsis announces that Ovechkin has signed the biggest contract in league history: a 13-year, $124 million deal that both sides might live to regret.

The Canadian Press /Luis M. Alvarez

Ovechkin knocks Crosby off the puck in their last head-to-head contest before the 2010 Winter Olympics, a nationally broadcast game played in Washington on Super Bowl Sunday. Ovechkin's hat trick led the Capitals to a win in overtime. By the end of their careers they might play head-to-head more often than any league-defining stars in modern sports history.

The Canadian Press /Gene J. Puskar

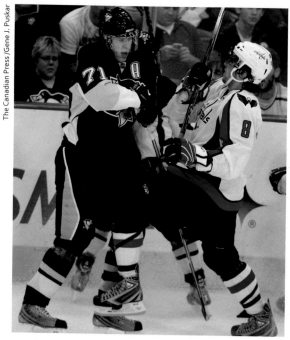

Ovechkin takes a run at Pittsburgh's Evgeni Malkin in 2008, at the height of their hostilities. Though they had played together on Russian national teams, an alleged fight in a Moscow bar between Ovechkin and an acquaintance of Malkin had poisoned the waters between them. The hard feelings were only put to rest at the 2009 NHL All-Star game in Montreal. The end of the feud was one of the reasons many rated Russia as the favorite for gold at the 2010 Olympic Winter Games.

The Canadian Press /Mike Carlson

Ovechkin celebrates his 50th goal of the 2008-09 season by pretending to warm his hands over a burning stick. To many traditionalists, opponents among them, the stick-on-fire routine crossed the line and amounted to taunting.

Bruce Bennett/Getty Images

The Russian Olympic hockey team went into an old Soviet-style lockdown at the Vancouver 2010 Olympic Winter Games under coach Vyacheslav Bykov. Seemingly, the lone expression of the players' individuality were these strange skates worn by Ovechkin for a couple of early games (but dispensed with by the quarter-final showdown with Canada). Ovechkin never fully explained why his skates featured an odd-looking ram—some described it as "demonic." Some in the Russian media have suggested that it was a play on the Russian work for sheep: *ovechka*.

ITAR TASS - Vitaly Belousov/The Canadian Press

Ovechkin's thunderous hit on Jaromir Jagr turned around an opening-round game at the 2010 Olympic Winter Games and seemed to be a portent of good things to come for Russia. Instead, it turned out to be Ovechkin's last good moment in Vancouver and his divided and dysfunctional team went home without a medal.

The Canadian Press/Nam Y. Huh

Ovechkin looks at Chicago defenseman Brian Campbell after he knocked him into the boards and broke his clavicle in a game in March 2010. The league judged the hit to be a dangerous play and handed Ovechkin a two-game suspension that cost him more than $200,000 in lost salary. Many thought the hit and the suspension forced Ovechkin to hold back for the rest of the season and in the playoffs.

Bruce Bennett/Getty Images

Montreal goaltender Jaroslav Halak celebrates as the Canadiens stun the hockey world by rallying from a three-games-to-one deficit and eliminating the Capitals in the first round of the 2010 playoffs. Ovechkin struggled throughout the series and couldn't beat Halak, an old nemesis, in the final two games of the seven-game series.

Ethan Miller/Getty Images for NHLI

For the first time in three years, Ovechkin wasn't voted the winner of the Hart Trophy as the NHL's most valuable player. But at the awards ceremony in Las Vegas, he did walk away with the Ted Lindsay Award, emblematic of league MVP as voted by the players.

as a great contract. "It's a ridiculous deal to lock up that long," one agent said. "With a top player like Ovechkin you want to get to the table to negotiate a contract as often as you can, so that his number [salary] reflects the market. When he signed the contract, his number reflected the market at the time but who knows what the market is going to look like down the line. You don't know what the collective agreement is going to look like or what position your team is in. You don't place that much value in long-term security that you sacrifice chances to get market value or move in free agency."

These weren't McPhee's concerns. McPhee had the franchise's owner and its chief executive on his side even if he was going to have to do a lot of explaining to his peers at the next meeting of league GMs. He knew he had done the right thing when he broke the news to a friend outside the industry and was told, "You basically just signed the Babe Ruth of hockey."

· · ·

A baseball signed by Babe Ruth can fetch $5,000 to $10,000 on the open market. Hersh Borenstein had a chance to buy up, in bulk, autographs from the "Babe Ruth of hockey" for $15 a pop.

IMG, the NHL, and the Washington Capitals reflect the business of Alexander Ovechkin on the grand scale. The agency, the league, and the team are big businesses. But the business of Ovechkin isn't all big business. Smaller operators have tied their fortunes to him. It's not a trickle-down effect either. These aren't, say, retailers in malls who are flogging licensed Capitals sweaters with his name and No. 8 on the back. These aren't Washington sporting-goods stores hoping Ovechkin's success will result in an uptick in the sales of hockey equipment. No, many smaller independent operators have been along for the ride with Ovechkin. He is a big business and many small businesses. Borenstein is representative of the latter.

Borenstein didn't get rich on Ovechkin. Before Ovechkin's rookie season a representative of his original agent contacted Borenstein to see if he had interest in an exclusive deal with the NHL's first overall pick of a year earlier. The deal was straightforward: a guarantee of $15,000 for Ovechkin to sign 1,000 autographs—either simple signatures or signed pieces for $15 apiece. "He told me that word around the office was that Ovechkin wasn't just one of the top rookies in the game but that he was actually one of the best players in the world. I congratulated him on his attempted up-sell and passed on the opportunity," said Borenstein, proprietor of Toronto-based Frozen Pond, a memorabilia retailer. Borenstein thought the price was outrageous and let the matter drop. "It was the worst business mistake I ever made," he said.

A Detroit businessman named Rich Sayig, owner of hockeyink. com, jumped at the chance. After passing on that initial opportunity, Borenstein had to negotiate with Sayig to get Ovechkin to appear for signings. In November 2005, Ovechkin appeared for Frozen Pond, which sold 274 tickets to the event at $39, plus had him sign another 130 pieces for the store's own stock. "He had no problem writing whatever people asked him to, which was nice since his English was obviously not fluent and words would have to be spelled out for him," recalled Borenstein. An appearance four months later, just after the 2006 Turin Olympics, was even more promising. The understanding was that if Russia made the medal round, Ovechkin would likely not make the February 27 appearance. The Russians did make it to the bronze-medal game, but Ovechkin came to the show anyway, flying from Turin to Madrid to Toronto, stopping at the Air Canada Centre to have an injured wrist attended to before making his way to Frozen Pond. More than 400 tickets were sold and he signed for almost five hours. "He was a dream guest," said Borenstein. "He talked to kids. He was friendly with adults. He did everything that was expected of him. I told him he was amazing and that it would have been completely understandable if he had cancelled on us. He told me, 'I said I would come, so I come.'"

Other shows for Frozen Pond went well. It wasn't just good-will that made Ovechkin the hottest name for the sports-collectors shows. He owned the territory because Sidney Crosby didn't do autograph sessions.

But the goodwill was in short supply by the time Ovechkin arrived at a signing for Frozen Pond in June 2008. Borenstein was disappointed with the show. Throughout the session, Ovechkin texted friends and watched TV, barely acknowledging those who had paid $59 each to get his signature. He wouldn't look at the camera when people asked him to pose, and refused to personalize his autographs for individuals. Borenstein got complaints, lots of them, one from a woman who had stood in line with her kids for four hours only to have Ovechkin essentially ignore her six-year-old child. Ovechkin had signed his $124-million contract five months before. Suddenly, a guarantee of $30,000 didn't seem quite so lucrative, at least it wasn't enough to buy his undivided attention for a couple of hours.

Hoping he had just caught Ovechkin on an off day, Borenstein set up another event, this time held in December 2008 at Wayne Gretzky's restaurant in Toronto. "Ovie was even worse than the last time," said Borenstein. "It was a really bad experience for us."

By 2009 Ovechkin was commanding upwards of $50,000 per appearance but doing fewer signings. This didn't seem to trouble Borenstein. "Ovie was not the same person," Borenstein said. "But he's not what he used to be. And it's doubtful if he ever will be again."

Borenstein missed out on a chance to tie his business to Ovechkin before his stock took off and their subsequent business relationship had soured over four years, but Borenstein didn't harbor hard feelings. He thought they were friends, especially when he crossed paths with Ovechkin at the 2009 NHL awards show. Ovechkin ran up to Borenstein and gave him a hug, but the businessman came away with a sense that Ovechkin had moved on, that he didn't have much time for those he had met and worked with on the way up. "I don't think he knew my name," Borenstein said.

• • •

In his first seasons with the Capitals, Ovechkin was a boon to the hockey media. He was usually accessible and often funny, sometimes unintentionally, other times just playfully. He was also self-deprecating, leaving it to others to take him seriously. He wasn't particularly analytical or insightful, but his fractured English often produced memorable and colorful phrases. "You can imagine a situation when you are running away from an angry dog," he told the *Washington Post* in a 2006 interview, describing the feeling of scoring a goal. "You've got a bit of adrenaline in your blood, right? Combine that with a sense of accomplishment, and you've got a goal." It made for good copy and winning sound bites. By comparison, Crosby and other young stars seemed rather bland.

By his fifth NHL season, it seemed like he dreaded the daily routine of talking to the media about his game. It was a strange turn of events—Abrutyn had brought Ovechkin on with IMG because of his irrepressible and natural charm just when the fun was going out of all the stuff that made him so marketable in the first place. When IMG had reason to get him out there, he started to withdraw, to protect his privacy, to guard his time.

In the fall of 2009, the *Hockey News*—a weekly Toronto-based publication founded in 1947 and for years known as the "bible" of the sport—named Ovechkin as the second-most influential figure in the game, behind only NHL Commissioner Gary Bettman. No Russian or European had ever been ranked so highly by the publication. It was an acknowledgment that Ovechkin's impact on the sport went beyond his superb skill—and just maybe a suggestion that he had more clout than Crosby. The *Hockey News* wanted to profile the Washington star. It was easy to arrange and it should have been easy to execute—the senior writer who drew the assignment, Ken Campbell, was a well-known 25-year veteran of the industry who had dealt with Ovechkin on numerous occasions over the years. At a party at the All-Star Game in Montreal 10 months earlier, a slightly looped Ovechkin approached, mussed Campbell's hair, and said "Hey, buddy." Campbell didn't anticipate trouble in putting together the story. "I thought I had a relationship with him," said Campbell.

The interview was set up on December 10 through the Capitals' media-relations department and the idea was that the *Hockey News* would get a day with Ovechkin to get an inside perspective on his career and life, or at least a good portion of a day. The *New York Times* had a 1 p.m. photo shoot with Ovechkin in full uniform on the ice at the Caps' practice facility, and the plan was that Campbell and his colleague Ted Cooper, producer of the *Hockey News* Web site, would tag along during the shoot, have some time to speak with Ovechkin afterwards, and then have a more extended session later that day in a luxury box at the Verizon Center during an NBA game between the Wizards and the Boston Celtics. It started badly. Caps coach Bruce Boudreau had cancelled the team's practice that morning, and Ovechkin, who lives about two miles from the Kettler Iceplex, showed up two-and-a-half hours late for the photo shoot without any apology. Just like a rock star. Campbell's initial interaction with the Russian star was disappointing. "When I walked out on the ice to watch his photo shoot, he didn't even acknowledge me. It was like I wasn't there," Campbell said. When the photographer was finished, Ovechkin dressed quickly and told Campbell he had to go but would see him at the Wizards game.

The interview at the basketball game went only slightly better. At tip-off, there was no sign of Ovechkin. Finally, with two minutes left in the first quarter, he arrived with his brother, Mikhail, and teammate Alexander Semin. The three made their way to the front of the box and sat chatting in Russian. "He shows up eating ice cream wearing a pair of pants that made him look like a homeless person. He was very nonchalant. He didn't say anything to me," said Campbell. Finally, worried that there wasn't going to be any interview at all after his company had absorbed the cost of sending him to Washington, Campbell approached Ovechkin and asked him if he could finally have some time for some questions. Ovechkin agreed, and they talked for about 15 minutes.

Campbell was encouraged. He thought that he might come away with scene-setting stuff over the course of the night. It didn't happen. "With two minutes left in the first half, he stood up and said, 'I gotta go.' And that was my day with Alex Ovechkin," said Campbell.

The veteran writer was one of a growing number of media people who had, in the previous months, suddenly found Crosby more engaging and willing to be interviewed than Ovechkin, a total change. "My sense is Alex takes on too many things, then he resents having to do them and then goes through the motions," said Campbell. "I thought we had a relationship he would at least respect. What happened to me typified the sentiment that he's changed. He's become jaded and worn down. He's feeling the burden of stardom. It's like it's no fun anymore. I still like the guy. But I've come to expect a lot less from him, as probably everybody has."

For Hersh Borenstein and Ken Campbell and others, it wasn't clear whether doing business with Alexander Ovechkin had changed or if the business of Alexander Ovechkin had changed him. For IMG it was a distinction without a difference. The task for Abrutyn and his team was twofold. First they had to get his name better known. Then they had to get people to warm to him—as a more likeable, trustworthy, and admirable figure, all the while maintaining his authenticity. If Abrutyn and IMG were successful, then Ovechkin's DBI numbers would swing from the negative to the positive.

●　●　●

Mark McCormack wouldn't have ever feared Palmer opening up. He wanted his client's story told—learning the game on the golf course where his father was the greens keeper, leaving Wake Forest after the death of a close friend, enlisting in the Coast Guard.

Palmer was accessible even in his prime when he was one of the best-known sports figures in the world. He genuinely seemed to enjoy talking to other people and telling them his story. He was downright loveable.

That, though, was Palmer in the 1960 and '70s. The sports world and the approach to branding were dramatically different by 2010. IMG had carefully micromanaged Tiger Woods—he wasn't an open book like Palmer, but rather an athlete cocooned in the game and sheltered by his entourage. The agency successfully steered Woods to hyper-celebrity, but a lack of authenticity became his downfall. Once the reality of his life was exposed as thoroughly out of sync with his thoroughly filtered image, the public felt betrayed.

In the run-up to the Vancouver Olympics, Abrutyn and IMG did sign off on giving a few media outlets access to Ovechkin. A *New York Times Magazine* profile rendered the colorful Ovechkin in a single shade of gray. *USA Today* also focused on Ovechkin the player and not his life story. It certainly wasn't the type of pre-Olympic rollout received by IMG's other winter-sports stars. Lindsey Vonn landed on the cover of *Sports Illustrated* in a skintight outfit that left nothing to the imagination, and she was around the set of NBC's *Today* show about as often as Al Roker. Shaun White graced the cover of *ESPN The Magazine* and was given the full profile treatment from *60 Minutes. Sports Illustrated* reduced Ovechkin down to sidebar status in its lengthy and glowing feature on Crosby.

Then again, Ovechkin's story was not like those of Palmer or IMG's Winter Olympic stars, or even Crosby. The circumstances of their lives were easy for the public to understand. Their stories weren't complicated. Not so Ovechkin's. It wasn't simply a matter of birthright. The public has warmed to other foreign-born celebrities. Ovechkin, though, was more foreign than most. He was born in a country where few in the West have travelled. Though he had come to North America eager to learn English and fit in with his teammates, he didn't embrace assimilation—he was steadfast in his Russian-ness. Abrutyn—who had worked in the marketing department of the Capitals earlier in his career—considered himself a hockey man but he could not have known the challenges that Ovechkin faced through the course of his young life. Abrutyn didn't know the story of the Russian players who paved the way to the NHL for his client.

But, then again, Ovechkin and his IMG handlers had to believe that Ovechkin could catch up and pass the others, Crosby too, with a victory and a great performance in Vancouver. If he scored a highlight-reel goal like he did against Brian Boucher and the Coyotes in his rookie season, if he celebrated a gold-medal-winning goal with a stick-on-fire routine, if he had an original and unforgettable signature moment, he'd be known and liked. The sports drinks manufacturers and fast-food chains would just be a start. In Vancouver he could go from hockey player to mythic hero and iconic celebrity.

chapter 8

Vancouver

"Like Gorillas out of a Cage"

IT WAS A MOMENT of perfect contact, the nearest thing to the meeting of an irresistible force and an immoveable object. It was also fraught with symbolism. It was a meeting of the current and former saviors of the Washington Capitals, a showdown between the best player in the world and another who once could lay legitimate claim to the title. It was hockey at its essence, beautiful and awful.

It happened in Vancouver, not quite two minutes into the third period of the opening-round game of the 2010 Winter Olympics between Russia and the Czech Republic. Alexander Ovechkin's team needed a victory to secure a favorable berth in the Olympic quarterfinals and was leading the Czechs 2–1. The Russians had to be encouraged by their play—they had dominated the action—but they also had to be fearful. If the Czechs scored a tying goal, all bets were off.

Jaromir Jagr carried the puck in front of the Czech bench and hesitated. This had always been part of his game. He waited for the other players on the ice to make their decisions so he could make his. They had to pick their spots and then he'd pick his, knowing his are usually better. Alexander Semin, Ovechkin's teammate on the Capitals, uncharacteristically hustled over to check Jagr, but Jagr slammed on the brakes and Semin went sprawling to the ice without having so much as bumped the Czech star. Jagr made him look foolish. *Olé.*

Jagr then stepped into the middle of the ice, passing a lazily back-checking and seemingly disinterested Ovechkin on the way. Ovechkin didn't even reach out with his stick to check Jagr. As it would turn out, Ovechkin was playing possum and Jagr didn't anticipate what was coming.

Jagr hadn't lost his game. He had left the NHL two seasons before and gone to Russia's KHL. Though 38 by the time the Olympics rolled round, he had looked as sharp and talented as ever, prompting discussion that he could return to the NHL and easily be the best player on a dozen teams. Maybe two dozen. He was no soft touch, no faded star, no easy victim. Maybe just a little less aware. Perhaps two years of competition in a league decidedly less physical than the NHL had shorted out his radar. Perhaps roaming large ice surfaces had given him a false sense of confidence. It was just at the moment when he presumed he was safest that he was, in fact, most vulnerable.

Jagr turned to his right to head up ice through the middle of the rink. He skated over the giant red, blue, green, and yellow inukshuk, the symbol of the Vancouver Games, that had been painted on the ice at Canada Hockey Place. Inukshuks are symbols of the Canadian Inuit culture, traditional stone monuments used as navigational aids for travel across the Arctic tundra. In this case, Jagr knew where he was going and what he wanted to do. *Let them catch up.* He just didn't anticipate what was coming.

Ovechkin had turned back to the middle of the ice, swooping towards the inukshuk logo. As Jagr moved the puck back into the center of his stride, he cut back against the grain, shifted his right shoulder back and turned his head to the right, dipping it slightly. Ovechkin abruptly turned hard to his left and drove his shoulder powerfully into Jagr's upper body. THWACK!

Jagr stopped dead in his tracks, tumbled backwards, and landed on his back. *Never been hit like that.* Ovechkin's left skate came well up off the ice but he kept his balance, perilously, on his right leg alone, like a figure skater. The back of his jersey was flipped up, the only evidence that he had collided with an opponent.

It was a spectacle of controlled violence. It was also an unforgettable sound. THWACK! The sound of two large bodies meeting, their armor pushed to its limits. The sound of Jagr's facemask cracking. The sound of all the oxygen in his lungs being emptied in a split second. Two enormous athletes travelling in opposite directions with different intentions, one without the puck and one with it, the impact of muscle and ligaments and bones. THWACK! A noise so simple yet so complicated that in an arena filled with 18,000 fans it was as if a prayer book had dropped in a silent church. "He hit Jagr, but it was like he hit all of us," said Ovechkin's Washington teammate Tomas Fleischmann, who was on the Czech bench at the moment of impact. "We all felt bad. Like we were dizzy." *That could be me next. That's what they have to be thinking when they're playing us in Washington.*

In hockey there's no immediate and ostentatious celebration of the big hit. Either the play carries on or it stops due to an injury suffered by the victim of the hit and, in that case, celebrating would just be bad form. Though this was one of the most memorable open-ice body checks in recent memory, Ovechkin did not celebrate. He couldn't, even though the hit immediately changed the momentum of an important game between two bitter international rivals.

The puck squirted back towards the Russian blue line and was quickly moved forward to Semin, who was back on his feet and heading down the left wing. Jagr, remarkably, had bounced back to his feet—he could have used a mandatory eight count to clear his head, but he still was giving a semblance of pursuit. That he was apparently unhurt, however, didn't lessen the effect on his teammates. As Semin carried the puck into the offensive zone, Czech blueliner Roman Polak kept glancing over his left shoulder, more concerned with Jagr than the Russian attack. *The play's not stopped?* Semin flipped a pass right through the slot to the far side of the rink and onto the stick of Evgeni Malkin, who fired the puck past Tomas Vokoun in the Czech Republic net to put the Russians ahead 3–1.

It wasn't just that Ovechkin had decked Jagr. That play had created a change of possession, which the Russians had quickly converted into a goal that they needed badly in a game they needed badly. It had shown the brute force that Ovechkin could apply to a hockey game, the difference he could make without ever touching the puck, the lethal combination that made him so different from so many other stars. Afterwards, Jagr was embarrassed, not for being the victim of such a sensational body check, but for giving the puck away. "The hit I don't really care about," said Jagr. "The mistake I made was turning the puck over and they scored. That hurt me the most."

Ovechkin had gone to Vancouver to help Russia recapture Olympic hockey glory for the first time in five Olympics, a drought that would have been unthinkable before the fall of the Soviet Union and the advent of NHL participation in the Winter Games. There were also other persuasive motivations for Ovechkin. He had assumed the role of national ambassador for his country in advance of the Winter Olympics going to Sochi, Russia, in 2014. The Sochi Games would be the first Olympics staged in his country since his hometown of Moscow had hosted the Summer Olympics in 1980. The Moscow Games had been boycotted by the top sporting countries of the West and, thus, they were forever diminished as was the gold medal won by his mother at those Games. The Games in Sochi would carry no asterisks. The 2014 Games were going to feature all of the best, and Ovechkin had made it clear to one and all that even if the NHL decided to end its involvement in the Olympic movement after Vancouver, he would go to Sochi on his own. His employer in Washington, Ted Leonsis, supported his franchise player's stance even though it was not the NHL's party line.

So Ovechkin arrived in British Columbia for what many believed would be the greatest tournament in hockey history as anything but a simple hockey player. At 24, he was possibly carrying the weight of more expectations and responsibilities than any other athlete at the Games. His hit on Jagr seemed to release all the fury, frustration, angst, and pent-up aggression built up by those expectations and responsibilities. It seemed to be his statement that he would not be denied. By the time the Czechs gathered themselves and began to compete again, the game was all but over, and Russia won 4–2.

What Ovechkin thought of his big hit was unknown. He and his teammates had gone into a media lockdown.

Russian coach Vyacheslav Bykov liked things out of the Cold War old school. With his practiced glower and a sense of style drawn from the KGB handbook, Bykov looked the part. He didn't volunteer much about his coaching philosophy, but he clearly believed that cloak-and-dagger had a lot to offer in team-building. Though national officials were supposed to release their final rosters weeks before the Olympics, Bykov declared his list of names was "preliminary" and reserved the right to make changes at his personal whim. Effectively, he treated the lineup for Vancouver as some sort of state secret.

Olympic athletes are supposed to be available for questions from the working media after competitions, and the NHL hoped participation in the Winter Games would elevate the game's profile, yet Bykov kept his players away from the cameras and microphones, almost a throwback to the days when the Russians regarded their best players as flight risks. Even friends and family were kept out of touch—when Leonsis called Ovechkin in his hotel room an unfamiliar voice at the other end told him that the player wasn't taking calls. It was a decidedly retro-Soviet approach to dealing with the public at the world's largest and most significant sports gathering.

Ovechkin's thoughts after the Czech game would have been an interesting footnote because, though no one knew it at the time, the devastating hit was going to turn out to be his best moment of the Vancouver Olympics. It would, in fact, turn out to be his last good moment.

• • •

The world's appetite for a Canada-Russia hockey showdown had been building for four years, ever since the Russians eliminated the Canadians from the 2006 Olympic Games in Turin, Italy. The Canadians had won gold in Salt Lake City in 2002, but the Russians sent the team organized by Wayne Gretzky home without a medal just four years later. Ovechkin scored the first goal in Russia's 2–0 win and celebrated with his Russian teammates that night in Turin. Few noticed that the Russians' Olympic run ended soon after with a loss to the Finns. Russia's moment was its victory over the Canadians. With the 2010 Olympics scheduled for Vancouver, the drumbeat towards the next Canada-Russia hockey confrontation, one that would almost certainly involve Crosby this time, started to build almost immediately.

In fact, a preliminary confrontation took place two years after Turin year in the gold-medal game of the 2008 IIHF World Championships in Quebec City. Canada led early and into the third period, but Russia, with Ovechkin on the roster after the Capitals had again missed the playoffs, stormed back and won the gold in overtime when an Ilya Kovalchuk blast eluded Canadian goalie Cam Ward. The result seemed to confirm the suspicion of many that Russia, not Canada, might be the favorite for Vancouver.

The Russians had an awesome array of offensive weaponry that included Ovechkin, Malkin, Kovalchuk, Semin, and Pavel Datsyuk. Guiding this group was Bykov, a former Soviet national team member and Olympic champion who had played his best seasons with Red Army before moving to French-speaking Switzerland for the final decade of his career. Bykov had been drafted by the NHL's Quebec Nordiques, but never crossed the ocean. Unsmiling and unable to speak English, Bykov was more European and Russian in his approach to the sport and certainly was not influenced by the NHL.

For years after the dismantling of the old Soviet hockey machine, Russia had seemed unable to get its stars on the same page, with many refusing to play internationally for the motherland because of one grievance or another. Bykov, however, had devised a formula for building a new cohesiveness among his country's top players, partly by assembling a roster made up of players drawn from both the NHL and the KHL. His approach was symbolized by his choice of Alexei Morozov as team captain. Morozov had been a one-time first-round pick of the Pittsburgh Penguins who had played seven years of mostly forgettable hockey in North America—he hit the 20-goal plateau once—before returning home. He played well for AK Bars Kazan, and year after year it was suggested that NHL teams had designs on bringing him back, but Morozov stayed put, eschewing the money available in the NHL to forge his career in Russia. For that loyalty to the country, Morozov was rewarded with the national team's captaincy—he wore the K even if he was a much less formidable heir than Russia's legendary captains, Boris Mikhailov and Viacheslav Fetisov. Bykov didn't necessarily regard it as a merit badge for officially sanctioned behavior. The coach had practical reasons, too. Ostensibly, Morozov could act as a liaison between Russian NHLers, with whom he had a shared experience, and Russians playing at home. Bykov pursued the concept that international success could be achieved by finding a way to get the two Russian solitudes to temporarily merge for major global competitions, and in Quebec City it worked. A year later, Bykov guided Russia to another world championships triumph in Bern, Switzerland. There were, however, still many possibilities for internal strife between those who stayed in the homeland and those who played in the West.

. . .

On the Russian team in Vancouver, the two most different personalities belonged to the two greatest talents. To the Russian public, Ovechkin, a Muscovite, is regarded as "street," a loud, brash character. He doesn't aspire to cool—he defines it. Malkin, on the other hand, is regarded as a country kid, quiet, modest, uncomplicated. In character, Ovechkin might have less in common with Malkin than with Crosby. That the two Russians would clash wasn't surprising. It might even have been inevitable.

A breaking point came in a bar in Moscow in 2007. Exactly what happened is a matter of some dispute. One version of events alleges that Ovechkin punched a Malkin associate named Gennady Ushakov, a balding, mustachioed 51-year-old former goaltender in the Russian league and an aspiring agent. According to this story, Ushakov was pushing Ovechkin to sign with him. Ovechkin has denied that he physically confronted Ushakov but Malkin confirmed it. "Yes," he told Joe Starkey of the *Pittsburgh Tribune-Review*. "Bad situation." Sergei Gonchar, Malkin's Pittsburgh teammate, was also drawn into the dispute.

If there even was a punch, how much damage was caused was unclear. A few went so far as to suggest Ushakov's jaw was broken. No matter the medical outcome, the incident set off a personal Cold War between Ovechkin and Malkin. They had been teammates in Grand Forks and roommates at the Turin Olympics, but for more than a year after the Ushakov incident they were barely on speaking terms. "I don't talk to those guys," Ovechkin said to a confidant one night when he passed Malkin and Gonchar at a restaurant.

The hard feelings carried over onto the ice, not that Ovechkin lacked for motivation when Washington played Pittsburgh. Ovechkin took runs at Malkin whenever he had a chance, as if he was out to maim him. The ugliest incident came on January 21, 2008—Malkin was circling behind the Washington net when Ovechkin came flying in. At the last moment Malkin twisted his body, and Ovechkin was travelling at such a high rate of speed that he was flipped onto his side in midair, his skates elevated two feet off the ice. Ovechkin crashed sideways into the boards, and when the whistle sounded and he got back on his feet, the two nearly came to blows. Malkin's agent, J.P. Barry, called it "very dangerous." After the game, Ovechkin was quoted as saying in a Russian interview: "But it is good that he is following [my movements] now. Because, if he puts his head down [again], I am not going to forgive him." Malkin, in turn, said: "So, it turns out that I am to blame now? What, I should be afraid to tell the truth? If a man does something wrong, he should make sure he doesn't do it again, right? Besides, everyone knows about [the agent incident] anyway, even if I didn't say anything. The whole world knows."

The fodder for the Russian tabloid press lasted through the 2008–09 season until both men arrived at the 2009 NHL All-Star Game in Montreal. With the Olympics slightly more than a year away, Olympic teammate Ilya Kovalchuk took matters into his own hands and arranged a meeting at a Montreal restaurant. Over vodka, the two shook hands. The next day at the all-star skills competition, Malkin handed Ovechkin a goofy hat and a pair of oversized sunglasses, and sent him on his way in the breakaway competition with a friendly squirt of Gatorade. "Those two guys are smart enough to do something like that by themselves," Kovalchuk told the *Hockey News*. "They're two great young players and sometimes miscommunications happen, but you have to get over it and that's what they did. These guys have always been friends." Ovechkin told the *Washington Times*: "It is enough. Like seriously—it is enough."

With the cease-fire arranged, everything was in place for Russia to take a run at Olympic gold. The consecutive world titles, both under Bykov, were compelling evidence that the Russians finally had their act together and could organize an Olympic team capable of winning again. All the top players were making themselves available, and while the number of Russians in the NHL was dropping dramatically, they were among the best in that league. Malkin went on to be named the Conn Smythe Trophy winner as the MVP of the 2009 playoffs. Kovalchuk had scored 189 goals over four seasons with Atlanta, while Semin had potted 34 goals in just 62 games with Washington in the 2008–09 season. In goal, Evgeni Nabokov was the No. 1 goalie for the perennial powerhouse San Jose Sharks, and in the months before the Vancouver Games Ilya Bryzgalov elevated his game, making the financially beleaguered Phoenix Coyotes a surprise playoff contender. Less known was the quality of players who would fill out the rest of the Russian roster, particularly with stars like Sergei Fedorov, Alexei Yashin, and Sergei Zubov having left the NHL. To most analysts, however, it didn't matter. Russia would be an offensive juggernaut with Ovechkin and the rest of the top two lines leading the way.

● ● ●

Everything in Russia, including sports, is filtered through a prism of politics. The Vancouver Olympic hockey tournament was a contest of talent on the ice and a contest of political wills behind the scenes. The Russian hockey culture was taking on the North American game's establishment and the International Ice Hockey Federation's officials were ineffectual intermediaries. The KHL and NHL signed an agreement on player transfers and other business matters in July 2008, but one day after the handshakes and goodwill, the KHL club Ufa announced that it had signed Alexander Radulov even though he was still under contract to Nashville. It was a deliberate and provocative act. The IIHF slapped Radulov with a suspension from international play but it didn't do Nashville any good. This almost guaranteed that others would follow Radulov's lead—and that the NHL might fire back.

The KHL was built out of the remnants of the former Russian elite league and had the official seal of approval from president Vladimir Putin—those wielding power in the Kremlin looked at the KHL not as a pro league like those in Europe and North America, but rather a development system for the building of a team for the 2014 Olympics in Sochi. The KHL's board of directors is headed by Slava Fetisov—though he had fought to gain his release to North America 20 years before, Fetisov had come back to Russia at the end of his NHL career and established himself as a rising star in the Putin government. Fetisov envisioned a league that would compete with the NHL for talent and would expand well beyond his country's borders.

The league was being underwritten by New Russian Jack, overnight millionaires and billionaires who had pulled the right strings and prospered in natural resources. Russian stars were coming home in part because the Russian teams outbid teams in the NHL and in part because of the promise of tax exemptions on their earnings. Despite the financial incentives, the KHL portrayed every Russian player who signed on with one of its teams as the author of a political statement, not just an endorsement of the league but a patriotic act. That was the impression that the political powers wanted to leave with the public—every returning player was a victory.

Still, the NHL didn't fret at all about most who had returned to Russia. Some, like Yashin, had North American careers marked by more contract controversy than excellence on the ice. Others, like Nikolai Zherdev, Ovechkin's former national junior teammate, were promising but ultimately unproductive.

NHL executives believed that their league's 28 Russian players represented the top end of Russian talent (Ovechkin, Malkin,

Datsyuk, and Kovalchuk) and most of the next couple of ranks of Russians below them. NHL general managers had no doubt that some Russians in the KHL were capable of playing in North America, but they were just as certain that none of them were up there with Ovechkin and the rest of the elite.

Coach Bykov was in an awkward position given Putin's support of the KHL. Going with an all-KHL team was not an option—it would have been outmatched against the top teams, closer to Latvia and Belarus than to Canada, the United States, and Sweden. The politics might have been right but the potential outcome eliminated it as a possibility. The coach couldn't go forward without Ovechkin, Malkin, and Co. and he knew it. Likewise, he knew he couldn't draw a team entirely from the NHL. His only option was finding a middle ground. He could help legitimize the KHL by making sure a sizeable chunk of the Olympic roster consisted of KHL players who played along with Ovechkin and the stars.

When Bykov named his team, nine of the 20 skaters were from the KHL, with all three goalies from the NHL. Some KHLers—notably Denis Zaripov, Sergei Zinoviev, and Morozov—had already served well on the back-to-back world championship teams. Still, some NHLers were shut out and not for lack of merit, including Frolov of the Los Angeles Kings, Slava Kozlov of Atlanta, Nikolai Kulemin of the Toronto Maple Leafs, Ottawa veteran Alexei Kovalev, Carolina winger Sergei Samsonov, and forward Artem Anisimov of the New York Rangers.

What was even more remarkable than Bykov's selection of the team was his approach to assembling his lines and managing his bench. Ultimately it was as though he decided to ice two separate teams within one squad, separating the NHL players from the KHLers in five-man units and spreading their ice time and responsibilities almost evenly. It was hard to imagine, but Bykov sometimes sat Ovechkin while his team was on the power play—Bykov went with a straight rotation of his lines. Ovechkin was used to getting 25 minutes of ice time each game with the Capitals, often more than that, but in Vancouver he was looking at 17 minutes and little more. It seemed like Bykov was intent on keeping his best players fresh for the elimination-round games, but Ovechkin's and Semin's and Malkin's body language told a different story.

The hockey world assumed the Russians would send a power-house to Vancouver. Instead the team became a political statement and an experiment in social engineering. Many thought that the Russian squad would be an updated and improved version of the Big Red Machine. In fact, the team was running no more smoothly than Mikhail Ovechkin's old Lada 6.

• • •

The subtext to the Olympic men's hockey tournament was the ongoing debate over the identity of the world's best player. Russia had Ovechkin, Malkin, and Datsyuk, the three Hart Trophy finalists. Canada had Crosby. Detroit's exemplary two-way forward Henrik Zetterberg and the Vancouver Canucks' league-leading scorer Henrik Sedin were Sweden's candidates.

Several fabled stars were participating in their last Olympic Games. It was like a championship fight where former champions are introduced before the bout . . . except in this case, players who had once laid legitimate claims to the title of the game's best were playing for their countries. Jagr was back with the Czechs, Peter Forsberg with the Swedes, and Fedorov for Russia. Each of the past stars had won Stanley Cups, while Jagr and Forsberg had led their countries to Olympic gold in the post-1998 NHL era. If Ovechkin, Crosby, and the others were to be considered as the best of their time, these were useful measuring sticks, if only by the memory of their greatness.

Jagr had left the NHL after the 2007–08 season, although he'd played all 82 games and scored 25 goals for the New York Rangers. Jagr wanted a two-year, $15-million-per-season contract to stay in Manhattan, while the Rangers, no longer getting contributions from Ted Leonsis, were offering a much lower salary on a bonus-laden one-year deal. Jagr bolted for Russia instead, signing with Avangard Omsk. "Once you make your decision, you don't look back," Jagr said in Vancouver.

Forsberg had been a hybrid player in his prime, known for fabulous offensive skills and perhaps for the most toughness pound-for-pound of any player of his time. He was acknowledged not for his ability to drop the gloves but his willingness to absorb incredible punishment to score points and help his team. That willingness shortened his career. Forsberg, only 36, had been forced out of the NHL by persistent foot and ankle problems and admitted he was no longer the player he had been. "It's a little frustrating," he said. "The young guys can go forever, but when you're older, you know where to go. That's the way I have to look at it. What you lose in speed you gain in experience. Hopefully that's going to show up in this tournament."

It seemed that among this old guard Fedorov had the best chance at gold and the best chance at making an impact. He wasn't far removed from the NHL game. The Capitals had acquired him from Columbus to serve as a mentor of sorts for their young Russians, notably Ovechkin and Semin—a well-compensated mentor at a $4-million salary. George McPhee approached Fedorov in the summer of 2009 to try to talk him into playing for less and extending his NHL career. Fedorov refused and, at age 40, the former defector returned to his homeland, signing a two-year deal rumored to be worth between at least $8 million with Metallurg Magnitogorsk of the KHL. To a significant degree, he had to keep playing, had to keep trying to draw a salary. He claimed he had lost $43 million to a former financial advisor Joseph Zada and was embroiled in a lawsuit.

When Russia opened the 2010 Olympic tournament against Latvia, Fedorov was there as the respected elder, although after picking up two assists in the 8–2 rout he joked that players were still calling him by his first name only, not the more formal Sergei

Mikhailovich they'd use if he were a much older man. "I have to goof off once in a while with them just to be part of that young, very electric group," he said. Fedorov seemed less convinced about the potential of the Russian team than many. "We have some talent . . . everybody gives us credit, but now we have to put it on the ice. Then you'll see, and so will we."

• • •

The first glimpse of the Russians' game in Vancouver told little about their chances of winning gold. Their opponent in their opening game, Latvia, had finished 12th four years earlier in Turin. The Latvians had only two NHL players in their lineup, Oskars Bartulis and Karlis Skrastins, and were hopelessly outmanned. Thirteen of their players were from the same team, Dinamo Riga, which sat 13th in the 24-team KHL. The game was given the last slot on the schedule of the day's games, 9 p.m., meaning that the game would air after midnight back in the East. The schedule-makers might have intended to bury a one-sided contest.

It was an after-hours type of crowd. As always, Latvian fans in maroon sweaters grew increasingly well-lubricated over the course of the game. The crowd was filled with Russian flags, and included a man in a gorilla costume wearing a Capitals jersey with "Ovechkin" on the back, and even a group of white-uniformed Russian sailors.

The Russians were exactly as advertised, explosive and prolific. Russian journalists cheered and clapped after every goal. The Russians came out looking as though each player wanted to score five goals. At the very least, they wanted to match the statement Canada had made earlier in the day with an eight-goal win over Norway. Zaripov and Radulov each scored for Russia in the opening eight minutes—Radulov gave it an extra flourish, "holstering" his stick after his goal. Ovechkin, playing on a line with Datsyuk and Semin, potted his first goal of the Olympics with 35 seconds left in the period off a feed from Semin.

It wasn't the first splash Ovechkin made that night. He went without his trademark tinted visor—illegal under Olympic rules—but wore a special pair of CCM skates with garishly painted blades. The images on the blades were unusual, a bug-eyed, gap-toothed sheep with a ribbon around its neck on each heel. Ovechkin later referred to them as "evil sheep." The skates were also adorned with a Russian flag and Ovechkin's No. 8.

The game was nothing more than an exhibition after the first intermission. The final 8–2 score flattered the Latvians. It ended up an easy win but one with midly troubling signs.

Ovechkin wasn't nearly as physical as he would usually be in an NHL game, as though he sensed a weaker opponent from a country that was part of his country when he was born. He would do just enough, no more. As the second period began, the Latvians actually created four or five good chances, and the Russians started getting bored and sloppy, firing long-bomb passes up the ice in hopes of engineering easy breakaway chances. Ovechkin didn't get a minute of ice time on a Russian power play, and Radulov and Viktor Kozlov barked at each other on the ice when their passes didn't click. Still, Malkin scored late in the period to make it 4–0. With just over a minute left before intermission, 35-year-old Latvian blueliner Rodrigo Lavins, all 5-foot-11, 185 pounds of him, took a run at Ovechkin inside the Russian zone. Lavins crashed to the ice, while Ovechkin barely wobbled.

• • •

Two days later, the Russians met the Slovaks in a game that figured to offer Ovechkin and his teammates more of a test than Latvia. It turned out to be a lot more than just a test.

Slovakia was a better team than Latvia. They had a contingent of NHL players, yet they were a very long shot to come out of Vancouver with a medal. The Slovaks had no single scoring threat who you could have mentioned in the same breath as Ovechkin and

Malkin—in fact, with the possible exception of Marian Gaborik, they didn't have a forward who would have made Russia's top two lines. Still, Slovak coach Jan Filc went in with a game plan.

Filc wanted his top blue-line pairing of 6-foot-9 Zdeno Chara and Andrej Meszaros out on the ice against Ovechkin as often as possible, with the checking unit of Michal Handzus between Richard Zednik and Lubos Bartecko also ready to hop over the boards. It was a self-evident strategy—it stood to reason that the Slovaks would want Chara, the winner of the Norris Trophy as the NHL's top defenseman the previous season, against the player who was the most potent scorer in the game, Ovechkin.

Filc also had a less heralded asset, a smaller man who would play a role equal to or bigger than Chara's in the game against the Russians: goaltender Jaroslav Halak. Halak was competing for but had not won the No. 1 job with the Montreal Canadiens before the Olympics, but he was the only near-elite goaltender available to the Slovaks. Little noted at the time was the fact that Halak had made life difficult for Ovechkin in an obscure contest at the world under-20 tournament six years earlier.

In the hours before the opening-round game with the Slovaks, the Russians had watched Canada struggle with Switzerland, eventually winning on a goal by Crosby in a shoot-out. If the Russians thought this game demonstrated that the Canadians weren't going to be quite as strong as expected, they took away the wrong lesson from a teachable moment. The Canada-Switzerland game proved that the gap between the first-rank teams and the next rank of contenders was closer now than ever before. For the Russians, Canada's narrow victory should have been a cautionary tale rather than a comfort.

When the Slovaks were caught with too many men on the ice, the Russians earned an early power play and sent out an outrageously talented five-man group that included Ovechkin, Malkin, Semin, Kovalchuk, and Gonchar. It was the hockey equivalent of the heavy weaponry wheeled through Red Square for the May Day parade. Ovechkin was stationed back on the left point, the same post he usually manned in Washington. The Capitals' power play had torn up the NHL all season and this looked like an immense upgrade, sure to light up the Slovaks—except it didn't happen. The Russians moved the puck around the perimeter and flashed some skill but to no real effect—they seemed to have no particular plan. The Slovaks killed the minor. It wouldn't have concerned the Russians too much at that stage, though.

The game was still scoreless late in the first period, and the Slovaks might have believed that Filc's plan had a hope of working. That hope was shaken when Ovechkin and Chara collided along the boards. It didn't have the sonic quality of Ovechkin's hit on Jagr, but it was bigger than anything you'd see in a month of NHL games. Chara dropped to a knee. Chara isn't just the NHL's biggest player, he's also regarded by most as the strongest, having trained with his father, a former Olympic wrestler. Yet strength-versus-strength it looked like Ovechkin had the advantage. *The other teams will be watching this one. It'll get in their heads.*

It looked like Ovechkin was prepared to take out the Slovaks' NHLers one by one. Early in the second period, Ovechkin steamrolled Slovak center Pavol Demitra, who was trying to come back from an injured shoulder that had kept him out of pre-Olympic action with the hometown Vancouver Canucks. The Slovaks, ranked eighth in the world by the International Ice Hockey Federation, were a banged-up team, with Gaborik nursing a deep laceration on his leg that left him limping. Another veteran, Miro Satan, was in the press box doing radio commentary for a Slovak network. But they hung in there even after Morozov put the Russians on the board and trailed only 1–0 going into the third. Bykov's squad was strong on defense but surprisingly quiet on the attack.

Ovechkin looked to be winning his individual battle with Chara. He wiped out the giant blueliner on one shift, then blew past him on a rush. The Russians appeared capable of nursing the slender margin to a victory, particularly after killing off a five-on-three disadvantage at the start of the third period. But with about ten minutes left in regulation time, a shot by Marian Hossa found a hole between Ilya Bryzgalov's legs to tie the game 1–1. A game that was supposed to be a challenge but eminently winnable had turned into a taut battle. Not exactly what the Russians had in mind with their high-powered offence.

Bykov's decisions behind the Russian bench then took a curious turn. For a power play late in the third period, he sent out a different unit than the one he'd used earlier in the game—no Ovechkin. And when Ovechkin did hit the ice for the final seconds with the man advantage, he was no longer assigned to the left point and instead wandered to the front of the net to look for tips and rebounds. It was not the role for a natural scorer—usually that dirty area out at the edge of the crease is reserved for the muckers and grinders. *I've got Knuble's job.* Bykov seemed to be relying on the players to figure it out on the ice as they played. All that talent and all those months of preparation, and the Russians were just tossing out five sticks for a power play.

None of the Russian lines seemed to click, and that continued into the overtime session. The one-on-one matchup between Ovechkin and Chara, meanwhile, had seen the giant Slovak take the upper hand as the game wore on. He blunted an Ovechkin charge down the right wing, then hit him hard into the glass. Chara then took the puck down the ice himself, swerved around Gonchar and nearly scored, forcing Bryzgalov to make a good stop. After a scoreless 10-minute sudden-death period, the game went to a shoot-out, and suddenly it wasn't a one-sided proposition. Slovakia had shoot-out specialists on par with the Russians.

Under the Olympic format for shoot-outs, three different players had to take the first three attempts for each country, and then it was wide open. The same player could take all the remaining shots, if a coach decided that was the best strategy. Halak had made 36 saves in regulation and overtime, looking anything but intimidated by Russian shooters he had seen before and stopped. The scene was set, and even with local time approaching midnight, the crowd was roaring, smelling the upset. The Slovaks shot first, with ex-NHLer Jozef Stumpel sliding in a nice backhand. Morozov's attempt to beat Halak on the blocker side was stopped. The tricky Demitra went next, but Bryzgalov knocked the puck off his stick with a pokecheck. Then came Ovechkin. He shot for Halak's five-hole. The puck hit the inside of the Slovak goalie's pad and dropped over the line. *Big relief.* After an aggressive Bryzgalov had stopped Hossa, Datsyuk had a chance to win the game for Russia. Halak waited in his crease, then uncoiled himself and delivered a perfect pokecheck. Now the shoot-out was going to sudden-death. As Crosby had done for Canada earlier in the day, Ovechkin could now shoot as often as Bykov wanted.

Russia now went first. Ovechkin bore down on Halak again and tried to make a forehand move on the snowy, rutted ice surface. No dice. Halak didn't even have to make a save as Ovechkin lost the puck. Stumpel's attempt to go five-hole on Bryzgalov was stopped. Kovalchuk came off the bench but shot wide. Handzus, with a chance to win the game, was stopped.

That gave Ovechkin his third chance. He took two short hops, then charged down ice. This time the deke would be to the backhand, but the shot was outside the left post. The greatest scorer in the game had been foiled twice by Halak with the game on the line and on neither chance had he even put the puck on net. *This shouldn't be happening.* Gaborik, the stylish winger, took his first attempt, but his shot went off Bryzgalov's right elbow. Bykov had seen enough of Ovechkin, and tapped Malkin to take the next shot. The Pittsburgh center's attempt was awkward. He swung well to the right wing, cut across the front of the net, fumbled the puck, and then flipped it harmlessly off the side of the net. In seven attempts, the very best shooters from the vaunted Russian attack had managed to beat Halak just once.

It was Demitra's turn again, this time with the game on his stick. He skated a wide arc to his left, along the boards, almost as though he had no intention of heading towards the goal. But he did. Skating slowly, the left-handed center held the puck as he meandered across the front of Bryzgalov's crease. Bryzgalov had stopped five of six shots and attempted several pokechecks. This time, he seemed frozen. Demitra dragged the puck behind his body and then, with a befuddled Bryzgalov finally forced to commit, he flipped the puck gently off the far post and in. Bedlam. The Slovaks had enjoyed little success against Russia, and now they'd beaten them at the Olympic Games. Canada Hockey Place was rocking, with the day's events surely having shown that this would be the best hockey tournament ever played. Canada had barely won, Russia had barely lost. Both had shown their vulnerabilities.

• • •

The victory over the Czechs had included Ovechkin's dynamic hit on Jagr, but he hadn't scored against either the Czechs or the Slovaks and struggled in the shoot-out. Other than serving as a pitchman for Sochi, he had remained elusive, unwilling to share his story with the world. "I'm trying to concentrate on my game, think about it more and not the media, my team and myself, just win the game, wanna win the gold. Keep my emotions, keep my strength, to myself," he told ESPN in a rare Olympic interview at Russia House. Suddenly he was sounding more like Crosby, no longer the swaggering superstar. Russia had two wins in three games heading into the quarterfinals against Canada, but had seemed unable to create the mesmerizing offence most had expected. Most of the KHL members of the Russian team wore green gloves from their club teams rather than Russian red, giving the team a mismatched look. This seemed to reflect the lack of cohesion in the Russian camp.

Canada, coached by Detroit's Mike Babcock, didn't seem much better off. The Canadians had lost to the United States in a 5–3 surprise, a game in which No. 1 goalie Martin Brodeur had struggled and made errors. Babcock decided to turn to Roberto Luongo, a move that played well with the Canadian media who seemed to blame Brodeur for Team Canada's defeat. Unlike Russia, Canada had to play an extra qualification game against Germany just to get into the quarterfinals. It was an easy 8–2 victory, with Luongo barely tested, but it had seemed exactly what the home team needed to get feeling good about itself. Like Ovechkin, Crosby's contributions had been limited, as if the pressure of leading the home team to victory was squeezing the life out of his game.

The game against Germany had allowed the Canadian coaches—Babcock and his assistants, Ken Hitchcock, Lindy Ruff, and Jacques Lemaire—to tinker with a few new ideas and combinations while outsiders focused on Luongo replacing Brodeur. Between them, the Canadian staff had coached 1,887 regular-season NHL games. Lemaire, Hitchcock, and Babcock had all won Stanley Cups as head coaches. In fact, Lemaire had eight Cup rings from his playing days, and 11 in total. This was the Olympics, not the NHL, but it was a game being contested mostly by NHL players on an NHL-sized rink. Canada had lost nine straight Olympic matches against Russian or Soviet teams, a drought stretching all the way back to the 1960 Games in Squaw Valley. But all those matches had taken place on the larger international rink, and most hadn't involved NHL players. That had been the case for Bykov as a player in 1988 and 1992 when he won Olympic golds. The situation in Vancouver, then, was far more foreign to Bykov than to the Canadian coaching staff, a group more attuned to making adjustments on the fly to suit the situation. Bykov went to Vancouver with an agenda and a blinkered vision of what his team had to do—while the Canadians were used to making more subtle changes over the course of a tournament.

The roster of the Canadian team had been forged amidst extraordinary scrutiny in North America, more than any other team in the tournament. In fact, the second-guessing had started the previous August at Canada's pre-Olympic camp, much of it surrounding the identity of Crosby's linemates. That Rick Nash would be one of them was a given. They seemed welded together from the start. First Jarome Iginla got a shot in the camp with the two, then Marty St. Louis. By the time the team was announced in Saskatoon on national television in late December, St. Louis hadn't even made the final cut, leaving Iginla as the obvious fit for Crosby and Nash. Other combinations seemed natural. Anaheim's Ryan Getzlaf and Corey Perry were a pair. The San Jose threesome of Joe Thornton, Patrick Marleau, and Dany Heatley would skate as a unit. Ditto for Chicago's talented young blue-line tandem of Duncan Keith and Brent Seabrook. In a short tournament, Canadian executive director Steve Yzerman theorized, it would help the team come together more quickly if some pieces were set beforehand.

To some degree, that worked. But it also soon became evident once the tournament started that Seabrook wasn't quite up to the Olympic challenge. Drew Doughty, the 19-year-old Los Angeles sophomore, moved in beside Keith. Iginla didn't seem to fit with Crosby and Nash and, when given an audition, Patrice Bergeron hadn't either. Scott Niedermayer and Shea Weber emerged as the top defense pairing, but players like Jonathan Toews, Mike Richards, and Brendan Morrow were finding themselves playing in different spots every game. Against the United States, the Canadians had scrambled and were prone to errors, while American goalie Ryan Miller stymied Canada's best shooters.

The qualification game against Germany, with little chance Canada would lose, served as a chance for Babcock and his staff to get in a little laboratory time. They had some ideas, most of them directed towards the combinations that would work against Russia, not Germany. Late in the 8–2 romp, Babcock tried a new line. Toews, who had been finding his stride increasingly during the tournament, would skate in the middle with Richards, usually a center with the Philadelphia Flyers, on his left side. Both were regarded as smart, tough, two-way players. Nash, meanwhile, was plunked down on the right side. Three young NHL captains. Only Nash had Olympic experience, and he'd been benched in '06. With the German game one-sided, media and fan discussion had by the third period turned to the Canada-Russia matchup. "We Want Russia!" chanted the sold-out crowd. Few noticed the new Canada line or what it might mean, but Babcock already believed he could put that unit straight up against Ovechkin, who was still playing with Semin and had been joined on a line by Malkin. *Eureka!* The focus was Ovechkin, and Babcock's idea was that the 6-foot-4, 230-pound Nash would present a physical impediment to the Russian star even though he wasn't generally regarded as a strong defensive player. In truth, because Nash played in Columbus and had only participated in the NHL playoffs once, his defensive talents were neither fully known nor appreciated. Hitchcock, stunned when the Blue Jackets had fired him just three weeks earlier, did know, however. "We believed that like a lot of offensively talented guys, if you told Nash what to do, he could do it," said Babcock. "He was a heavy body who could make it tough for Ovechkin." Behind Nash would be Weber, the 6-foot-4, 240-pound blueliner. "Weber wasn't going to give up an inch, and neither was Nash," said Babcock. "Nash was told never to forecheck off a face-off in the offensive zone. He had to bump Ovechkin. We didn't want Ovechkin to get the puck."

The Canadian plan was set, but it had one problem attached. Russia had the better record and so was the home team with the advantage of last change. Bykov, if he quickly recognized what was happening, could make it difficult for Babcock to get the Toews line out against Ovechkin. Russian coaches, however, rarely match lines in the same way as North American coaches, preferring instead to play five-man units, often just rolling them out, even on power plays. Moreover, Bykov wasn't familiar with NHL players. He might have seen Nash as just another offensive player that Ovechkin could exploit. So the quarterfinal game began with Canada getting those five players—Toews, Richards, and Nash up front, Weber and Niedermayer on the back end—out against Ovechkin. The trap had been sprung. "Right away, I liked what was going on," Babcock said. "I liked how much time we were spending in their zone."

Bryzgalov, who started the game on the bench as the Russian backup goalie, would later say that Canada charged out "like gorillas out of a cage." It was a colorful line repeated around the world, but it was a bit exaggerated. The actual facts were more strategic, almost surgical. There had been no media discussion of Canada's new checking line because Babcock had successfully cloaked the change. Even his own players were in the dark. "I didn't know until we got on the ice," Richards said. "We really didn't have a heads-up beforehand where we could talk among each other and say this is what we have to do. We just more or less got out on the ice and played against him. Those guys from the West [Toews, Nash, Weber, and Niedermayer] may not have played against him as much but I knew what his plan was, so we just suffocated him with pressure."

As the puck was about to be dropped, TV commentator Pierre McGuire noticed the new matchup of the Toews line against Ovechkin's unit. "Canada is showing their [sic] cards early," he said. McGuire, a former coach, seemed to notice the change more quickly than Bykov. Play-by-play announcer Chris Cuthbert, meanwhile, noted the Russians had been "sedate" in their pre-game warm-up and that Ovechkin had left the warm-up early. Still, it was the Russians who gained the offensive zone first, with Ovechkin charging down the right side against Niedermayer. The Canadian captain used his stick to easily knock the puck away, and there was a whistle a few seconds later. Ovechkin and his linemates, Malkin and Semin, left the ice.

Before they returned, Canada had the lead. Defenseman Dan Boyle had wheeled into the Russian zone, gone around Anton Volchenkov, and backhanded the puck in front. Getzlaf, not the fleetest skater in the NHL, had cruised past a half-hearted Viktor Kozlov and easily tapped the puck into the open side: 1–0 Canada after only 2:21 of play.

Bykov quickly deployed his top line and Babcock managed to roll out the Toews line again, with Weber and Niedermayer. Ovechkin took a pass along the boards deep in the Russian zone and spied Richards lining him up. This time Ovechkin wasn't trying to play through a shoulder injury, like he had been when Richards slammed him at the world juniors five years before. Still, instead of "eating" the puck and taking the hit to make a play, Ovechkin got rid of it quickly. *There's lots of time.* Ovechkin ended up flipping the puck into the middle of the ice and right on to Nash's stick. A moment later, Canada nearly scored. The home country was generating offence, Russia wasn't. On Ovechkin's next shift, he did little again against the Toews line, and when he left the ice the change was so sloppy the Russians were nearly caught with too many men on the ice.

Just past the six-minute mark, the Russians iced the puck, and Bykov had Ovechkin's line out for the defensive zone face-off. Babcock sent Toews, Richards, and Nash over the boards. "[Bykov] is playing right into Babcock's hands," said McGuire. "I wonder if he'll ever change out of it." The puck came around to Ovechkin on the left boards and this time he hurriedly one-handed the puck away to avoid a hit by Weber. Nash again intercepted it, but too late to hold the zone. No room for Ovechkin, just as Babcock has planned. *We've got him. No time. No mercy.*

Seabrook took a penalty at 7:58 when the officials fell for a rather obvious Morozov dive, and the Russians went on the power play hoping to tie the game despite the fact that their extra-strength unit had scored only twice on 16 chances in the tournament. Once more, it was a hodgepodge of talent. Up front it was Ovechkin, Malkin, and Datsyuk, this time with Gonchar and Fedor Tyutin on the back end. Ovechkin was bodychecked along the boards by Weber, and the impact broke his stick. When he went to the Russian bench, he first had to wait for a new stick and then was given the wrong one. Total confusion. The next time down the ice, Ovechkin drove along the left boards and tried to spin back towards the boards. Doughty was ready. He drove his left forearm into Ovechkin's lower back, crumpling him to the ice. Ovechkin's head hit the boards. *No mercy. No time. No respect.*

Still, it was a one-goal game, and Russia managed four shots on the power play. Canada had the lead, but the Russians were in the game with the first period more than half-over. At 10:26, Volchenkov again had difficulty handling Canada's speed to the outside and was forced to pull down Crosby and take a penalty. The Russians had nearly killed off the penalty when Boyle took a drop pass from Heatley and took a wrist shot through a screen supplied by Marleau that beat Nabokov and made it 2–0. Three San Jose players had combined to put one past their own Sharks goalie, who looked decidedly tentative. At the next face-off, Bykov predictably sent out Ovechkin, Malkin, and Semin, and Babcock again responded with Toews, Richards, and Nash. No response at all from the Russian coach even though his line hadn't created a scoring chance and had surrendered several to the forwards who were ostensibly there to check them. "I can't believe Bykov hasn't changed out of that matchup," said a disbelieving McGuire. "If they don't change out of that matchup they're going to get lit up like a Christmas tree."

Ovechkin finally received a pass in the neutral zone without Nash in his face and headed towards a backpedaling Weber. He cut into the middle of the ice, sensed that Weber was holding the line and that there was back pressure from a hard-skating Nash, and flipped a pass across the ice to Semin, who was turned away by Niedermayer. Malkin scooped up the puck and circled high in the Canadian zone towards the middle of the ice with Toews nipping at his heels and hacking at his stick. Richards was waiting for him, and Malkin coughed up the puck. The Canadians rushed up the ice, aided by the fact defenseman Denis Grebeshkov had inexplicably gone too deep into the Canada zone, leaving only Red Army captain Konstantin Korneyev back.

As Toews carried the puck over the Russian blue line, Nash churned up the ice, his long strides eating up huge chunks of real estate. Toews flipped a backhand pass into the slot and Nash grabbed it at the hash marks. Nabokov, a shutout hero over Canada four years earlier in Turin, panicked. He hadn't been out challenging

Toews, but when the puck moved back into the middle of the ice, he readied himself for a pokecheck and dove feet first to his right, stacking his pads. Nash easily flipped the puck high into the net to make it 3–0. Two Canadian goals in 46 seconds and a building gone berserk. It had all unraveled so quickly for Russia. Bykov called a timeout. His players heard his words but one thought had to go through their heads. *The game's over. There's no getting the gorillas back in the cage.*

Nabokov was thoroughly rattled, but he stayed in the game—again, another dubious decision by Bykov. As soon as Dmitri Kalinin made it 3–1 with a long wrist shot, Canada's Brendan Morrow made it 4–1. By the fifth minute of the second period, it was 6–1. On the sixth Canada goal, three Russians—Semin, Ovechkin, and Malkin—had congregated to contest a loose puck along the boards in front of the benches against Richards, who was sitting on the ice. Still, Richards won the battle, setting up a slap shot goal by Weber. Nabokov was pulled with tardy mercy, and Bryzgalov went into the Russian goal. Partway through the second, Fedorov replaced Malkin on Ovechkin's line. It was more a symbolic act, a little star turn for the fading veteran, than a meaningful move.

The Russians had lost the strategic battle, their goaltending had gone south and their stars had been neutralized. At some point in there they had lost the will. The final score was merely mathematics, 7–3 for Canada; their first victory over Russia at the Olympics in 50 years and a compete humiliation for Ovechkin and his countrymen. Two-time-defending world champions, and they wouldn't even get to play for a medal.

• • •

At his home in Alexandria, Capitals defenseman Brian Pothier had some explaining to do to his six-year-old boy, Jake, as father and son watched Canada annihilate the Russians. "Jake said, 'Alex is on your team, but you're sitting on the couch,'" Pothier said. "He couldn't understand why I wasn't playing. I tried to explain it to him but then I just said, 'Son, just watch the game.'" Pothier, from the Boston area, claimed to be indifferent to the result, but he wasn't really. "Selfishly, I knew if the Russians lost we would get our guys back earlier instead of playing two more games. Selfishly, I felt that would be good for the Caps' season," he admitted. "This way they get five or six good days of rest before we play Buffalo next Wednesday." Tomas Fleischmann, playing for the Czech Republic, had also seen his country eliminated, as had Nicklas Backstrom with Sweden. All the Caps' Olympians had tasted the same bitter wine of early defeat.

Pothier was unsparing in his analysis of the Canada-Russia game. "Canada just played much better, much more aggressively, and much smarter. The Russians just turned the puck over and over, all in the important areas. They tried all these crazy passes and they just ended up creating chances and two-on-ones for the Canadians," he said. "I thought Canada was borderline flawless. I was so impressed with Weber, the way he played against Ovie, finishing every check and making it really hard on him. He played a phenomenal game. I thought he was the best Canadian player. It's a tall task to go out and compete with a guy like Ovie." If there was an upside, Pothier figured, it was that Ovechkin and Semin, in particular, had learned a hard but invaluable lesson. "I thought it was a great example of what to do in the playoffs to be successful. If you don't play smart hockey, you're not going to win. There's not enough room on the ice to toe drag and try to beat guys one-on-four."

Like Pothier, Bruce Boudreau had watched the game from his couch. It was a game he had eagerly anticipated. "My sense of it was I wanted Canada to win, but I wanted Ovie to do really well because of all the scrutiny and pressure he was under," Boudreau said, protective of his star player. "But I don't think he had his finest hour."

Before the game, Boudreau wasn't sure what impact a Russian victory or defeat would have on the Capitals. "Was it better for us for the Russians to lose so we'd get our players back earlier? Or if they won, would it motivate our guys even more to win the Cup?

We over-analyzed it to death." As a coach, he saw the result as the correct one. "Before the game, people were asking me who's gonna win? Who's gonna win? I said I didn't know. But when the game was over, it made so much sense that Canada won. When you looked at the KHL players the Russians had and some of the older Russians, I thought, wow, of course Canada should have won."

Boudreau felt Ovechkin would return and quickly readjust to the NHL. "I think we'll get the same Alex back. It'll take him a week to get over it. He's a very proud man and I guarantee you he would love to go back and play that team again," said Boudreau. "It was like he was the torchbearer for the entire Russian Olympic team. He loves his country. There's no doubt in my mind he felt the pressure of the Olympics. His mother had been an Olympic champion, and he wanted to do well for that, as well."

What Boudreau had seen, however, was his captain stripped of the joy and passion that had defined his on-ice persona. "Against Canada, I didn't see that excitement. I saw, 'Oh man, this is not what I expected.'" Getting that joy back in Ovechkin's game, Boudreau knew, would be critical to Washington's season and the playoffs.

As expected, at home there were repercussions to the Russian defeat.

"Disaster . . . like end of the world," said Bryzgalov, bracing for the worst.

There was anger. "It was the worst game in Russian history," said the Toronto Maple Leafs' Nikolai Kulemin, one of the Russian NHLers left off the team.

Bykov had little explanation to offer after the game. "Everything was just bad . . . nothing helped," he said. The Russian coach bristled when asked about rumors that his charges had been enjoying Vancouver's nightlife a little too much. "Let's get the guillotine or the gallows out, yeah?" Bykov sneered at *Sovetsky Sport*. "We have 35 people in the squad. Let's cut them all up on Red Square."

That it was a disaster and an embarrassment to a country that had not enjoyed much success at the Vancouver Games outside of hockey either was a theme picked up by Russian media. "Nightmare in Vancouver," read a headline in *RIA Novosti*, the state-owned news agency. "Red Machine Runs into Maple Tree," said *Pravda*. After the Olympics, the head of the Russian Olympic Committee quit after being told he should resign or he'd be fired.

Crosby, who hadn't shone that game either, chose not to gloat. "That's for you guys to decide," said Crosby when asked if it was another win over Ovechkin in their rivalry. "We won a game. It happened to be against Russia."

Ovechkin went without a goal in Russia's final three games after potting two in the easy win over Latvia. Other than the crushing hit on Jagr, he hadn't distinguished himself, but then neither had Kovalchuk, Semin, Malkin, or Nabokov, the other big-name NHLers who were supposed to lift Russia to gold. More than anything, they all looked like individuals, nothing like the well-oiled Soviet teams that once ruled the Olympic world. Even Semin and Ovechkin, who played together in the NHL, had looked more like strangers than linemates. Ovechkin had been no worse than his mates, and no better.

Where he was notable was in his unusually brusque, nearly secretive approach to the media and the public in Vancouver. The day after the Canada defeat, he was caught on video in an uncharacteristically menacing fashion confronting a woman with a video camera, grabbing the camera and apparently knocking either her or her camera or both to the ground before stalking away. The 22-second clip made it to YouTube and was viewed around the world. Supposedly Ovechkin had been set up by the Russian tabloid press—this woman was looking to provoke him like a Hollywood paparazzo would Britney Spears or Lindsay Lohan. It was probably a measure of his celebrity in Russia that he would be targeted by scandal sheets. Still, just months after the Tiger Woods debacle, it was another branding nightmare for IMG. For the Caps, all the hard work they'd put into building the Ovechkin persona in D.C. over the previous five years had been, to some degree, damaged.

McPhee mused wistfully afterwards that he should have sent Nate Ewell, the team's capable media relations executive, to Vancouver to look after Ovechkin.

For Leonsis, it was a familiar problem. Leonsis had been suspended and fined by the NHL six years earlier after an altercation with a fan, and in Ovechkin's Vancouver incident he saw the same unfortunate realities. No matter how many positive interactions there had been with fans and media over the years, one negative moment would be the image that lasted. "I thought, something is up there, because I'd never, ever seen him like that. Never. I think it was a Russian documentary that was supposed to be 24/7, and it was like, could you just get out of my face for a second," said Leonsis. "His body language and even his facial structure looked different. I think he realized I'm fighting invading armies with knives and forks." Leonsis told a story about getting an e-mail from a fan who had seen the Capitals play in New York with his children and had waited by the team bus afterwards hoping to get an autograph. Ovechkin walked over, introduced himself, got a picture with the kids, and then got on the bus. "The e-mail said, 'Twenty-two other players walked on the bus. No one saw that. Alex didn't have to do that. He's a great guy and my kids are going to be fans of the Washington Capitals for the rest of their lives. They feel like a billion dollars. The greatest player in the world saw them in New York City and gave them an autograph.' Now I'm sure during one of his trips to Edmonton or Calgary or something he didn't sign somebody's autograph. And there will be a big stink about it. But that's the responsibility that comes with this bigger-than-life, greatest thing."

When Ovechkin returned to Washington after staying in Vancouver for the closing ceremonies, he met with the Caps' owner at the Kettler Iceplex in Arlington, Virginia, the team's practice facility. The two men hugged, Ovechkin sat on a leather couch in Leonsis's office and Leonsis pulled an armchair over so he could have an intimate debriefing with his $124-million superstar. "He was shattered. Just shattered," said Leonsis. "I think he felt like he personally had let down everybody because they didn't win. The ending didn't turn out the way he envisioned. And he had envisioned a lot. The Russians put a lot of responsibility on him. He was the ambassador, the spokesperson, the closing ceremony guy, and I think he was tired and jet-lagged. All those things. And now it's over and there's nothing you can do about it for four years."

Leonsis's own experience with his first Winter Olympics—he left Vancouver before the Canada-Russia game—had been a decidedly mixed bag. He had signed on with his fellow NHL governors to be part of the Olympic family, yet while he was in Vancouver he was cut off completely from Ovechkin. "I'm thinking I've got five players here that represent a couple of hundred million dollars in contracts. I've shut down my team and ultimately I've lost some of my players for a month. About a week before the Olympics they kind of checked out and went to the Olympics. My thank you was two tickets to a suite for every game. That's what I got back out of it. I [can't even upload] the Ovechkin hit on Jagr on my website [because of the IOC's broadcast agreement]. I got two tickets. And so, analytically, you'd say, that's a really bad deal."

Leonsis had endured the questions from his fellow owners about Ovechkin's vow to go the 2014 Olympics in Sochi, Russia. "I just hope if we go back again the players really know what they're in for. It's really easy now to say of course we have to go, the last one was great. I remind people, what if that final was Slovakia and Belarus. How would we feel? I'm still a proponent for us to go. I want to support Alex. I just want our eyes to be open. I don't want there to be this reaction of, 'Of course we have to go.' Because it's complicated. Much more complicated than we think."

At their debriefing, Leonsis said he told Ovechkin he would have to be more demanding of the Russian hockey authorities. "I asked Alex, what was up with the power play? And he said the coach told us, 'You guys figure out how you want to play.' I said to him, 'This is your decision. They're using you like the face of the Olympics. You need to be demanding that if it's going to be in Sochi and you're going to insist on playing that they can't embarrass you and the other players. They have to be very committed to it. They have to make the investment. They have to really care about the deliverable and the end product. It's nothing to take lightly, to think, well, just because we're playing in Russia we'll win.'"

• • •

In the aftermath of disappointing performances by Russian athletes in many events in Vancouver, the nation's Olympic officials blamed systemic dysfunction. "If we make a list of all those who should be held responsible," Gennady Shvets, a Russian Olympic Committee spokesman, said on Russian radio, "then it would be half the population of the country, because, unfortunately, many took part in the destruction of athletics or passively looked on. In the 1990s, everything was destroyed. When stadiums were turned into markets and pools into VIP saunas, athletics collapsed." If Shvets is right, then Ovechkin might turn out to be the most prominent member of the last class that benefited from the traditional sports institutions like Dynamo that survived the fall of the Soviet Union for a decade or so but won't be developing athletes for Sochi.

Ovechkin spelled out problems with his team for Leonsis but otherwise avoided the topic completely. He broke his silence three months later in an online chat with Russian fans through *Sovietsky Sport* and seemed more perturbed with the reaction of people in his homeland than with the team's failure and his own performance. "I understand that the fans will long remember how we failed in Vancouver. But we tried. We didn't just go there to get the Olympic uniforms for free and then go back to our clubs and play hockey. We have not succeeded. What can we do about it now? People who have poured mud and said bad things are not real fans. This is the crowd who behave like the weathervane. If everything is good with us today, they are with us, if tomorrow it's bad, they turn away. I think this is stupid. I do not understand these people. The real fans will never cast a stone at you when you're struggling on the ice and trying to defend the honor of your country. You can't win all the games in a row. At this time there were these circumstances. Yes, we lost. But, guys, don't turn away from your team. This is our team, there's no other one."

But there was another team, one that offered him another shot at one of those moments worthy of myth and becoming an icon.

chapter 9

Buffalo

"This Is a Crazy Business"

OVECHKIN COULD HAVE gone back to Washington immediately immediately after the loss to Canada, but he stayed four extra days in Vancouver—he wanted some downtime, and he wanted to represent his country in the closing ceremonies at B.C. Place. When he saw Canada win the hockey final against the Americans on Sidney Crosby's overtime goal, he had to be reminded of what might have been. Racing from the boards to the front of the U.S. net, finishing with sure hands, throwing his gloves in the air, waiting to be mobbed by his teammates: Crosby again had something that Ovechkin wanted, Olympic gold. Maybe more than that, Crosby owned another unforgettable moment, one that would be replayed thousands of times over the next four years.

In a baby-blue Sochi sweatshirt, Ovechkin paraded with the athletes at the closing ceremonies—the musical headliner was Neil Young, somebody who'd never show up on Ovechkin's playlist in the Capitals' dressing room, though Ovechkin would probably agree with the idea that it was better to burn out than fade away. Ovechkin waved to the fans in the stands and worked hard to smile. It would have been easier if he knew for sure that he was going to be at the Winter Games in four years' time and that he'd have a chance to beat Canada and Crosby, and all the other best players in the world.

When Ovechkin arrived in Washington for practices before the NHL reopened for business, he seemed drained, physically and emotionally. He wasn't hurt but he seemed wounded. It was the same when the Capitals arrived in Buffalo for their first game back together after an almost three-week break.

● ● ●

The start of the game was held up for an obligatory ceremony: the introduction of the Sabres who had played in the Olympic tournament. As expected, Ryan Miller, the Sabres' goaltender, was introduced last and received most loudly for his heroics on behalf of the American team that lost to Canada in the gold-medal final. The cheers rang unhappily in the ears of those on the Capitals' roster who had no medals at all to show for their own trips to Vancouver—Ovechkin, Semin, Varlamov, Backstrom, and Fleischmann. Each carried the disappointment of their country. For his part, Miller already seemed weary of the attention and acknowledged the cheers with a raised stick but nothing more. He had already moved on. *Forget the Crosby goal. Never thought he'd shoot from there.* Playing for gold had given way to playing for a shot at the Stanley Cup. For Ovechkin, meanwhile, this night was going to be his own painful re-living of his Olympic experience. The first two periods of this contest against the Sabres felt like the fourth and fifth periods of Russia's blowout quarterfinal loss to Canada.

Ovechkin wasn't pouring down the left wing against Canada's Shea Weber—Canada's best on the blue line was back in Nashville, back in the distant Western Conference. No, Ovechkin was skating into the chest of Tyler Myers, a 6-foot-8 20-year-old rookie defenseman. Everybody had watched the Olympics and seen the punishing puck-denying job that Weber and Rick Nash had done on Ovechkin, and everyone included Lindy Ruff, the assistant coach charged with managing the Canadian Olympic blueliners who was now back coaching the Sabres. Myers wasn't Weber—not now, maybe down the line—but he was another oversized, long-armed body who offered a different set of challenges for Ovechkin. Ruff hadn't just seen the Canada-Russia game, but also Slovakia's earlier upset of the Russians, and in that game the success of Zdeno Chara snuffing out Ovechkin's fire. Again, Myers wasn't Chara. He wasn't quite as tall, not nearly as tough or experienced. But Ruff could coax a passable impression out of him.

The Washington captain looked like a dragonfly dive-bombing right into the maw of a Venus flytrap, swallowed up into the tangle of Myers's oversized limbs. More than a dozen shifts through two periods played out just like that. Ovechkin had looked physically spent even in his first few attempts to squeeze by Myers along the boards or to somehow toe-drag his way to open ice. He seemed to slow as the game went on. Ovechkin wasn't, as Brian Pothier had described it, the Incredible Hulk, getting stronger as he was getting madder. He couldn't generate a scoring chance at even strength. The lessons of Vancouver weren't lost on Myers and his teammates. *Put a body in front of him. Put a body on him. Bump him. Don't let him get a pass.* The state of Ovechkin's game and his spirits that night were as plain to them as the number on the back of his sweater. *Don't back off. Go at him when he's vulnerable.* Patrick Kaleta, a Buffalo-born winger of no great distinction, treated the league's most feared player with disdain, as a mere target. Ovechkin skated down the wing, heading into what looked like yet another lockup by Myers. Instead of trying to skate by him, Ovechkin pulled up just inside the blue line, steps in from the boards. At that moment, standing dead still with the puck, Ovechkin didn't spot Kaleta steaming in from the middle of the ice. Ninety degrees to Ovechkin's right shoulder. He never saw it coming.

It wasn't a dirty hit—not in the back, not with an elbow high, not a drive into the boards. It was an open-ice hit by a player who was giving away 20 pounds to Ovechkin, a player who remembered being illegally driven into the boards by the Washington captain in a game in November. Ovechkin was tossed out of that earlier meeting with Buffalo, but the NHL opted not to suspend him. Kaleta didn't have to bend or break the rules to get retribution and leave Ovechkin in a heap on the ice. Kaleta floored Ovechkin like Ovechkin had floored Jaromir Jagr in Vancouver. As Ovechkin lurched back to his feet and made his way to the Washington bench from the far side of the ice, he looked like a beaten boxer searching for his corner at the end of a round. Kaleta got an ovation from the Buffalo crowd second only to Miller's that night. Ovechkin looked exhausted. If it had been a blind test with no numbers and names on the sweaters, you couldn't have picked out the guy on the ice who had won the Hart Trophy. It might have been his most desultory performance all year.

Yet the Capitals won the game. Efficiently. Clinically. Easily. The final score was 3–1, but the Sabres posed almost no threat, generating only four shots in the second period and only 23 for the game. Miller kept Buffalo in the contest into the third period, turning aside 37 shots. The fans who had cheered Miller before the game booed the home team off the ice at game's end. After the game, reporters gathered around Washington's head coach Bruce Boudreau. "I just told [the players] that that was our best game in 10 games," the coach said.

• • •

Any team with Alexander Ovechkin in its lineup would be tempted to lean on him too much in a time of need. *Okay, big man, it's your time.* Basketball offers a star talent a slim chance at ultimate success with a mediocre supporting cast. Kansas won a U.S. collegiate basketball title with "Danny and the Miracles," player of the year Danny Manning and four other guys as forgettable as Smokey Robinson's backup vocalists. The same phenomenon has played out in the pros, with Portland winning a title with Bill Walton, the game's best center for a stretch in the late '70s, and four journeymen on the court at any given time. In hockey the nearest thing to a star winning a Stanley Cup with modest support came back in 1999 when the league's most valuable player and its best goaltender, Dominik Hasek, singlehandedly took the Buffalo Sabres within a couple of games of a championship, even though they didn't have anyone else resembling an all-star on the roster. In all games, though, and in hockey, in particular, history shows that a star needs talent around him.

Whenever Wayne Gretzky and Mario Lemieux raised the Stanley Cup they were able to hand off the trophy to teammates who would go on to be inducted into the Hockey Hall of Fame. Ray Bourque was the game's best defenseman for a generation, but he didn't win a championship until late in his career when he joined the Colorado Avalanche, a team that featured other future Hall of Famers Joe Sakic and Peter Forsberg.

George McPhee drafted Ovechkin and assembled other talents through the draft, trades, and free-agent signings. That's the big picture. Often over the years, though, even the most individually talented teams have hit the rocks, undone by the day-to-day stuff. Arguably the most difficult job was making stars and the chorus work together—not just driving them to play industriously night after night, but identifying roles for them, finding the right fits and coaxing them to buy into the team program. Ovechkin, the star talent, was spotted and identified years out, back in Selkirk. The fellow who could bring the most out of him and his teammates was the most unlikely figure, someone the NHL had managed to overlook for 20 years.

• • •

Bruce Boudreau's stories inevitably position him as either the butt of the joke or the bewildered onlooker. And he loves to tell stories. If he doesn't start telling you a story when you cross paths with him, that only means you've walked into the middle of him telling another epic tale of his hockey life. He comes by the nickname Gabby honestly. Some of his stories have grown better over the years and seem almost too good—or bad—to be true. Sometimes the facts get twisted—he riled his mother when he credited her with an extra year on the planet in his folksy 2009 autobiography, *Gabby: Confessions of a Hockey Lifer.* "She called me and said, 'Your book is filled with mistakes,'" Boudreau said. The story of Boudreau landing the job as the Washington Capitals' head coach in 2007 seems too good to be true on a first pass. A career minor-league coach toughing out millions of miles on buses finally landing an NHL job: it was Horatio Alger doing hockey. It needs no enhancement.

Boudreau became the 34-year-old playing coach of the Fort Wayne Comets back in 1990, and for the next 17 years NHL teams expressed no interest in him as a head coach. His credentials were indisputable. He had more than three decades playing and coaching in the minors. As a coach, he'd won championships, developed players, more than paid his dues. Yet over the years that had resulted in just one sniff of an NHL job. In 2003, while working as the head coach of Los Angeles's farm team in Manchester, New Hampshire, he had been interviewed for an assistant coaching job with the Kings. Boudreau thought he had the inside track. Instead, the job had gone to another veteran minor league coach, John Van Boxmeer.

Effectively, he had been branded. NHL executives just looked at him as a minor-leaguer. Boudreau ruminated about what might have been and what he might have done differently. If he had a do-over, maybe he wouldn't have skated as an extra in *Slap Shot.* It seemed like the people who might have hired him didn't realize it was just a movie, like his single scene left him hopelessly typecast as a guy who couldn't hope for more than the Charleston Chiefs.

This was consistent in all Bruce Boudreau stories: he was the butt of hockey's cruelest joke. He had played 141 NHL games along the way and 30 in the World Hockey Association, but they'd been spread over a decade, just enough to tauntingly remind him how close he was and what he was missing. "Of course, I was the same guy who was playing in the minors at 38 years old still hoping I'd get called up to the NHL," he said. "I'd always told myself that a fella named Connie Madigan had played as a rookie for the St. Louis Blues when he was 38. I just never wanted my dream to die."

Still, Boudreau did not consider himself a victim—in fact, luck surely looked his way when he switched off one of the doomed 9/11 airliners back in 2001 at the last minute—he had clear eyes about his plight. He partly blamed himself, just as he always did for not getting further as a player, for lacking the personal discipline to translate his skill into a big-league job with big-league per diems. As a coach, he figured that while he knew what to do, he didn't look the part and didn't know the right people. Enough people had told him that. He had lots and lots of friends. Just not the right ones. He was chubby, always had been, even when he played, and had let his weight balloon up to 242 pounds at one point, way too much for his 5-foot-10 frame. Becoming diabetic in 1997 didn't help that. He was bald and wore suits in a way that suggested either they were poorly fitted or he was impossible to fit. He called himself "the Columbo of coaches," after the Peter Falk character in the television detective series from long ago. He wasn't a superbly coiffed man in a $2,000 suit like so many of those NHL types, and he didn't communicate his ideas in theorems, but rather in old-fashioned, common-sense hockey talk. With lots of stories attached. For NHL teams looking for something or someone to sell as much as a coach to coach, he just wasn't part of the conversation.

Boudreau embraced the laissez-faire, common-sense style of George Armstrong, his coach with the Toronto Marlboros a junior dynasty. Armstrong had played for the Leafs for 21 seasons and captained four Stanley Cup champions in the 1960s. Nicknamed "The Chief" for his native heritage, Armstrong took over the juniors who played out of Maple Leaf Gardens and turned them into national champions in the 1970s, among the greatest teams in junior-hockey history. Armstrong was old school and his style was quiet and simple. His players loved him for it. Some practices he would just throw a puck out on the ice and tell the players to play "hog," which meant keep the puck as long as you could, and when you lost it, figure out a way to get it back. "He allowed us to do things with the puck," said Mike Kitchen, a teammate of Boudreau with the Marlies and eventually an NHL head coach in St. Louis. "He was quiet, but if you ever asked a question, it was more than answered. He would sit at the front of the bus and some of us, Bruce and myself and Trevor Johansen, would sit up with him and listen to his stories." That had a lasting impact on a generation of players who came through the Marlboro organization and endures to this day.

• • •

In 2005, George McPhee and Doug Yingst, the general manager in Hershey, received 82 applications from hockey men who wanted a shot at the head coach's job with the Bears, Washington's AHL affiliate. After several interviews, they chose Boudreau, who had been fired as the coach of Los Angeles's minor-league affiliate. "You could tell he was an honest guy who knew his stuff about players," McPhee said. "It felt less formal. He just talked. You didn't get a lot of that in interviews. He was a guy's guy, a really likeable person."

Boudreau had immediate success in Hershey, but, like the others who had bypassed Boudreau before, McPhee had reservations about him, not on substance as much as image—he just didn't look like an NHL coach. McPhee doesn't come off as a hard-ass boss or any sort of executive despot, but he knows something about the power of persuasion. He had once coaxed one of his scouts, Eddie

McColgan, to quit smoking as a condition of a new contract. At the Capitals' training camp in the fall of 2007, McPhee decided to sit down with Boudreau and try to have a similar discussion with him about his weight. "I said, 'You're a good enough coach. You can coach in the NHL. But your appearance might be holding you back.' I was hoping it would [work] but afterwards, I really felt like I had hurt Bruce's feelings. I really felt bad after."

The decision that finally delivered Boudreau to an NHL bench, the decision that turned the Caps from a youthful squad with potential into immediate winners, would eventually be viewed by others as a stroke of genius by McPhee. It wasn't. It was made hesitantly. It was more like a tentative half-swing on a golf course, with the ball ricocheting off a tree, hitting a rake lying in a sand trap, and bouncing onto the green.

The Capitals had a plan that called for patience in the first two seasons after the lockout but significant progress in year three. That was advertised in the team's slogan going into the 2007–08 season: *New Look. New Season. New Attitude.* "We wanted our players to develop a work ethic and good defensive habits in the first couple of season because they were going to be around for five or six years," says Glen Hanlon, a former NHL goaltender who had taken over as Washington coach from Bruce Cassidy 26 games into the 2003–04 season. Hanlon has been characterized as a defense-first coach, something he bristles at. "That's the farthest thing from the truth, Hanlon says. "In those first two years after the lockout, our best chance to win was [goaltender] Olaf Kolzig. He gave us a chance to win 2–1 games if we limited chances. I think my approach wasn't all defense—I wanted our players to score—Ovie scored 50 goals. I wanted them to play aggressively. We needed all the goals we could get."

New Look. New Season. New Attitude. The promise of change looked like a bad joke by November 2007: the Capitals didn't get nearly enough of those desperately needed goals and had just six wins in 20 games, and it looked like a fourth straight year out of the playoffs was in the offing. To McPhee's mind, it wasn't that Hanlon had the wrong approach to the game but rather that he simply had lost the room—it seemed like the Capitals players were tuning out a disciplinarian coach. On the night before Thanksgiving, the Caps were hammered 5–1 at home by Atlanta. With the club off to its worst start in 26 years, McPhee decided to fire Hanlon. The general manager had two candidates for the job (one rumored to be former Washington captain Dale Hunter). But he needed someone behind the bench right away, someone to get on the ice with the team at practice the next day.

The next morning, a ringing phone woke up Boudreau at his home in Harrisburg, Pennsylvania. Yingst was on the line telling a bleary Boudreau to expect a call from McPhee in five minutes. "I thought I was getting fired," Boudreau recalled. Quite the contrary. "George said, 'We want you to coach the Washington Capitals.' I said, 'Oh-oh-kay.' Meanwhile, my wife is waking up and rubbing her eyes. I'm trying to play it cool, but I'm pointing my thumb upwards towards the sky. I'm going up, I'm trying to tell her."

McPhee swore Boudreau to secrecy because he hadn't yet told Hanlon. But Chloroform couldn't have kept Gabby quiet. His wife, Crystal, obviously knew, but Boudreau was bursting with the news. In short order he made his promotion hockey's hottest rumor. He quickly told his three kids from his first marriage. Daughter Kasey was in Ottawa working for the Senators, while sons Ben and Andy were both pursuing pro hockey careers in the minors. His son from his marriage to Crystal, Brady, was still sleeping. As he drove from Harrisburg to the Kettler Capitals Iceplex for his first practice as the Caps' coach, he called John Anderson, a former teammate with the Marlies and a career minor-league coach who was also waiting for his first NHL shot. It was a call out of the blue and Anderson was suspicious that something was up after reading about the Capitals' loss the night before. "Is this the new coach of the Washington Capitals?" Anderson asked his old friend. "Yes it is," Boudreau told him. In fact, McPhee had only named Boudreau interim coach, but he didn't want to ruin the moment with the details.

• • •

The record shows that Boudreau worked out far beyond McPhee's limited expectations and even beyond the general manager's wildest imaginings. The Caps posted a 37–17–8 record under him in that first season, a surge that won the Southeast Division and returned the club to the postseason for the first time in five years. Boudreau won the Jack Adams Trophy as the NHL coach of the year.

The remarkable thing wasn't what Boudreau did but rather what he didn't do: he didn't make sweeping changes to the lineup. "Yes, they had talent," said Yingst. "But they'd had that same talent before he got there."

Boudreau just worked the Capitals' dressing room. He was a complete professional and emotional counterpoint to his predecessor, Hanlon. A tense, grinding man with a shock of fiery-red hair, Hanlon had been a professional goaltender for 14 years, the first in the minors but the rest in the NHL with Vancouver, St. Louis, New York, and Detroit before retiring in 1991. A few years later he had made his way back into the NHL with a job that Boudreau had longed for: a gig as an assistant coach with the Canucks. After four years there, Hanlon had come over to the Washington organization, first serving as the head coach with the AHL affiliate in Portland, Maine, for three seasons, and then joining the Capitals as an assistant. Most of Hanlon's adult life had been spent in the NHL, where veterans are accorded the respect reserved elsewhere for tribal elders, where young players were expected to defer and not make waves. As Washington's head coach, Hanlon had liked his veteran players and been hard on some of the youngsters. One of the players Hanlon had been hardest on was Mike Green.

It's easy to see how Green wouldn't have been a favorite of Hanlon, how he'd frustrate a coach. The Calgary native wasn't brash, just a curious character who seems young for his years. Even after a tough practice Green looks like he just woke up—not just the bed head, but also the seeming obliviousness to things going on around him. On game days, he'll walk out of the dressing room in a suit that might have been left over from his high-school formal. Sometimes his shirt is untucked. Sometimes his pants aren't even done up. A lot of coaches would think that he's too clueless to be a NHLer—harsh but true. Green's game was the antithesis of the values that Hanlon was trying to instill in the team. "We wanted our defensemen to support the rush, not lead the rush," Hanlon said. "We didn't want [our defensemen] to stop behind the goalline at the other end of the ice with his skates stopped. I didn't want to pay some forward to play defense for us 30 sec of 45 second shift while a defenseman is [freelancing] with the puck." In describing what he did not want his team to do, Hanlon pretty well provided a thumbnail description of Mike Green's usual game. Under Hanlon, Green was a talent at risk of falling through the cracks, a prospect who might never have panned out.

The change in the Capitals under Boudreau was evident from the first day. "That first practice was a memorable moment," said Brian Pothier. "Green, Steckel, Gordon, Laich, all these guys who had played for him in Hershey, they were just flying in practice all of a sudden. They were different players."

No one was more different than Green. From Boudreau's first day in Washington, Green was like a prisoner unshackled. "It was like an anvil was lifted off his shoulders," Pothier said. "He was trying to find his game, find out what kind of a player he was going to be. Bruce said, 'Just go.' I never thought he could be that explosive, that amazing. And it was overnight." Green had been a productive offensive defenseman in junior hockey. "But even in junior I had to hold back," he recalled. He'd gone on and showed promising signs in the AHL, but not much in the more confined, restrictive environs of the NHL, partly because Hanlon was preaching defensive responsibility and not turning the puck over ahead of offensive creativity.

"We weren't allowed to do what we could do," Green said. "When Glen Hanlon was here, no offence to him, but we had a lot of the same players and we didn't get the same results."

In Hanlon's final 21 games, Green registered three goals and four assists. In his first game under Boudreau, Green scored the winning goal in overtime in Philadelphia. At home the next day against Carolina, he scored again. "[Boudreau's] system is to be very aggressive and it fit my game," Green said. "He encouraged me to get up the ice. I'd get up the ice and create a play and pass all the time and he was the one who told me to shoot the puck. If I had gone somewhere else I probably wouldn't have had an opportunity to play like Bruce gave me here."

Over Boudreau's first two full seasons behind the Capitals' bench, Green led all NHL defensemen in goals and scoring and in adventurous and nervy rushes up the ice. He'll go a month before he sees a forecheck that he can't beat, a rolling puck sliding back to the blue line that he can't control. He plays with a confidence that sometimes borders on recklessness. Green scored the winning goal, a snap shot from the high slot, midway through the third period against Buffalo in the Capitals' first contest after the Olympics. Against the Sabres, Green had played his usual game, leading the Capitals in ice time with almost 26 minutes, four more than Ovechkin.

If Hanlon had stayed on in Washington and Green never had a chance to show his skills with the Capitals, maybe another team would have taken a chance on him, bringing him in as a project. Most of the other young Capitals would have been given a look somewhere if things didn't work out for them with the Caps. Like Green, Jeff Schultz, Boyd Gordon, and Eric Fehr had all been first-round draft picks of Washington. Tomas Fleischmann and Brooks Laich had been acquired in trades for frontline NHLers, so they were going to get a long look. The one player who might have been completely out of luck was David Steckel. A 6-foot-5 center with an ungainly skating style, Steckel was a project that Boudreau started in Hershey and saw through to completion in Washington. If Green can thank Boudreau for a chance to make the most of his gifts, then Steckel owes the coach for having a career at all. But for a handful of games in Washington with Hanlon, Steckel has played his entire professional career with Boudreau—three teams in two organizations. "The joke is that Bruce is my father," Steckel said.

Truth is, some fathers would have bailed on Steckel. The Los Angeles Kings drafted the Milwaukee native with the last pick in the first round of the 2002 draft based on his impressive freshman year at Ohio State. Steckel stayed on with the Buckeyes until graduation, but it turned out that his first season with the team was his best. The Kings signed Steckel, but after a 10-goal rookie pro season with Boudreau's AHL team in Portland they decided to let him go. After the Capitals hired Boudreau, he recommended that they pick up Steckel, a 23-year-old free agent, ostensibly as an organizational player, someone to fill out the Hershey roster. In Hershey, though, Steckel made strides as a player. It was nothing like the overnight transformation of Green, but still Steckel realized what his role would have to be in the NHL: *face-off specialist, grinder, no-maintenance team guy.*

When Boudreau arrived at his first practice in Washington, no one was happier than Steckel. He had never been more than an afterthought to Hanlon. With Boudreau, Steckel knew he had the coach's confidence. His role with the Capitals was far from glamorous and it consisted of stuff that almost never shows up in the stats summary, but it was exactly as Boudreau had laid it out back in Portland and Hershey.

Not that there's only drudgery—Steckel had scored in overtime of Game 6 of the Pittsburgh series the previous spring—but still the post-Olympic game in Buffalo was his typical night's work. In the final five minutes, with the Capitals protecting a tenuous one-goal lead, Boudreau kept Ovechkin and the other Olympic stars on the bench and sent Steckel, Gordon, and Matt Bradley over the boards whenever there was a face-off in the Washington end of the rink. Steckel beat the Sabres' Tim Connolly on a face-off to Jose Theodore's right with less than four minutes to go. With 90 seconds left and with Miller pulled for a sixth attacker, Gordon beat Derek

Roy on a draw and seconds later Steckel stepped in front of Myers's slap shot from the point. *That will leave a mark.* The checking line, along with Tom Poti and Shaone Morrisonn clogged the passing lanes and kept the Sabres out on the perimeter. And with just over a minute to go, Gordon fired the puck off the boards and it travelled 170 feet into the open Buffalo net to seal the victory.

Despite the success of the pluggers and grinders, Boudreau's job and the Capitals' performance rode largely on his ability to work with Ovechkin. "The only reservation I had was that Bruce hadn't had the opportunity to handle million-dollar athletes," Yingst said. McPhee had questions along the same lines. "Would he be himself, or would he be intimidated by Ovechkin and other players?" the general manager said.

Boudreau knew the rank and file in the Capitals dressing room from their stints in Hershey. Fleischmann, Laich, Gordon, Green, Schultz, and Fehr had played for him when Hershey won the AHL title in '06. But he didn't know the stars, the players who never had to ride the buses in the organization, those who jumped directly to the NHL. He had coached players making $400 a week in the East Coast league, never someone who'd sign a contract paying him $100,000 a game.

"George said to go in and talk to the players," said Boudreau. "So I'm walking around, looking at all the name plates, and I see Ovie's name. And I think, 'Holy shit, I'm coaching Alex Ovechkin now!' And I thought, I better get him on my side right away. I better show him I know what I'm doing."

There didn't seem to be any common ground. Boudreau had played beside a few Hall of Famers, Darryl Sittler, Lanny McDonald, and Denis Savard, but as a coach he had never worked with anyone who had been a first overall pick. He had coached a couple of East European players, the first being Igor Malykhin in Fort Wayne. For a hockey lifer, this was *terra incognita*.

As the club went on the ice and began a drill, Boudreau noticed Ovechkin wasn't just doing it incorrectly, he was making big, wide turns, out of either uncertainty or indifference. Boudreau blew his whistle. He knew this was the moment. If all those years of laboring in the minors were going to be worth anything, he had to make a stand right away, and he had to make it with a player who was already among the biggest stars in the NHL.

"I called him over and gave him shit. I had to let the players know that I wasn't just some minor-league guy, that they had to take me seriously. You know, the words aren't right, but it was that head-of-the-snake idea." Ovechkin looked at the new coach, a rotund, balding stranger. Ovechkin knew nothing about his history—not George Armstrong, not the bus leagues, nothing. The two men eyed each other. Boudreau had waited so long for a shot at an NHL job but knew the trapdoor could have opened beneath his skates just on the franchise player's whim. After a couple of nerve-racking seconds, the tension broke. "He said, 'Yup, okay,' and he went out and did [the drill] right," Boudreau said. "Our relationship grew from there."

Ovechkin had been deeply disappointed by the firing of Hanlon. "I've never been in this situation in my life, with coach getting fired. If we lose, guy who will be fired is coach. If we win, nobody's talking about coach. If we lose, everyone talks about coach," he told reporters in his developing English.

Boudreau knew enough to tread carefully. "I didn't want to bust in like the new wife," he said. "I needed to give him some space. I don't think we even had a conversation for the first week."

Right away, Boudreau was drawing on the lessons learned as a teenager under Armstrong. "It really wasn't about what George taught you as a player. It was how he taught you to treat people," Boudreau said. "We were more worried about letting him down than we were about losing a game."

Boudreau's bedside manner worked in the room with Ovechkin and those who had come up from Hershey. Still, it was Hanlon's tough medicine that delivered an improving franchise player to his coaching successor. Hanlon's emphasis on defense had limited Green but was going to serve Ovechkin well in the long run. "He was raw in his own end. He was raw at playing a defensive style of the game," said former teammate Jamie Heward, who was with Ovechkin in his rookie year in Washington. "He was coming from a place where a coach said to him, 'You can score goals. Go score goals, don't worry about everything else.' The one thing that I'll give the organization credit for is they made Alex a responsible player on and off the ice—they made him aware that there were some things that he was going to have to do to be responsible, complete, and with that winning was sure to follow. They made him responsible in his own end—he wasn't handed 35 minutes a night and told, 'Score five goals and if you give up four, so what.' They drilled it into his head that he had to be good in his own end. That he got the message, accepted it, and worked with it got the respect of his teammates. Respect that he took it as a challenge to be a better player in his own end, be a good defensive player. And with his skating ability and his ability to read the play on the ice and his hockey sense, we all knew that he'd figure it out. And he knew that [Sidney] Crosby was good in his own end—if he's competing with Crosby he'd have to be able to compete with him in all aspects of the game."

Ovechkin was stuck with the stereotype of a dangling, one-way winger, and he was still no threat for the Selke Trophy as the league's best defensive forward. Yet he has improved his plus-minus numbers in each of his first five seasons. Hanlon's bad-tasting medicine was still paying off years after his firing. And even though he couldn't generate any offence against the Sabres in Buffalo, Ovechkin didn't make any egregious gaffes that led to a scoring chance. He wasn't on the ice for a goal for or against that night and that was good enough to hold on to his league lead in plus-minus.

• • •

It wasn't just that Boudreau had freed up Green or had the back of Steckel and the Hershey alumni or even won Ovechkin's confidence. Boudreau helped his team develop an identity, a swagger. If an opponent was going to score four goals, they believed—no, they knew—they were going to score five. It was a game familiar to Boudreau, who had once upon a time registered 165 points—including 69 goals—playing for Armstrong with the Marlies. Wayne Gretzky saw similarities between that junior team and Boudreau's Capitals. "It goes back to when he played for George Armstrong with the Marlies," Gretzky told ESPN.com. "He loves that transition, head-manning the puck and going to the net. It's very similar to the way the Marlies played."

The Caps scored 242 goals in the 2007–08 season, and increased that total to 272 the following campaign. By the 2009–10 season, they'd surpassed that number by the 70-game mark, amassing 20 percent more offence than any other team in the league while running away with both their division and the Eastern Conference. Boudreau had been the perfect fit. "I don't think you could have had a guy like Claude Julien or Jacques Martin in that environment," Pothier said. "You'd be making those guys play a game they're not going to be very good at." Nothing slowed the Washington machine, not suspensions or injuries to Ovechkin. By December 26, they moved into first place overall in the NHL and stayed there. "Is this what I thought it would be?" Boudreau asked. "Well, I've got a vivid imagination. I imagine things on a grand scale."

On the grandest scale, the franchise player wouldn't just score goals. He wouldn't just be defensively responsible. He wouldn't just be professional. He'd be the leader of the team, but it wasn't something that was up to Boudreau and Ovechkin. It was going to require a shuffle and a gut check for management.

Sensing the possibility that the Caps might be able to take a serious shot at the first Stanley Cup in team history, George McPhee made a bold move in late December '09. He traded Chris Clark, the Washington captain since the lockout, and young defenseman Milan Jurcina to Columbus for winger Jason Chimera. Clark, who had been named captain by Hanlon, was devastated. "I didn't see it coming at all," he said. "At the trade deadline anything can happen but at that point in the season I didn't expect that. I knew my time would come eventually, but I would have liked to finish what we had started. I'd hoped to be part of it." On its face it wasn't a huge deal. Clark was an oft-injured grinder, Jurcina a big Slovakian defenseman low on the Washington depth chart, and Chimera was a journeyman forward who had never put up significant offensive numbers. It wasn't the type of trade that loads up a Cup contender for the playoffs. It wasn't a matter of addition so much as subtraction. Clark had been injured so often he was more of an off-ice presence than on-ice contributor under Boudreau. "It was tough for Bruce," said Clark. "He didn't know me that well as a player or a captain. I never got back to where I wanted to be." With Clark gone, Washington's captaincy was vacant, one clear motivation for the deal. "I don't know if that was the reason I was traded," said Clark. "But I knew Alex would be captain when I left."

After Clark packed off for Columbus, the team spent a week considering various candidates to wear the "C"—or, at least, that's how the official story goes. Ovechkin, really, was the only choice, if only because he was under contract through the 2020–21 season. Naming another player captain would only forestall the inevitable and put that player on the clock. Moreover, while the captaincy in hockey doesn't come with quite the gravitas it does in soccer, where it's bigger than in any other sport. It would have been an insult to name any other player captain. Atlanta had made his Russian compatriot Ilya Kovalchuk captain the previous season. Crosby, younger than Ovechkin, was captain of the Pittsburgh Penguins. Finally, Ovechkin's desire to raise his profile through the spread in *Men's Journal*, his new marketing deal with IMG, and his willingness to cooperate with virtually every league-initiated promotion dictated that he be seen as the unquestioned alpha male with the Capitals. There was no way the team could choose another captain. It had to be Ovechkin.

When Ovechkin was named the team's new captain, no one was surprised. "The players were really happy when I told them this morning," Boudreau said. "This doesn't happen too often, but the group got up and cheered. I had talked to a lot of them in the last couple of days and they said that Alex was the only choice; he's our leader, he's our guy. I think the thing that really sort of shows how he was ready was, when I talked to him a few days ago, he said, 'I would accept the responsibility, but only if my teammates want me to.' So he was already thinking about the team rather than thinking of himself, which is what good captains do."

Still, the Caps wanted to make it at least appear that they'd gone through a process of choosing a new leader, and that Ovechkin was at least somewhat reluctant. In a political town where perception is everything, it was important to make sure Ovechkin wasn't portrayed as grasping for the captaincy or, in the worst scenario, demanding it even if it meant Clark had to be traded. The Capitals had enjoyed local success portraying their players as different from those in other sports. With the Redskins, star running back Clinton Portis had publicly criticized starting quarterback Jason Campbell during the season, while filthy rich defensive lineman Albert Haynesworth had ripped the scheme installed by the defensive coordinator. The NBA Wizards, meanwhile, had fallen into a mess initiated by star Gilbert Arenas, who was revealed to have brought as many as four handguns to his dressing room locker and would ultimately be suspended from the team and convicted of a criminal offence. The Caps certainly didn't want Ovechkin portrayed as just another selfish athlete. So the move to name him captain was announced quietly. At the Verizon Center on January 5, 2010, Ovechkin simply skated out for the pre-game warm-up against Montreal with the "C" stitched on his Capitals jersey. The team's media department sent out prepared comments from Ovechkin, Boudreau, and McPhee. It was all very restrained, very non-Ovechkin-like. None of the city's major newspaper columnists wrote about it. The process of transferring the official leadership of the hockey club from a hardworking, good guy American to a rich Russian rock star had gone smoothly. If Ovechkin had secretly desired the captaincy, there was nary a whiff of that in the public domain. Clark, while disheartened by the trade, endorsed his successor. "He's one of the guys whose heart is with the team no matter what," said Clark. "Off the ice, he cares for all the guys." Still, there was no farewell. Clark left town without a word from the new Capitals captain.

●   ●   ●

Boudreau was in a buoyant mood after the win over the Sabres—his team had come off the Olympic break with one of their tightest defensive games in a couple of months, something even Hanlon would have trouble finding fault with. The coach held court for a few minutes and then the reporters fanned out, looking for players to comment. Chimera who scored the first goal. Green who scored the winner. Theodore who was further establishing himself as the Caps' No. 1 goaltender in the stretch run. For his part, Ovechkin made a point of keeping his distance. He had his back to teammates and reporters, stripped down to his stretch shorts, identifiable only by the tattoos on his back. He had his cell phone pressed to his ear, his hand cupped over it so that the music in the room didn't drown him out. Reporters read the body language and the situation: bad game, bad mood, no quotes forthcoming. They didn't have to be too cynical to suppose that he was on the phone bitching about the game to someone in his posse. Or maybe mom. However, Ovechkin hadn't keyed in the number of a member of Team Ovechkin on his cell phone, but rather an ex-member.

"I'm sorry it happened," Ovechkin told Pothier, who had been shipped to the Carolina Hurricanes by McPhee earlier that day, prior to the league's 3 p.m. trade deadline. Pothier had just arrived at the airport in Charlotte en route to Raleigh and his new team when he heard his cell phone ring. He had been on the Capitals' roster since 2006, signing as a free agent when the Caps were wallowing at the bottom of the league, but he had missed almost all of the previous season with a concussion after being hit hard by Boston's Milan Lucic. For months, every trip to the neurologist made it feel like his career was over, but it turned out to be a simple fix: glasses and contact lenses. After a lost regular season, he'd played in 13 of Washington's 14 playoff games in the spring of 2009, right through the epic series with Pittsburgh. But this season he had found himself pushed further down the Capitals' depth chart, a vulnerable place to be on a team that was looking to tinker, looking to add a final few pieces for a run at the Cup. The game in Buffalo fell right on the NHL's trading deadline and so Pothier had spent a few days working out with teammates that he'd never play with again. Early that morning, he was moved to the Hurricanes, the team with the league's worst record, along with a second-round pick and a prospect named Oskar Osala. Coming the other way was another American-born, right-hand-shooting puck-moving defenseman, Joe Corvo, a player similar to Pothier but with the ability to take a shift or two on the point of the power play when necessary. "If they trade you and a pick and prospect for another guy, obviously they feel that player can bring more to the table than you do," said Pothier, hurt but philosophical. His departure from the Caps was just a footnote the next day—one Washington columnist didn't mention him at all in summing up the Capitals' moves—as the story was all about the players McPhee was bringing in for a run to the Stanley Cup. Pothier no longer mattered, except to Ovechkin.

The cell phone call caught Pothier off guard. He thought that eventually he'd see Ovechkin a week later when the Hurricanes went to D.C. for a game, maybe talk to him after the game. His closest buddies were other peripheral types, Tyler Sloan and Quintin Laing, but he liked Ovechkin. He liked how he asked about Pothier's pickup when both knew it wasn't the kind of expensive vehicle Ovechkin would ever park in his own driveway. Still, Pothier didn't expect a call that night around 9:30. *He has to still be in his equipment.* "He said, 'Potsy, I'm so sorry. This is a crazy business. It could happen to anyone,'" said Pothier. "I know he has this crazy rock star image, and he can be an eccentric, wild person, but at the same time he's a thoughtful guy who cares about his team and his teammates. He's special. That he called meant a lot to me."

Ovechkin hadn't called Chris Clark but, then again, he hadn't been named the Capitals' next captain at that point. Those little courtesies weren't yet part of his job description. But the call he placed to Pothier was evidence that he was taking the C seriously, that he was starting to look at the big picture and not just in the mirror. For Ovechkin, it had been a rocky start to the home stretch of the regular season and still he had the presence of mind to look after this bit of business. As bad as he felt, he knew he had a shot at a Stanley Cup, while Pothier might never have another one. The call meant something to Pothier, but it was also something that Ovechkin's teammates would pick up on, something that they could respect.

One game into the rest of their regular season, the Capitals had reason to feel good about themselves. They had beaten a tough conference foe in the Sabres and, on the deadline, they had acquired Corvo and Eric Belanger, a useful center who offered them depth for a long playoff run. Against Buffalo, those who had only watched the Olympics on television had stepped up to lead the Capitals. Ovechkin's team had won the game even though he contributed very little. Soon the Capitals were going to face a tougher test, having to win without him at all.

chapter 10

Chicago

"I Respect Everybody, but on the Ice It Can't Be Everything"

THE CAPITALS' SCHEDULE after the Olympics looked like a forgiving one. If McPhee and Boudreau had drawn it up themselves it could hardly have been more favorable for delivering a rested and ready team for a long, grueling playoff run. The Capitals had eight road games, but only three against teams that were going to make the playoffs. They had two away games against Eastern Conference teams that they might meet in the postseason: the first game out of the Olympic break was in Buffalo and the last was Game No. 82, the eve of the playoffs, in Pittsburgh. The third road game against a contender represented a possible preview of the Stanley Cup final: a date on a March Sunday afternoon in Chicago against the Blackhawks, possibly the Western Conference's most exciting collection of talent. The Chicago game was the first of four games on the Capitals' last road trip of the season.

From Chicago the Capitals were heading to, in sequence, Fort Lauderdale to play the Panthers, Raleigh to play the Hurricanes, and St. Petersburg to play the Lightning. All the teams on the Sunbelt leg were bound to miss the playoffs and were somewhere between weak and dysfunctional. Four games over the course of a week, no games back to back, only one change in time zones: on paper it looked like a tough game followed by a team-building vacation in the sun. For the league's best team, anything less than six points out of those four games would have been a disappointment. For Ovechkin, the road trip should have been a chance to fatten his stats and, in doing that, solidify his case for the Hart Trophy. It was like the Capitals were leading the race and driving the second-last lap under the yellow flag. They were virtually guaranteed the top seed in the Eastern Conference and just about as sure of the league's best record.

The game against Chicago seemed like the best opportunity to measure the Capitals in the weeks leading up to playoffs. It was an obvious choice for NBC programmers: two success stories. A playoff preview. The Hawks' young stars, Jonathan Toews, Patrick Kane, and Duncan Keith against Ovechkin and the light-show offence of the Capitals. NBC had all kinds of story lines to work with for the broadcast.

All these story lines were lost in the aftermath. They were eclipsed by another Ovechkin moment, another of the black clouds that so often blow over the NHL shield. Instead of trumpeting success in the television ratings, the league went into its familiar crisis-management mode.

Ovechkin was kicked out of the game. Face of the league, sent to the showers. Roll-out of the brand unavailable, we now return you to your regular programming.

Just by itself Ovechkin getting tossed might not have seemed a big deal, especially in a regular-season game. Albert Pujols could argue balls and strikes and get the heave and it would be a couple of lines in a wire-service story. Kobe Bryant getting a couple of Ts would get a good run on the sports highlights but not much more.

If Brett Favre was pulled or somehow reconsidered his retirement at halftime, again, it would be good for a single news cycle. None of it would hit the commissioners' desks.

This, however, was different. It was a problem for Ovechkin and it also dragged out for public consideration an ongoing problem for the NHL.

• • •

It went down 12 minutes into the opening period. The game at that point was 1–0. Chicago had taken the lead on a goal by Toews. Ovechkin was on the ice with Mike Knuble and Tomas Fleischmann, two-thirds of the way through a line change. Chicago defenseman Brian Campbell had chased down the puck in the Blackhawks' end and was skating towards the back of the net. He saw Ovechkin chasing him. *They're looking to lay the body on me.* He had already sucked up hits from Brooks Laich and David Steckel. Campbell was looking to throw the puck off the boards and reverse it around to his blue line partner Nicklas Hjalmarsson.

Exactly what happened depended entirely on your vantage point.

From Campbell's vantage point: You are going back for the puck and Ovechkin is pouring in full speed on the forecheck. He is 230 pounds, maybe more. You are 5-foot-10 and describe yourself as "not even a middleweight." You are stopped in your tracks. There's no need to do the math, no opportunity to calculate the physics. You're in trouble and for any player in the NHL, at some point your job boils down to managing trouble. It's especially true of NHL players who have to dig out pucks dumped into their own ends. You know the game is faster and the hits are bigger since the NHL rewrote the rulebook after the lockout. You've said: "Players don't have to skate through hooks and holds. They're carrying more speed up the ice." You've told people that the biggest hit you ever laid on a guy back in Buffalo, a knockout blow against R.J.

Umberger in the playoffs against Philadelphia, wasn't malicious. You're asked if the Umberger hit was dirty and you explain, "I was standing still."

From Alexander Ovechkin's vantage point: There is the puck. There is the player carrying the puck. There is no other context. You've said that scoring is like "running from an angry dog." When you're chasing the man with the puck you *are* the angry dog. Who can say what's instinct or what's impulse? There's no history here. It's not a matter of retribution. You don't owe Campbell anything. There's no history between the two of you. There are no messages to send to him. Put the fear into him for the Stanley Cup final? You don't think that way. Shouldn't you be worried about the big hits that have you explaining to the league office why you shouldn't be suspended? You *can't* think that way. Not if you're going to play your game. You have no problem hurting people, but doesn't the thought of injury cross your mind? No, the game happens so fast and you can't imagine ever getting hit hard enough that you can't skate away. And this seems like a little hit.

From the vantage point of the trainer on the Blackhawks' bench: You know Campbell's hurt by the way he goes into the boards head first. From the bench your view is blocked by the net and by passing players. You hope it's not a spinal-cord injury or a concussion. You start going to the gate to get on the ice before the whistle is blown.

From the vantage point of the referee: You blow the whistle. It is boarding. It's a hit from behind. You head over to the scorer at the penalty box. It's five minutes and a game misconduct.

From the vantage point of Pierre McGuire: You don't realize that he's being tossed. You tell the NBC viewers that the hit is "another demonstration of the skill and the size of Ovechkin."

After the hit, and after Campbell was helped off the ice and Ovechkin was ejected, Chicago ran out to a 3–0 lead on a second goal by Toews and another by John Madden, but the Capitals stormed back with three goals in the third period—by Backstrom,

Laich, and Fehr—and went on to win in overtime on a second goal by Backstrom. There was plenty of skill and speed, in the game, but at the end of it one image stuck in the memory of those who watched in the arena and at home: Ovechkin knocking Campbell into the boards.

It would have been like Mariano Rivera intentionally beaning Ken Griffey Jr. Or Kobe undercutting Steve Nash. Or Brian Urlacher spearing Peyton Manning out of bounds.

From Campbell's vantage point it had been a gratuitous shot, a late hit. By the end of the game he wasn't around to give an account of events. He had been rushed to hospital and was being treated for broken ribs and a broken collarbone. His teammates were left to give their versions of events. "So much of that stuff going on now, it's pretty frustrating that the players don't take a stand against something like that and say we have to respect ourselves a little bit more and know it's not all about the flashy hit," Toews said. "You've got to know when there's a dangerous situation where you could really hurt somebody, and be smart about it."

Ovechkin was surrounded by reporters after the game. He had the demeanor of a perp, a multiple offender, just before he was going to be charged again. He didn't wait for questions to start rationalizing. Ovechkin said that he "just pushed" Campbell. "It was not a hard hit," Ovechkin said. "I just pushed him. I respect everybody, but on the ice it can't be everything. We play for our team and make some hard hits and sometimes you get hurt. It's a hockey game. He fell bad, and that's probably why it looks bad."

Boudreau had his take on Ovechkin's hit on Campbell. He said that he had seen plays like this happen before and injuries "happen when players try to make plays to avoid the hit."

There were shades of gray: Late or not late? Intentional and malicious or just part of a game played by big, fast men? Some things weren't open to interpretation. This was the third game misconduct of the season for Ovechkin and it could have easily been the fourth. He had slew-footed Atlanta's Rich Peverley in October—the dirtiest of hockey plays to many—and been fined $2,500—it likely would have been more but Ovechkin got off with just a minor penalty and the fine after a league review because Peverley was able to skate away. In November he was hit for his first gamer when he slammed Buffalo's Patrick Kaleta face-first into the glass—Kaleta got his payback in Buffalo after the Olympic break. And just days later he was ejected for his knee-on-knee hit on Carolina defenseman Tim Gleason, which the NHL's director of hockey operations Colin Campbell, aka The Sheriff, deemed an intentionally reckless play and slapped Ovechkin with a two-game suspension. IMG was looking at him as an iconic figure, but a wrestling promoter would look at him as a heel, a rules-breaker. While Ovechkin claimed to respect everybody, it seemed like respect was, if not in short supply, a sometimes thing.

It wasn't just Ovechkin, though—for the league it had been the season of playing dangerously. The NHL had a spate of ugly hits, blind-side head shots, that had sent players to the sidelines for months with concussions. Brian Campbell was lucky enough not to be carried off on a stretcher, but still, because of Ovechkin's own history and recent events around the league, the hit was guaranteed to get a long, critical look at the NHL's offices.

• • •

Many inside the game, those who were around to see him play, believe Gordie Howe was the forerunner for Ovechkin. What Pierre McGuire said about Ovechkin's skill and strength after the hit on Campbell was said of Howe with a grim regularity. The Gordie Howe hat trick: a goal, an assist, and a fight. He was capable of a vicious turn almost out of the blue; maybe the strongest player in the game in his day. A player known more for his elbows than any other player in league history.

The comparison is true as far as it goes. In Howe's prime, players were smaller, shifts longer, and the pace of the game often a walk compared to the modern game's dead sprint. And while players, including Howe, suffered head injuries and concussions, in retrospect it was remarkable how few there were considering that helmets were rare up until the '70s. It's seemingly not just a matter of size and speed but also of culture. Violence has always been a component of the game and in Howe's day bench-clearing brawls were a regular occurrence. Now, though, the worst aspect of violence comes not when two willing participants start punching, but rather when a player targets an unsuspecting opponent with a shoulder or elbow to the head.

Earlier in the season, Philadelphia's Mike Richards blind-sided David Booth of the Florida Panthers and left him on the sidelines for months with a concussion. Richards wasn't suspended. Pittsburgh's Matt Cooke, one of the worst of the league's bad actors, delivered a similar hit on Boston's top center, Marc Savard, with a similar result. Both were considered to be part of the action not illegal in any way. That latter hit compromised the Bruins' chances of getting into the playoffs and prompted the league to rewrite the rules on checks with contact to the head, a measure unprecedented in the middle of an NHL season. Supposedly it was going to be a crackdown on dangerous play.

Ovechkin couldn't have known what the outcome would be of his hearing with Colin Campbell. Campbell's experience as a tough guy on the ice with five NHL teams colors his administration of justice. He interprets and applies not only the rule book but also the game's "code," the unwritten etiquette that players abide by. Campbell, no relation to the Chicago defenseman injured in the incident, has to tune out the background noise when making these rulings. Wirtz, the Blackhawks' owner, was calling for Ovechkin's suspension for the remainder of the NHL regular season, 13 games in all. "If you're really going to hurt a player . . . and [he's] out for the season, then let them suspend that player for the rest of the season," Wirtz said. No one inside the game imagined that it was going to come to that with Ovechkin. Campbell can maintain that justice is justice, nothing less, but history shows who you are does matter—fourth-liners whose jobs called for them to rough up and intimidate opponents inevitably faced harsher sentences than first-line stars. And in this case it was the league's top scorer and most valuable player over the past three seasons—a suspension like that suggested by Rocky Wirtz would not only hurt the Capitals in the short run but also damage the league's image. A stain on the NHL's brightest star would be a stain on the league.

Ovechkin hoped for a walk. He hoped that the league would see it his way—that it was just a push that had gone horribly wrong. He could claim, rightly, that he'd been on the end of even more reckless and dangerous plays—the run that Pittsburgh's Craig Adams took at Ovechkin in the Super Bowl Sunday game just being one example. Ovechkin hoped Campbell would see the big picture, the historical context. Howe had hurt players just like this and did so with intent in his day. Ovechkin hoped that Campbell didn't believe that he had a mean streak like Howe's.

● ● ●

Jamie Heward doesn't think of Ovechkin as a mean player—just a dangerous one. Some might presume Heward would give him the benefit of the doubt because he was a defenseman with the Caps when Ovechkin first came to Washington. He became a good friend of Ovechkin that year—he was one of the veterans who went out of their way to help the young Russian get used to life in Washington and in the NHL. Yet no one would have a greater reason to hold a grudge against Ovechkin than Heward. Ovechkin after all, ended Heward's career in the NHL.

It was a hit that Heward remembers nothing about, a hit he has only seen on video. It's like a whole day in his life has been lost. It happened in St. Petersburg on January 1, 2009. Heward had moved on from the Capitals. He was with the Tampa Bay Lightning, the seventh NHL team he had played for. With about 13 minutes left in the game, the puck came around the boards behind the Tampa Bay net. Heward was chasing it with Ovechkin going full speed behind him. Heward has only his best guess at what he was thinking at that moment.

"I knew he was behind me," Heward said. "Instead of keeping the puck going, if I could just do a little quick turn-back and he just did a fly-by, maybe I could get the puck away from him. I knew he was in the zone by himself. The puck slowed down coming around the boards more than I wanted so I actually had to turn back to get it in order for him not to get it. As I turned he was right there, full steam."

The hit seemed to bear out Boudreau's later observation about the big hits Ovechkin landed that injured opponents: Heward was trying to make a play to avoid the hit. In Heward's case the play was a little too cute, a guess that didn't work out.

Ovechkin took Heward into the end boards and Heward's head slammed into the Plexiglass. He lay facedown on the ice, motionless, for five minutes while the Lightning's team doctor checked him for catastrophic injury. Ovechkin skated over to check on Heward before he was turned over, placed on a backboard, lifted onto a stretcher, and wheeled off to an ambulance. There was no penalty on the play.

Heward had been told by his Tampa teammates that Ovechkin had waited outside the Lightning dressing room asking for word on his former teammate's condition. But Ovechkin never called Heward in hospital, though Matt Bradley, Brooks Laich, and other members of the Capitals did, along with their team doctor and George McPhee. And Ovechkin didn't call Heward after he was released and went home. They only crossed paths by chance, months later, when the Capitals went to the Air Canada Centre to play against the Toronto Maple Leafs.

While he was out with post-concussion syndrome, the Lightning had traded Heward and other veterans to Toronto in a move to dump salaries. Heward and Ovechkin passed each other in the hall at ground level outside the dressing rooms. Some have described their exchange as heated but Heward says it wasn't the case. "I talked to Alex about it," Heward said. "We're good. Totally fine."

Weeks later Heward had read Ovechkin's comments after the game. "I didn't know what to think," Ovechkin told reporters. "I saw him and he turned around and . . . I didn't mean to hit him. Sure, you're concerned. I want to know how he is. It was an accident and I'm very sorry. I never want to hurt somebody, especially my old teammate. It's hard and I'm very sorry, but it's a game and it's a moment. He turns and I have speed. . . . I hope he is okay."

Heward wasn't okay. Through the summer and into the fall he was still feeling the effects of the concussion. The 38-year-old, who was making the league minimum salary of $475,000 at the time of his injury, had hoped to be ready in time to sign on with another club for a final season. He hoped that it would give his young son a chance to see him play. He didn't recover quickly enough or fully enough.

Many outside the game would expect Heward to have hard feelings. He doesn't absolve Ovechkin, but he remains philosophical about it. "Part of it was my fault," he says. "Part of it was his fault."

The first part: Heward acknowledges that for a split second he had to have made a mental error. "I got myself into some trouble. I was thinking I could get away. I didn't think I was vulnerable. He comes up on you so fast that even when you anticipate him coming he's on you before you're ready. He's making a play better than most guys can. You're putting yourself in a vulnerable position because you're trying to make a play that you've made a hundred times before but not against an elite player."

The second part: Heward's not suggesting that it was a matter of intent, but rather Ovechkin's inability to rein in almost uncontrollable force. "He could have let up a bit. He could have got to the inside and pushed in a different direction. Fifty other guys in the league could have hit me that way but because of the way it happened I couldn't claim that there was malice even with them. Most of them, if they hit, I would have been able to skate away."

Ovechkin had to hope that Colin Campbell saw the hit on Brian Campbell the same way that Jamie Heward saw the hit that ended his career.

• • •

By the time Colin Campbell started considering the incident, the Capitals had already checked into the Ritz-Carlton out near the arena in Fort Lauderdale. The possibility of a suspension to Ovechkin was the first topic of conversation among hockey fans and the media, but apparently it was no great concern to the Capitals. This was a speed bump. They owned the league's best record. The swagger they played with on the ice carried over off it. They'd say the right things when asked, resorting to clichés about taking nothing for granted, but they had to believe that they were charmed. They had to believe that the talent in their lineup and their level of play this season made games against non-contenders little more than a formality. Boudreau had bemoaned the lack of practice time for the team when the Capitals lost three games in a row on their last extended road trip before the Olympic break, but now there was no finding fault with their play. He let the players know that there'd be no practice the next day—a discreet way of telling them that they were free to have a few beers or a few more than a few. The players broke into groups and went out for dinner and beers in restaurants at the upscale mall across the road.

At breakfast on their off-day the players organized a team outing: a round of golf. It was a spontaneous idea—none of the players had brought clubs or even golf shoes or gloves on the four-game road trip. It was a collective impulse, what frat boys with trust funds would do on spring break. By the time the players made it back to the Ritz-Carlton, Colin Campbell had handed down his decision, but Ovechkin either had his cell phone off or not with him.

Tarik El-Bashir, the Capitals beat reporter for the *Washington Post*, approached Ovechkin in the lobby and asked him for a reaction to the suspension.

"I don't know," Ovechkin said. "What is it?"

El-Bashir broke the news to him.

"It's two games, Alex."

Ovechkin drank it in. He looked exasperated. "It's hard to lose $100,000," he said.

"The way it works out, it's more like $220,000," El-Bashir said.

Ovechkin didn't react at first. He seemed to be calculating what the number meant—converting it into sports cars or putting it up against the money that he saw from his equipment deal. When it finally sank in, he walked away shaken. There were no gap-toothed smiles, no jokes.

It seemed strange that he automatically converted games into dollars—the games themselves didn't seem to factor into his thoughts. He didn't express any concern about being out of the lineup or about maybe losing ground in the races for the Hart Trophy and a scoring title.

Ovechkin was out of pocket a good chunk of change, but his suspension didn't seem like it would affect the Capitals' season at all. He missed two meaningless games on the road trip: a one-sided win over the Panthers and a loss in overtime to the Hurricanes.

* * *

Brian Campbell wasn't around after the Sunday afternoon game to say what had happened. That had to wait until the Capitals were halfway through their road trip. He spent most of the week after the Hawks' loss to Washington on a couch in his living room or in bed, doing "a lot of staring at the TV or ceiling." At night he slept in a chair. It was the only way he could get comfortable.

Campbell had always been soft-spoken. He wasn't a trash talker on the ice. He wasn't much for entertaining reporters with stories after games. He gave the impression that his life would be just fine if his name didn't show up in print. That last bit was even more true when he signed a massive contract with Chicago and struggled, making him the least-favorite player on a team that the fans otherwise loved. Still, when he finally made it back to the Blackhawks' dressing room for the first time after the injury, he didn't mince words.

"Whatever [Ovechkin] says isn't going to change the fact I'm not going to be playing for a little while," Campbell said. "I think the intent was there. If the intent is there, I don't think you can really say you didn't mean to do anything. So for me, I don't need anything from him."

Campbell laid out in detail what happened on the play and what happened on the ice that the television cameras and commentators didn't pick up.

"The puck bounced over my stick so I was going back to get it," Campbell said. "I knew [Ovechkin] was on me. I'm just reversing the puck. I don't mind if he rides me in the boards or hits me. But he pushed me from behind. I had nowhere to go. I was going into the boards trying to protect myself but it was hard to do."

Almost impossible as it turned out.

Campbell knew immediately he was seriously injured. He had reason to think that it might have been worse than a broken clavicle. "I couldn't move my arm or the right side of my body very much," Campbell said. "I rolled over and had a tough time breathing. So I tried to take some time and lay there to see if something may correct itself. The pain just got worse and worse."

Campbell didn't need to see the play again on tape. While he was still down on the ice, he thought Ovechkin had crossed a line. "I just looked up at Ovechkin and I was like, 'What are you doing?'" Campbell said. "I was shaking my head."

Campbell had missed 10 games in 10 years of pro hockey. The game against Washington was Campbell's 388th straight in the lineup. He had been an all-star. He had been personally burned by Ovechkin, but it's not unfair to assume that he was speaking for a lot of NHLers, maybe even the majority, when he criticized him.

"[Ovechkin] is a great player and works hard but obviously he does some stupid things. I don't think it's anything against me personally or anyone else needs to seek retribution for. You know the most frustrating part for me? I'm sitting on the couch watching hockey and he's going to play this weekend. . . . I feel like I've hurt my team."

"You come off the Olympics and you have such a great high for hockey and then you have these things. Parents see this and are probably like, 'I'm not putting my son or daughter into hockey, I can't risk that.' I know people say players have to police it themselves but how that happens is through tougher suspensions and fines. It takes the league to step up like the NFL has."

If you thought of it only as two games missed, it wasn't a big deal. But the suspension, the loss of $220,000 the way Ovechkin saw it, had a drastic effect on Ovechkin and the Capitals' season.

chapter 11

Washington, Montreal

"It's Not Going to Happen. It's Not Going to Happen."

IN THE SUMMER when Alexander Ovechkin was 12 years old, he was still playing soccer in his free time, pickup games with his friends on the pitches around his apartment block. Before he had ever started skating or picked up a hockey stick, he had been a goalkeeper, his height and raw athleticism well suited to the position. Originally, his mother had the idea that her son had a brighter future in soccer than in hockey, that there were simply more opportunities in the game. That summer, Coca-Cola sponsored a soccer tournament open to sandlot players, Olé Coca-Cola. To get into the competition the players had to collect 30 bottle caps. Ovechkin and his friends scoured the gutters beside the sidewalks in the neighborhood to hit their quota and then filled out the paperwork required by the sponsors. For days in the run-up to the Olé Coca-Cola. tournament it was all that kids talked about, and they worked out, practicing plays off corner kicks and other set pieces, believing that they were going to win the championship. Then their parents readied their uniforms—Ovechkin had his goalkeeper's gear laid out the night before. On the day of the competition, the kids were up before dawn and piled into a minivan with their bag of bottle caps. They had to cross over to the other side of Moscow, and the boys were in the ecstasy of expectation.

It all came apart within minutes of their arrival.

Olé Coca-Cola featured a soccer tournament along with a bunch of skills competitions. The paperwork filled out by Ovechkin's team was for the penalty-kicks contest only, not the tournament. They didn't even get to play a game, and not long after they had arrived they were piling back into the minivan in tears for the long drive home.

Given the innocence of a 12-year-old, it's hard to imagine that any defeat would have hit him as hard. Or ever could.

• • •

By the time the 2010 Stanley Cup playoffs arrived for the Capitals, it could no longer be described in traditional terms as their second season. It was their third. The team had clinched a playoff berth on March 11, one month before the final day of the regular season. By Game No. 82, the Capitals had racked up 121 points, the most any team had accumulated in the past four years. The team had all but lapped the rest of the NHL field during the season, largely by pounding the weak Southeast Division. The period between clinching and resuming meaningful competition represented a season of purgatory for Washington. They were on top but at the same time on the outside.

The feeling was captured by Ovechkin one morning during his suspension for the hit on Brian Campbell. Ovechkin isn't the only star who hates practice and lives for games, but his loathing of the former matches his passion for the latter. For almost a week he had only practices and a seat in the press box for a couple of nights—that in and of itself constitutes cruel and unusual punishment. His frustration mounted and finally peaked when he was kept on the ice to skate line drill sat the end of a game-day practice in Carolina. At every level of hockey there are Black Aces, players who are healthy scratches on game days, and it's business as usual to have them slog through a hard skate long after the frontline players have hit the showers before lunch. Only a few minutes in Ovechkin started griping. He yelled at assistant coach Dean Evason: "Is this the NHL or the KHL?"

It was a joke—the session was hardly punitive and in no way comparable to KHL practices, which are somewhat less grueling than a death march. Still, it hinted at an issue for the team. With the acquisitions at the trade deadline, the Capitals had more bodies around than open places in the lineup. Boudreau had to sit out groups of four or five players every game, some of whom had been with the team just for a few weeks, some of whom had been with him going back to Hershey. Ovechkin's suspension gave him a chance to see how the other half lived and played—they were members of the league's best team but didn't always feel like a part of it. On top but on the outside, again.

Between March 11 and the playoffs, the Caps had little or nothing to play for save pride and individual statistics. It was as though for those weeks their season had been reduced to a fantasy-league competition. Team goals had taken a backseat to individual ones. How many 20-goal scorers would they end up with? (Seven) Could Nicklas Backstrom crack the 100-point barrier? (Yes, by one point.) By what margin would Mike Green lead all NHL defensemen in scoring? (By seven points over Duncan Keith.) There was also Ovechkin's drive to capture the Art Ross Trophy as the league leader in scoring and the Rocket Richard Trophy for racking up the most goals. Both were still in play late in the last weeks of the 2009–10 season. He had to make up for lost games, having missed a total of 10 games to injury and suspension that season. Effectively he had spotted those 10 games, an eighth of the season, to Vancouver center Henrik Sedin in the race for the Art Ross Trophy. He was also giving up the same head start to Sidney Crosby and Tampa Bay's 19-year-old Steven Stamkos, for the Rocket Richard hardware.

This created a conundrum for coach Boudreau. He knew Ovechkin was most effective when playing between 20 to 22 minutes a night, and the team tended to perform better when No. 8 was on the ice that much. He also knew from his own playing days that there was no quicker way to earn the animosity of a scoring star than denying him precious minutes to pad his numbers in meaningless games. Boudreau wanted Ovechkin to win the scoring race, and, with his own contract hurtling towards its final year, it was in the coach's own interest to make it happen—to a point. That point was reached on March 30, when Ovechkin played a fairly outrageous 28 minutes and 28 seconds in a loss to the Ottawa Senators, producing one measly assist. Boudreau brought Ovechkin into his office to explain his beliefs about his minutes and productivity. "The trick is to make him happy with a lower number of minutes," Boudreau said. All the Russian star could see, however, was that he wasn't scoring or getting points. In the final week of the season, Sedin surged past Ovechkin to win the scoring title and both Crosby and Stamkos passed him in goals. Ovechkin wasn't going to be posing with three trophies at the NHL awards in June. He'd have to count on love from the media to be voted the one award, albeit the biggest of all: the Hart Trophy, for the league's most valuable player.

The stalling in Ovechkin's production concerned some of the Capitals' staff. It wasn't just his embarrassment from losing both the scoring races. He'd looked fatigued at times. Worse, the suspension earned for injuring Brian Campbell had taken the starch out of his physical play. Everyone thought so, including Boudreau.

If some in the hockey industry thought the Capitals were heading for any kind of early playoff trouble, only one went on the record about it: Columbus' R.J. Umberger, a journeyman forward on a non-playoff team whose career highlight had been getting knocked cold on a legal check leveled by the not-so-threatening Brian Campbell. Umberger had never won a Stanley Cup and never made an all-star team, but that didn't stop him from going for the short sell on the Capitals' chances in the postseason. "They play the wrong way," said Umberger after a late-season loss to Washington. "They want to be moving all the time. They float around in their zone, looking for breakaways and odd-man rushes. A good defensive team is going to beat them in the playoffs." These were interesting observations but, again, they were coming from a guy who was nobody's idea of an authority.

Where Umberger saw flaws, others found good signs, signs that the Capitals were capable of making a memorable run. They were remarkably healthy going into the postseason. Their power play ranked first in the league and was seen as so powerful it could overcome any of their shortcomings. Jose Theodore had lost only one game since mid-January. They weren't in quite the form that they'd displayed during their 15-game winning streak earlier in the season. Still, they looked like they could get there at the point when it mattered most. And the best sign of all for the Capitals came at the end of the last weekend of the season: the Montreal Canadiens were going to be their opponents in the opening round of the playoffs.

• • •

In their last regular-season game, the Montreal Canadiens had needed one point at home against the lowly Toronto Maple Leafs to clinch a spot in the 16-team Stanley Cup tournament. The Leafs owned the second-worst record in the league, but they pushed the Canadiens to overtime and won the game. The point for the overtime loss was still enough to get Montreal in. The Canadiens finished in the eighth and final playoff position in the Eastern Conference, much closer to the Edmonton Oilers, dead last in the entire league, than they were to the Capitals. It wasn't a proud entrance worthy of the franchise's history, but it was a ticket to the dance, and the Canadiens were going to be able to check their pride at the door.

Washington and Montreal had never before met in the NHL playoffs. In fact, the only significant sporting link between the two cities was the relocation of the Montreal Expos to Washington in 2004. Though the Expos often played before little more than family and friends at Olympic Stadium, the loss of the baseball team remains one of the darker events in the modern history of Montreal sports, a bit of American imperialism. It was a stretch to believe that the Canadiens were going to pose a threat to set things right between the cities. Even R.J. Umberger might not have gone that far.

The Canadiens had endured a very difficult 12 months. After hosting the 2009 NHL All-Star Game as part of their centennial season, a weekend during which Ovechkin had been feted like the international celebrity he and his handlers desired him to become, the Canadiens had crashed and lost in the first round of the 2009 playoffs. General manager Bob Gainey decided to overhaul the roster, including jettisoning popular captain Saku Koivu. Owner George Gillett, meanwhile, decided to sell the team, or at least the global financial crisis created by the sub-prime mortgage meltdown in the United States had decided it for him. The Molson family bought out Gillett for $500 million. This seemed to signal a return to the franchise's former glories, the Molsons having owned and operated the Canadiens for most of the back half of the 20th century. But with new players like Scott Gomez, Brian Gionta, and Mike Cammalleri carrying weighty contracts, some believed the Canadiens were headed in the wrong direction. That seemed to be borne out by Montreal's struggles over the course of the 2009–10 regular season. Gainey had been an icon from his playing days and his number had been retired, but the team's struggles and increasing public criticism prompted him to step down from the GM's post in February, handing the reins to his assistant, Pierre Gauthier. Gainey's resignation had been effectively an admission that his vision for the team had failed.

Part of that vision was the coach Gainey had handpicked the previous summer: Jacques Martin. No one in the game chooses his words more carefully than Martin and, thus, he's a hard man to dislike. Martin's all-encompassing caution and his seemingly emotionless presence behind the bench also makes him impossible to be excited about—one scribe labeled him the Least Interesting Man in the World, a play on a popular Dos Equis television commercial. Points of style aside, Martin hardly lacked experience, having coached 1,200 NHL regular-season games. What he did lack were results: his career playoff record was under .500, and the most talented teams he took into the postseason had inevitably underachieved.

Making matters worse for the Canadiens was their goaltending issue. The old hockey saying seemed to apply: a team with two No. 1 goaltenders doesn't have one it can count on. Former first-round pick Carey Price had started the previous two playoff campaigns in the Montreal crease, and he had been a Gainey favorite. Over the course of the 2009–10 season, Price had been outplayed by Jaroslav Halak—but not to such a degree that one couldn't envision Price taking over if Halak struggled in his first exposure as a playoff starter. Little noted in the run-up to the series was the fact that Halak had a record of success against Ovechkin dating as far back as the 2004 World Junior Championships and as recently as two months earlier in Slovakia's shoot-out victory over Russia at the Olympics. Maybe Halak knew something, maybe he didn't. Martin didn't seem to identify him as any kind of unique antidote to Ovechkin and the Washington attack. In the last regular-season meeting between the two clubs, just before the Olympics, Martin had given Price the start, and he'd been good enough in a 6–5 overtime victory. And in that crucial final game of the regular season, Halak had looked lousy against the doormats of the Eastern Conference, the Maple Leafs.

• • •

The Capitals had their own goaltending questions: Jose Theodore, their first choice during the regular season, or Semyon Varlamov, the rookie who had played so well in the previous year's playoffs? Theodore owned the long unbeaten streak that looked particularly flashy if you could ignore the number of goals he had surrendered. He was also an inspirational figure—he and his wife Stephanie Cloutier had lost their son Chace to respiratory illness in late August, just 54 days after his premature birth. Theodore had planned to spend the off-season in intense training, trying to recapture the form that won him the Hart and Vezina trophies in his days in Montreal, but instead he and Stephanie spent the summer in Children's National Medical Center, where Chace was clinging to life on a ventilator. Going into the season, the Capitals had reason to suspect that Theodore would struggle to cope with his son's death—no one could have blamed him for bringing his heartbreak to work. But it turned out that the dressing room would be his refuge and pouring himself into the game would give him temporary escape from the pain. Theodore's regular season was perhaps his best since his All-Star days with the Canadiens and, if the Capitals hadn't counted on him going into the season, they ended up needing him. Expectations had been high for Varlamov going into what was his first full year in the NHL, but injuries kept him on the sidelines for much of the season while Theodore seized the No. 1 job. The team couldn't have known how long that was going to last, though—how long Theodore was going to be able to keep it together when he had been emotionally spent for so long. The Capitals had to believe that, in the first round anyway, their firepower was going to be enough to compensate for the occasional bad goal while Theodore and Varlamov sorted themselves out.

Still, in the final days before the series, the Capitals seemed more on edge than confident and especially so when reporters pressed Boudreau on the goaltending question. Out of exasperation he finally announced Theodore as his Game 1 starter two days before the series began—a bit out of the usual routine of keeping opponents guessing.

Montreal reporters asked Canadiens center Tomas Plekanec about Washington's goaltenders and he made a frank assessment. "It's not as though we are facing [Martin] Brodeur or [Ryan] Miller," Plekanec said. "They don't have a dominant goaltender. When you look at the goaltending matchup in this series it favors our team. I just believe that our goaltending is more solid than theirs. I'm not saying their goalies are bad. I'm just saying our goalies are better."

Plekanec might have intended a spitball, but the Capitals viewed it as a verbal grenade. "Tomas who? Jagr? Oh, Plekanec. OK. I thought you meant Jagr," Theodore said. Then Boudreau, who had sat at home the previous night and watched four other playoff favorites lose the opening games of their first-round series, got involved, and his comments were incorrectly interpreted as taking a shot at Price and Halak. "I don't mind the controversy. Just get it fucking right!" the normally affable coach thundered at the morning skate before Game 1.

Instead of the first-place Capitals coming in with a swagger, they seemed tentative, or at least disinterested in getting into a contentious battle. They just wanted it to go nice and easy, to let the obvious trends and realities of the series play themselves out. They knew there would be hard stuff to deal with later on, just not yet.

. . .

He looked like the same Alexander Ovechkin from the middle of winter, but then the puck dropped and it was all different. Ovechkin wasn't himself. *If I wait for it, it will come to me.* It looked like he was still feeling the effects of an Olympic hangover, still put off his game by the suspension for the hit on Brian Campbell, and, maybe, a little shaken by losing the season's scoring races. As the captain, he was expected to set the standard for his teammates—he had to show them a commitment and passion that they'd try to match. Yet all through Game 1 he appeared to be either unwilling or unready to engage in the kind of intense struggles that even average NHL playoff series can require. The Capitals lost the opening game at home by a 3–2 overtime score, a disappointment, but more troubling was his play. Statistics rarely tell the entire story, but his struggles could be measured by a number: 0. For only the second time in his career Ovechkin didn't register a shot on goal. It was as if he was waiting for it to happen rather than making it happen. Worse, Plekanec scored the overtime winner for the Canadiens. Ovechkin and Backstrom were caught up ice, executing a lackadaisical line change. It was a disconcerting start for Ovechkin, particularly since many were still discussing his ineffective play for Russia against Canada at the Olympics.

Boudreau didn't candy-coat the critique of the captain's performance. "He didn't play good," Boudreau said. That was as harsh as any coach would go with his franchise player—when that coach's contract was winding down.

The game was nothing like North Dakota in '05, when Sidney Crosby, Mike Richards, Patrice Bergeron, and Dion Phaneuf were looking to knock Ovechkin's head off. It wasn't the Olympic scenario, where layers of Team Canada talent blocked his way to the net. This was different. The Canadiens just weren't as talented as those teams, not even remotely, but they were spirited and their defensemen were blocking shots like the pucks were made of sponge. Their small veteran forwards like Gionta, Cammalleri, and Gomez were both surprisingly combative and shockingly confident. There was Halak again, stopping 18 of 19 shots in the first period and looking very good the rest of the way. None of the shots he'd faced in the game had come off Ovechkin's stick, but the Montreal goalie was off to a positive start.

At the Olympics, Ovechkin had been able to dodge questions and refuse to speak English with Coach Bykov's approval, but the day after the loss in Game 1 he had to step forward. "I didn't play my game at all," he said. "It's not about Montreal, it's all about me." Clearly, the intent was to be a stand-up guy, to provide the leadership on an off-day that he hadn't provided on game day. He dismissed suggestions that the captaincy was weighing heavily. "I don't think when I'm on the ice that I'm the captain and I have to do something differently. I just have to play better. I don't know why but last game I didn't feel that power or something, I don't know what. Maybe it was the first game and before the game I said everybody is nervous, shaky and too excited. This is the playoffs and this is a fun time."

Ovechkin's demeanor made it seem like anything but fun. He wasn't quite like Vancouver again. He wasn't rudely dismissive and glowering. Still, Ovechkin seemed under strain. He was giving rote answers, like they had been laid out by the Capitals' staff to put the best possible spin on the situation. His team needed passion, but in the wake of the Game 1 defeat Ovechkin offered only memorization.

●　●　●

It was as though the NHL playoff schedule was specifically designed to keep the personal game of H-O-R-S-E between Ovechkin and Crosby going. Going into Game 2, Ovechkin had seen all the highlights from the second game of the Pittsburgh-Ottawa series from the night before when Crosby had constructed a brilliant setup for the winning goal. On that play, Crosby eluded Jason Spezza behind the net with a series of reverses, like he was running a three-man weave by himself, before feeding Kris Letang for the clinching goal. Crosby also made the key defensive play for the Penguins earlier in the game, batting a loose puck away from the Penguin goal line. So the standard was again set, or lifted, for Ovechkin as he stepped out on the ice for the second game against the Habs.

I have to be better. He was at the start. He raced down in the Montreal zone in the opening moments, flattened Canadiens defenseman Marc-Andre Bergeron and launched himself into Russian countryman Andrei Markov, sending him spilling to the ice. *I respect him but on the ice that is not everything.* The visiting team didn't seem rattled—in fact they promptly took the puck down the ice and scored. Then they quickly scored again, forcing Boudreau to yank Theodore from the net—the coach's reassurances that the veteran goalie would not be "on a short leash" proved to be empty. Boudreau realized that the series and the season might already be on the line. And he owed little loyalty to Theodore who was going to be a free agent at season's end and was unlikely to be signed to another contract. Theodore didn't try to conceal his disappointment and disgust, throwing down his gloves and stick in a fit of pique.

Winger Eric Fehr restored some sense of equilibrium to the proceedings with a breakaway goal. But by the latter part of the second period, despite all of Ovechkin's most rambunctious physical efforts, the Caps trailed 4–1 as their fans squirmed uncomfortably in their seats.

That it was the Capitals doing the celebrating by the end of the night was, if not shocking, seemingly an indication that the ambush the Canadiens had sprung on their favored opponents had worked initially, but ultimately failed. Three straight goals, including Ovechkin's first of the playoffs, over the final minutes of the second period and early part of the third, tied the game. And when Plekanec gave Montreal one last lead with just over five minutes to play, the NHL's highest scoring team erased that, too, on a wrist shot by rookie defenseman John Carlson. *You score five, we'll score six.* In the first minute of overtime, Nicklas Backstrom completed the first hat trick of his NHL career to tie the series 1–1 before a joyous sellout crowd. *Game on. Game back on.*

The Canadiens had enjoyed their moment, but now it seemed to be time for Washington to assert its supremacy. Afterwards, in the Verizon Center hallway outside the family room, Tatiana Ovechkina held court with family and friends, most wearing red Capitals home jerseys. It was the same scene you see played out at minor hockey rinks on countless days and nights around the world, the parent of the best player enjoying the same adulation as the child, soaking up the glory created by a winning goal or a winning effort. It was the same scene that had played out at the Moscow Dynamo arena when her Sasha was the young phenom. Ovechkin's mother was happily basking in the reflected light of her son's glories and those of his teammates. The most valuable player and the most valuable parent. "Boys . . .boys . . . all of the team," she smiled, as if to magnanimously share her son's spotlight with his less-talented colleagues.

Ovechkin had responded to the criticism about his flaccid Game 1 performance with a goal, three assists, and six shots, all in 20:22 of playing time, the amount preferred by his coach. While Boudreau conducted his post-match press conference in the Wizards' practice court, which had been converted into a media center for the playoffs, Ovechkin and Backstrom shot hoops, the echoing sounds of the ball hitting the floor causing Boudreau to look over his shoulder. *Lots of energy left for those boys*. Halak had been solved, the Washington offence had kicked into gear, and the embarrassment of falling behind 0–2 to an inferior opponent had been avoided. More important, the Capitals had won without being particularly good. Against this opponent, their "C" game had been enough.

●　●　●

It just wasn't like Ovechkin to talk trash, let alone to talk trash in the middle of a deadlocked playoff series. Sure, he'd been part of that rowdy Russian team that had mockingly lobbed one f-bomb after another at Team Canada during the 2003 World Junior Championships. He'd seen it done. He enjoyed the image of the bad boy, the rebel; he liked wearing the tinted "Darth Vader" visor and was pleased at the way he'd been able to "gangster up" his $370,000 car. On the rare occasions when he seemed to boast, however, it appeared to be only a product of a poor command of the

English language. But as the series switched from Washington to Montreal for Games 3 and 4, Ovechkin decided to make the curious observation that he had spied rattled nerves in Halak during the Game 2 comeback. When Halak had gone to drink from his green water bottle after being beaten by Fehr on a breakaway, according to Ovechkin his hand was "shaking." Or at least Ovechkin believed he had detected that nervousness when he watched the game on replay. "I watched the replay when Fehr scored the goal and [Halak's] arm was shaking when he drank water," Ovechkin said. "So, he's nervous. He knows all the pressure is on him and that's a good sign for us."

It came out as an innocent observation, or at least he claimed it was, but given the pre-series goaltending snipes, the words seemed anything but innocent. To the Canadiens, Ovechkin's verbal volley was ridiculous. "We all kind of laughed because that's not Halak at all," said Montreal blueliner Josh Gorges. "Any player, any professional, to have a comment made like that about you, it's a challenge."

Ovechkin was responding in kind to Plekanec's knock on the Capitals' goaltending, but he had no grounds for any charge that Halak was actually quaking. Any reasonable examination of the videotape suggested that if Halak's hand was shaking, it was simply from squeezing the bottle in the midst of physical exertion. He wasn't trembling. It was as if Ovechkin was reaching for answers, searching for belief. If it was gamesmanship, it was weak. It was also at odds with the transformation regular Ovechkin watchers had witnessed over the preceding months, a fairly astonishing transition from the open, relaxed, and sometimes cheeky Ovechkin with whom the city had fallen in love to a more uptight and cautious version, a player no longer willing to speak his mind. The season had taken its toll. The compilation of complicating factors—the captaincy, the Olympics, the threat of another suspension—had sucked the life and sense of joy out of the star, resulting in a deterioration of the very image his new IMG handlers had hoped to cash in with. Over the course of the final weeks of the NHL season, the personality had gone and the game had followed, as though they were linked. Then, suddenly, the shot at Halak, his tormentor from Vancouver. Shaking? Really? Why would the goalie who had backstopped the out-manned Slovaks to a fourth-place finish at the Olympics be shaking? The truth was that all the pressure was on Ovechkin and he knew it, even if he wasn't talking about it.

•   •   •

The Canadiens have often mined their colorful history to provoke emotional responses from their fans, and they dug deep for the third game of the series. Over the course of a century they had achieved complete and total command of their brand. They did things right. Before the teams took to the ice for Game 3, the lights at the Bell Centre were turned down and a small boy in full Habs garb skated out onto the ice with a torch in his hand, the same torch that had been used to close the old Montreal Forum in 1996. It was a bit of theater that IMG would have had to admire. It was a powerful piece of iconography inspired by the words from a First World War poem, "In Flanders Fields," that had adorned the team's dressing room at the old Forum for decades. "To you from failing hands we throw the torch. Be yours to hold it high." The atmosphere was electric. Then came the national anthems, first *The Star-Spangled Banner*, then *O Canada*, which two decades earlier produced boos in Montreal from separatist-minded quebecers but in the new century elicited a more joyous response, an entire arena singing as one. On the massive video screen, the visage of a great Canadiens hero, Jean Beliveau, was flashed as the final words of the anthem were completed. It was greeted with a roar, as fans had not seen Beliveau in his usual seat since suffering a stroke three months earlier. The building was stoked like a roaring fire, leaving only the question of how Ovechkin would be greeted.

Fourteen months earlier, at the 2009 NHL All-Star Game, Ovechkin had been the most popular player in town, greeted as a rock star and heralded for his personality, particularly when, during the breakaway portion of the skills contest, he donned a hat and joke-shop glasses, given to him by Evgeni Malkin after their much-publicized reconciliation, and tried to score with a stick in each hand. On a weekend in which Crosby attended the events but didn't play due to injury, Ovechkin stole the show and won over the crowd as much as any visiting player could. Certainly, no Russian had ever evoked such a response, not in a city where the Soviets had stunned an entire nation back in 1972 by strolling into the Forum and humiliating Team Canada, and certainly no Russian who skated for another team and had never played for Montreal. Meanwhile, a December swing through western Canada during the early part of the 2009–10 season, seemed to confirm the notion that hockey-loving Canadians somehow viewed Ovechkin differently, embracing his passionate personality, YouTube moments, and exuberant goal-scoring celebrations. "I feel like a movie star," said a thrilled Ovechkin in Vancouver. It was delicious news for his IMG handlers who, on signing Ovechkin a few weeks earlier, had boasted that his popularity had separated him from other hockey players.

For the 2010 playoffs in Montreal, however, there had been a decided sea change. Maybe it was the suspensions, and perhaps it was Ovechkin's decidedly unfriendly, no-speak-English attitude at the Vancouver Olympics. Or perhaps it was simply strategic. Whatever the reason, boos rained down on Ovechkin every time he came anywhere near the puck, let alone touched it. "They don't really mean it," theorized *Sports Illustrated* writer Michael Farber, a Montreal resident. "It's like singing *O Canada*. They don't really mean that, either." Nonetheless, Games 3 and 4 in Montreal produced the most hostile environment Ovechkin had ever faced as an NHL player. During lulls, the 21,000-strong crowd would break into thundering "Ovie Sucks!" chants. It may simply have been fans trying to knock an opposing player off his game, but it resulted in an atmosphere more akin to that produced when an athlete who had demanded a trade returns with his new team to face his former club. No more special treatment for Ovechkin, no more comfy movie-star status. The reception showed that Ovechkin's relationship with the rest of the hockey world had been altered. He was now the enemy.

Ovechkin seemed to hear each and every catcall in Game 3. He was as ineffective as he'd been in the series opener. "It's the worst stretch I've ever seen him go through," a worried McPhee said. During off-days and pre-game skates, the media atmosphere around the Washington star had become tense. *Washington Post* beat writer Tarik El-Bashir had always been Ovechkin's favorite member of the media—he'd think nothing of asking El-Bashir to borrow his computer at the arena at practice. In Montreal, however, their history meant nothing. El-Bashir said, "Hey Alex," and Ovechkin chilled him with a look and abruptly told him that he was only going to be talking to the media in an organized scrum setting.

It seemed that there was soon going to be a reason for the tension to break. Neither Ovechkin's struggles nor the hostile atmosphere in the games assisted the home team. The Caps swept Games 3 and 4 by 5–1 and 6–3 scores, forcing Halak to be pulled from Game 3 and then humiliating his backup, Price, who was given the start in Game 4. Price took a pair of unsportsmanlike penalties, one for shooting a puck into a pack of Capitals celebrating a goal, the other for trying to reach from the Montreal bench and clip Backstrom with his stick. "Gotta let 'em know you're there," said an unrepentant Price. His teammates weren't amused. "You gotta grow up a little bit," Cammalleri said. The Habs, losers of both home games, suddenly seemed to be fraying at the edges.

The constant booing of Ovechkin had been unpleasant, per-haps, but the vaunted Washington offence had come to life and the Caps had put a 3–1 stranglehold on the series. A few hours later there was an omen, miles away from any arena.

• • •

Once or twice a season a pro sports team has some sort of travel nightmare. It's true of anybody who travels weekly on business, even those who have their own charters. Pittsburgh's came on the Saturday night and into the wee hours of Sunday in the lead-up to the Super Bowl Sunday game in Washington. The Capitals' came after Game 4 of the series with Montreal. The team managed to get away from Montreal in good time, but when they were almost home the pilot got word from the ground at Reagan National Airport that fog had rolled in. The flight would have to be rerouted to Baltimore.

That would have been an inconvenience in most circumstances, but this was particularly bad. Because the Capitals had departed from the other side of the border, the team needed to pass through customs and there were no customs officers on duty at the airport after midnight. The charter landed but the Capitals were stuck on the plane for hours while calls were placed to get customs officers to the airport.

"I had a bad feeling about it," McPhee said. "Our guys would have been sleeping in their own beds but they weren't getting home until 4:00 or 5:00 in the morning."

McPhee wanted the incident hushed up—the Capitals announced that they wouldn't have an off-day skate at the rink but gave no reason. As it turned out, though, the news of their travel problems did leak out because one of the players Tweeted about them while on the tarmac. What the Capitals would have liked to have hushed up was making the rounds on Twitter in real time.

• • •

The Capitals needed a strong first period in Game 5 at the Verizon Center, a chance for the favored Caps to put the reeling Montrealers away and end the series quickly, usually a necessary component for a serious Stanley Cup aspirant during the long postseason grind. With everything on their side—home ice, a roaring crowd, a healthy team, goaltending questions on the other side of the ice, Boudreau's team played one of the worst games of their season.

By the eight-minute mark of the first period the Canadiens had grabbed a 2–0 lead and, in the end, it was all that they would need. Halak was back in the Montreal net and allowed only one goal. Boudreau went from concerned to outraged over the course of three periods. "We had Game 5 in our building and we played like crap for the first 10 minutes. Game's over," he shouted. "We're not getting 20 guys playing every night. We're getting 13 or 14." *No names. They know who they are.*

The power play had gone from brilliant to awful, falling to 1-for-24 in the series. The Canadiens had effectively taken away Washington's most lethal weapon. Green hadn't scored and looked confused, as though all the talk of his defensive shortcomings had left him unwilling to take a chance—it was like Glen Hanlon was in his ear. Even the news that he had been named a finalist for the Norris Trophy didn't settle him. *It should be easier than this.* Semin hadn't scored either, and was moving further away from the Montreal net and making more sensational attempts to score, rather than embracing the down-and-dirty style of NHL playoff competition. He hadn't scored at all the previous spring in the second round of the playoffs against Pittsburgh, leaving him goal-less in 12 playoff games. He'd been nearly useless for Russia at the Olympics, too, showing himself to be a one-dimensional player who, if he wasn't scoring, wasn't doing much else. *It will take a big play and I'll be the one to do it. I know that I can do things the others can't.* It was as though the Washington arsenal was disarming itself piece by piece.

The Caps had let the Habs back into the series, although with two more chances to advance to the next round, it seemed a safe bet that Boudreau would find the right combinations to get his team through, even though some of the players who had done a great deal for the team during the regular season were either sitting out or taking a backseat to late arrivals like Joe Corvo and Eric Belanger.

Given a new life in the series, Halak again haunted Ovechkin. With the noise level at the Bell Centre cranked up to a new level for Game 6, the Slovak had a game for the ages, a magical 53-save performance in a 4–1 Montreal triumph that sent the series back to Washington for Game 7, a match that would have seemed unthinkable just a few days earlier. It was vindication for Halak, and an extraordinary achievement for a player selected 271st in the 2003 entry draft. *Who's shaking now?* Comparisons were made to Ken Dryden's remarkable 1971 playoff effort against the powerful Boston Bruins and to Patrick Roy's magical work in both the '86 and '93 Stanley Cup championship efforts. This time, Ovechkin and Backstrom joined Green and Semin in their inability to get the puck past Halak. The entire Washington attack had been grounded. In three days, the Caps had blown a 3–1 series lead, putting themselves in the potentially humiliating position of crashing and burning in the first round of the playoffs after the best regular season in team history.

• • •

Dean Evason, one of the Capitals' assistant coaches, was a nervous man as he rode the Washington subway system to work in the late afternoon before Game 7. His players were nervous about losing the game, but the stakes were even bigger for the 46-year-old Evason. He was worried about his job. He was worried that a loss would result in wholesale changes on the coaching staff. He was worried about having to start over somewhere else.

Evason's a hockey lifer. A native of Flin Flon, Manitoba, he played more than 800 NHL games for five teams. He could have been financially set up for life but his career had ended with Calgary in 1996, just before the money started getting really good for the checkers and grinders like him. He ended up in Europe, playing in the Swiss and German leagues—he's best remembered for captaining a Canadian team to the 1997 World Championship, wearing the "C" though he was the only non-NHLer in the lineup. The notion that Evason would have left the game behind for a job in another field probably never crossed his mind. He had worked six seasons in the junior leagues in western Canada before he was hired as an assistant to Glen Hanlon after the lockout in 2005. It was a better life than he might have had in the lower levels of hockey—NHL assistant coaches' salaries vary from team to team, but they're well short of even a middling NHL player and more in line with what a doctor or lawyer might make. The difference is that doctors and lawyers have a lot more job security than assistant coaches.

Evason and his wife had bought their home in the D.C. suburb of Alexandria, Virginia, five years earlier, and they had watched as the local housing market suffered the sledgehammer-like effect of the sub-prime mortgage collapse over the previous 12 months. The stunning Montreal victories in Games 5 and 6 had him worrying about not just his hockey team, but his family, too. He didn't know how he'd pay the mortgage if a total Washington collapse ended up costing him his job. He didn't have any illusions about landing the top job if Boudreau were terminated—he had already been passed over for Boudreau when Hanlon was fired. Another assistant's job with another team was no sure thing. Back in the Western juniors? A job in Europe? Those were options he'd have to investigate if worse came to worst. "If I get fired, I'm screwed," he said grimly, getting off at the Verizon Center stop.

Evason wasn't the only one worried, just one of those with a large financial stake in the game. The sellout crowd that gathered for a Game 7 none had believed they'd need tickets for was tense and nervous. A murmur of uncertainty was rippling through the stands from the warm-up on. Their team had been exposed in the previous few days, weaknesses and vulnerabilities made plain after a season in which they'd dominated the entire league. Boudreau made more roster moves, inserting 36-year-old veteran Scott Walker for his first game of the playoffs in place of Tomas Fleischmann, a 23-goal scorer during the regular season who had been even less effective than Semin against the Canadiens. Tom Poti, the reliable veteran blueliner, had been lost with a facial fracture after being struck in the face with a puck in Game 6. Rather than giving veteran John Erskine a shot, or tapping Tyler Sloan for his third game of the series, the Caps coach called up former first-round pick Karl Alzner from the minors and dressed him. Montreal had made the same move with 20-year-old P.K. Subban for Game 6 and received a boost, so maybe Alzner could do the same. Still, those decisions were indicative of a team that had lost faith and was searching for answers. Maybe Walker could add some grit and savvy. Maybe Alzner would surprise people. Maybe, maybe, maybe.

For most of the first period, the Capitals looked like they were in good shape. Ovechkin fired a shot from the left wing just before the three-minute mark, and hammered both Maxim Lapierre and Ryan O'Byrne with heavy checks on his next shift. *Get out of my way.* He hadn't been this engaged since Game 2. The home team's play was better but their luck stayed the same. With just over eight minutes left in the first, Laich fed a perfect pass to Semin in the goal mouth, but Semin's redirect fluttered upwards and then off the crossbar. Still 0–0. With less than a minute remaining, in the period, Green snared the puck and jumped forward into the play, making the kind of bold rush he'd avoided for the entire series. As he crossed the Montreal blue line, he fumbled the puck, losing it off the end of his stick into the corner. Rather than chasing it, he turned towards a backpedalling Markov and cross-checked him in the chest, sending Markov tumbling to the ice. It was an inexplicable play, a penalty that wouldn't have been forgiven in an exhibition game, let alone the deciding game of a seven-game series.

During the regular season Boudreau had sent out David Steckel in this sort of situation—a penalty-kill face-off in the Washington end. But despite his work in this valuable if limited role, Steckel was a healthy scratch—instead Boudreau opted to dress Belanger, who, like Walker, had been added to the roster at the trading deadline. Steckel was "Boudreau's son" and he had scored clutch goals in the previous year's series against Pittsburgh, but the coach opted for pieces that McPhee had traded for when making out his lineup.

Maybe things would have worked out differently with Steckel. Maybe he would have beaten Montreal center Scott Gomez on that important draw after the penalty to Green. Instead, Gomez controlled the face-off and the Canadiens circled the puck back to Marc-Andre Bergeron at the point. A veteran defenseman no NHL team had wanted until the Habs signed him after training camp the previous fall, Bergeron hammered a slap shot past Varlamov to give the Canadiens the first goal of the game for the fifth time in the series. It wasn't a collective groan that went up in the arena, more like a low hum, 18,000 muttering under their breath in disbelief. They were thinking the same thought as the Capitals. *How can we outplay Montreal and yet keep falling behind? It can't end this way.* It was as though Games 5, 6, and now 7 had been joined into one long, agonizing sequence.

In the second period, Green again drove into Montreal's zone and looked to put the puck in front only to find three teammates hovering far from net, unavailable to receive a pass. Or unwilling. Just past the halfway point of the period, with Plekanec off for tripping, the Washington power play unit entered the fray and looked even worse. Only Corvo, suddenly the quarterback, seemed to want the puck. All season, Ovechkin had played the left point with Green manning the right, and the extra-strength unit had flowed through them. Most of the time, Ovechkin stayed out for the entire two minutes. Now, with Boudreau looking for offence, Ovechkin had moved to other positions—it looked like he was taking a page out of Coach Bykov's book. Still, the Canadiens were able to isolate Ovechkin and take him away. Semin and Backstrom looked like they couldn't get rid of the puck fast enough. Green was booed, and loudly.

Trailing 1–0 going into the third, having already tested Halak 24 times without success, the desperate Capitals poured it on. Just 24 seconds into the period, Ovechkin whipped a shot at the net from the left boards and, as the building gasped, the white twine behind Halak bulged. It was a goal, one that pulled Washington back from the brink, one that was going to be replayed for months. A tie game. Bedlam ensued, and Ovechkin skated across to the other side of the rink and hurled himself into the glass. His standard celebration: He kissed his glove and reached heavenward, his way of recognizing his late brother. *Everything will be alright now.* But Ovechkin's expression quickly went from joy to bewilderment. Referee Brad Watson had waved off the goal and there wasn't going to be a replay. Watson had detected winger Mike Knuble encroaching on Halak's blue crease. There hadn't been significant contact. *I didn't touch him.* There wasn't a penalty assessed but there was just enough, in Watson's judgment, to wave off the goal. It was a stunning, heart-wrenching setback. Their leader, the star who was supposed to produce at exactly this moment, had done so, then seen that moment cruelly reversed.

Sitting in the Capitals' management box, McPhee said to no one in particular: "It's not going to happen. It's not going to happen."

He knew his team was going to lose or, at least, he was girding himself in case of a loss.

The rest of the period and the rest of the season slipped through the Capitals' fingers like a handful of sand. A John Carlson chance in the slot was deflected high into the netting. More blocked shots. A big hit by Ovechkin on Gorges, leaving the much smaller blueliner woozy. With four minutes left, Ovechkin churned down the right side, his opposite wing. A hard, low shot. Deflected away by Halak. With 3:36 left, Montreal center Dominic Moore, another player left unsigned the previous fall until Florida gave him a contract before later trading him to the Habs, put the

Canadiens ahead 2–0. But just 80 seconds after that, Laich finally broke Halak's shutout, setting up a wild finish. Moments later, with the Caps pushing ferociously, Ovechkin prepared to one-time a slap shot from high in the zone. Snap. *It can't be. This doesn't happen to us.* His stick shattered for the second time in the game from the same spot. There would be no more scoring chances for the home team, even with Varlamov removed for an extra attacker. The clock ticked to zero. The upset no one had seen coming had happened, and it was difficult to decide who was more shocked, the victors or the vanquished.

The Canadiens had blocked an amazing 41 shots on the night, with 15 players blocking at least one. They had fought an uphill battle as one. The Canadiens did not have a captain—no replacement for Saku Koivu had been named during the season. Still, despite their lack of a designated leader, Montreal had won with a greater sense of cohesiveness than a team captained by one of the most celebrated players in the world.

• • •

The victors were barely able to settle themselves for the obligatory post-series handshakes. The Capitals looked like zombies. When Ovechkin shook the last of the Canadiens' hands, he looked for his teammates, wanting to have one and all lift their sticks in recognition of the fans, something that had become commonplace around the NHL in the post-lockout years, a gesture from millionaire athletes to their customers to suggest appreciation. Ovechkin's center Nicklas Backstrom stood beside him. Also joining in were veterans who had worked their way up from Hershey to Washington, Eric Fehr and Brooks Laich. So did Varlamov and Alzner. Theodore did also, sensing that he had played his last game for the team. Walker waved, wondering if he might have played the last game of his NHL career. The gesture was half-hearted and barely acknowledged by the crowd. More telling was the fact that most of the Capitals had bolted. They had already gone down the hallway to the dressing room, focusing on getting out of the building as fast as possible.

After an elimination game in sports, the post-game dressing-room sequence becomes almost surreal. The athletes pretend to try to explain what just happened, win or lose, but usually they're still trying to understand it themselves, particularly in defeat. What these scenes usually express is the pecking order and understanding of responsibility within a team setting. When the Pittsburgh Penguins lost the last game of the 2008 Stanley Cup final to the Detroit Red Wings on home ice, Sidney Crosby sat at his stall with his equipment still on answering wave after wave of questions while Ryan Malone sat beside him, head bowed, crying quietly. Crosby knew that's where he had to be as captain, if only to spare others the task of answering all the questions. He didn't have to be found. He was waiting for the media when reporters entered the room.

For the Capitals after their Game 7 defeat to the Habs, it was a very different story. The first player out to greet the horde of more than 50 media members was Knuble, a veteran but hardly the first among equals. He stood in the middle of the room and patiently answered questions, many of them surrounding the disallowed goal, others the once-feared power play that had gone 1–33 in the series. Then came Jason Chimera, sitting at his stall, followed by Alzner, and then Fehr. No Semin. No Green, who was so upset he wouldn't talk for several days. No Backstrom. After about a 15-minute wait, Ovechkin emerged with a white towel draped around his naked shoulders and buried himself within an enormous scrum around his stall. It was an absurd situation, with the star player mumbling quietly, no microphone to amplify his voice, no riser to make it possible to see or hear him. He dealt with 17 questions, answering seven of them with "I don't know" and three with terse one-word answers. Suspects in a crime are more expansive before their lawyers arrive. Usually IMG's iconic figures owned moments like this, the good and the bad. Palmer and Nicklaus and Federer and others: they were always gracious in victory and defeat. But Ovechkin had descended into a deep pout.

The Washington season was suddenly, shockingly over, and for Ovechkin, it had been more about what hadn't happened than what had. There had been no YouTube moment, no stick-on-fire creativity, no Olympic triumph, and now a disastrous playoff performance. In the wake of Game 7, there was only a disallowed goal, two shattered sticks, and a mumbling, 17-question press conference that made him look like anything but the game's next great ambassador or a player who could transcend his sport. He had five goals and five assists in the series, but no goals in the final two games. His performance had, in many ways, mirrored that of the Olympics; a superb individual player unable to alter the momentum of a competition, stifled by the team approach of the opponent. It was less about his skill, his commitment, or his effort, and more about his lack of imagination and inability to adapt his game to the circumstances. The Habs had figured Ovechkin out and identified his inability to effectively use his teammates or use his backhand to make plays and get shots on goal. He had been predictable. Time and time again, he had bulled his way down the left wing only to be turned away by Jaroslav Spacek, Gorges, or Bergeron, none of whom would be regarded as elite defensemen.

In the Montreal dressing room there was no trash talk, no return of fire for Ovechkin's claim that he saw Halak shaking. Instead, the Canadiens defensemen explained how they had shutdown Ovechkin, how they had rendered hockey's most dangerous man as safe as milk. Josh Gorges made it sound so simple the wonder was that no one else had seemed to pick up on it before.

"Generally, you know what's coming," Gorges said. "When he comes in on the off-wing, he'll try to step to the middle and shoot through you. You can bait him into that." As the Habs prepared to move on and play the Penguins in the next round, Hal Gill explained the difference between defending against Crosby and defending against Ovechkin. "Sid's got a pretty good repertoire of moves," Gill said. "He's got a pretty good backhand and he sees the ice with his backhand. You can't overplay him. That's the biggest thing. I think against him [Crosby] and more than anyone else, you have to be really good as a team. You let somebody slip through the cracks and he'll find him. [Ovechkin]'s very different from Sid in that respect. Sid has so many moves. He's resourceful." In defeat, the player who most NHLers would have identified six months earlier as the game's top attacker had been reduced to a player who could be controlled, if not shut down.

For Ovechkin, this was the ultimate indignity—in defeat he was again being compared to Crosby and again found wanting.

• • •

In the days following Montreal's upset triumph, the predictably harsh judgments came in on Washington's playoff demise, both from within the Capitals organization and from without.

"Collapse with a Capital 'C'" read the headline on the main sports page of the *Washington Post*. Columnist Tracee Hamilton called the series a "referendum" on Ovechkin's status within the sport, and, picking up on a theme opened by Gill after Game 7, suggested he was now clearly running second to Crosby. She questioned Ovechkin's decision to blow off an optional workout the day before Game 7, something a team leader, in her opinion, would not do. Another *Post* writer, Mike Wise, suggested the absence of meaningful postseason results for Ovechkin, including being part of a team that had lost three of four Game 7 matches on home ice in the previous three years, was in danger of putting him into an unhappy stratosphere. "If he doesn't hurry and hoist something besides another Hart Trophy, he's A-Rod or Wilt the Stilt in training, pre-championships." Another media voice, Michael Wilbon, took the flaying of Ovechkin to another level on ESPN's *Pardon the Interruption*, using the Caps' defeat to comment on NBA star LeBron James. "If LeBron James is going to be something other than the NBA version of Alex Ovechkin, which is to say a transcendent talent who collects all kinds of individual hardware but cannot win a championship, he needs to lead his team past Boston, and he should," said Wilbon. IMG would have been thrilled with having Ovechkin described as a "transcendent talent," but the subtext was that he was more Dominique Wilkins than Michael Jordan. That is, a celebrity within a niche and nothing more. Forever relegated to the quadruple-digits on the DBI.

Two days later, when the Capitals made it out to their training facility to empty their lockers, Ovechkin was more expansive than he had been immediately after Game 7. He had been advised and warned about what was coming.

"Maybe we just thought it was a done series," he said. "Especially after couple playoffs and what we do in the season, I think everybody knows we can win the Cup, we can be on top of everybody. But when you get the lead 3–1, you think, okay, maybe they're gonna give up and maybe we just gonna win easy game and be ready for next round."

These were not the words of a seasoned, hardened playoff performer. It was an admission that he had expected the playoffs to be easy when they never had been, even for the greatest in the history of the game.

Mike Green was even more forthcoming about his failures, admitting that he had paid too much attention to what was being said and written about his suspect defensive abilities. "I think mentally I was preparing myself for the playoffs to play strong defensively," he said. "When all season you're an offensive-minded player and you get criticized about your defensive play, you adjust to become that complete player. Going into the playoffs I wanted to play strong defensively. Maybe that [hurt] my offense."

Green was mournful, even lost, but the seemingly irrepressible Ted Leonsis was inconsolable. In his first blog entry after the defeat, the Caps owner said his team's "hockey I.Q. seemed low in the series" and wondered about its mental toughness. That immediately produced a flurry of speculation about the job security of Boudreau, although McPhee quickly shut that down by saying the coach would be back.

To a large degree, many of the post-series assessments lacked perspective, or at least a reasonable understanding of hockey history. Most of the top hockey dynasties of the previous 30 years—the New York Islanders, the Edmonton Oilers, the Detroit Red Wings—had suffered stunning playoff defeats before their star players matured and began to understand the personal and group sacrifices required to win championships. The Isles had lost to the Maple Leafs in the 1978 playoffs. In the "Miracle on Manchester," the 1982 Los Angeles Kings had eliminated Wayne Gretzky and the Oilers. The Red Wings, loaded with talent, had lost stunning playoff decisions to Toronto and San Jose in the early 1990s and been swept by New Jersey in the 1995 Cup final before finally figuring it all out in 1997. Steve Yzerman, regarded as one of the greatest leaders in the sport, was 32 years of age when he first lifted the Cup. Ovechkin was only 24 after the loss to Montreal, yet some were saying he would never win a title. Part of the problem was that the playoff defeat had followed so quickly on the heels of the Olympic debacle in Vancouver. The Penguins meanwhile were as young as or even younger than the Caps, and they'd won the 2009 Cup. As well, franchises in Tampa, Raleigh, and Anaheim had come out of nowhere to capture the Cup in the first decade of the new century. So while hockey history suggested that even in the wake of defeat the Caps were on the right path to success, other teams had accomplished more in shorter time periods.

As a team, the Capitals had lacked playoff experience, team structure, and the necessary nastiness to brush aside a lesser opponent. In the hours after Game 7, Laich had stopped on the way home to help a stranded motorist change a tire, a lovely humanitarian gesture. Laich, to a large degree, epitomized the

Capitals, classy, well-meaning, and unfailingly decent. The team, however, didn't need Boy Scouts. No, there was a crying need for physical menace. In the parlance of the game, they didn't have enough guys who were hard to play against. No one who inspired dread. The New York Islanders' championship teams had Clark Gillies, one of the NHL's toughest players in his time, and maybe the toughest first-liner. The Oilers had the often vicious Mark Messier, and Detroit needed to find players willing to respond to the likes of Claude Lemieux before winning it all became possible. McPhee's first team in Washington had only a fraction of the skill on the current roster yet that squad went to the 1998 Stanley Cup Final largely on playoff-quality toughness—players like Dale Hunter, Mike Eagles, Steve Konowalchuk, Esa Tikkanen, Mark Tinordi, Craig Berube, and Chris Simon weren't worried about showing respect to opponents, only inspiring their fear. In the 2010 playoffs, the teams that advanced to the second round had players who would make opponents' nights unpleasant. Vancouver's Alex Burrows, Pittsburgh's Matt Cooke, Philadelphia's Dan Carcillo, and Chicago's David Bolland caused mayhem when they were on the ice. By running their mouths or rubbing their gloves in stars' faces or slashing opponents out of the referees' sight, they knocked very good players off their games. The Capitals had no such sandpaper. They were the biggest team in hockey, but they couldn't intimidate or otherwise dissuade the Canadiens, the smallest team in the playoffs.

Ovechkin seemed to understand part of what was missing, if not all of it. "I think everybody wants to win not regular season, we want to win Cup," he said. "We all played great in season, but in the playoffs something missed. We just have to concentrate more about playoffs, more about how we have to play in the playoffs, not about [regular] seasons. We just have to be ready for the playoffs and be ready for that kind of pressure, what it's gonna take."

Most analysts believed the Caps still had the talent and organization to succeed, and the franchise as a business concern had made spectacular gains in just five years, going from a team with 4,500 season tickets to one of the leaders in the sport. The Ovechkin brand, however, had indisputably taken a major hit. "Aside from Caps owner Ted Leonsis, the biggest losers are the Caps' Russian superstar Alexander Ovechkin and sports marketing powerhouse IMG," opined *Forbes* magazine. "Ovechkin and IMG signed a deal about five months ago hoping to cash in on Ovechkin's global appeal. This will be harder now." A season of enormous promise had deteriorated into one of defeat. Hockey's most dangerous player had been humbled.

Las Vegas

"He Is Not Alone Over There"

IT SEEMED STRANGE that the National Hockey League gathered its stars in Las Vegas, where the radiant late June sun and the nuclear heat hardly seem a fit for the winter game. For years, the NHL staged its annual awards show in Toronto, home of the Hockey Hall of Fame. The move to Las Vegas was the antithesis of John Collins's masterstroke, the Winter Classic, an outdoor game evoking the game's roots. But the strategy was founded on the belief that show biz can sell the game, serving its established audience and building a new one in the U.S.

The NHL's host for the awards show, the Palms, did its level best to make the hockey people feel at home. The air-conditioning was working overtime, cold enough to frost glasses. The white noise of the casino floor the binging and bonging of the slots paying off and the chatter at the tables, could have passed as the sounds of an arena crowd, and the pulsing neon signs could have symbolized a thousand goal lights. There was certainly glitz—showgirls, diamonds as big as glass doorknobs, a parking lot full of pimped-up rides, and a pool lined with girls who could have passed for Cheyenne Tozzi, the model from Ovechkin's *Men's Journal* shoot the previous fall. Glamour, though, was in short supply. It wasn't just the retirees feeding nickels into the slots for hours on end. It was also the horde of guys in hockey sweaters who were leaning over the velvet ropes, looking to get autographs on photos and hockey cards that would be posted on eBay within hours. That was about as glamorous as a mid-season bag skate.

The NHL tried its level best with the 2010 awards show, but the league was only able to recruit an unfunny comedian named Jay Mohr as host and "celebrity" presenters who merely aspired to the B-list. Mohr might have been behind Alexander Ovechkin on the DBI. None of their numbers were going to change at all as a result of this show—it would end up drawing 750,000 viewers in Canada but only 206,000 on the NHL network in the U.S.

●　●　●

Ovechkin didn't seem put out about this command performance in Las Vegas, but he didn't seem enthusiastic either. When the league officials brought him into a ballroom for a press conference, he didn't smile as he settled in behind a microphone. He had been pulled away from a poker table and had $500 in the pocket of his cargo pants. "Winnings," he said. Sporting a plain red T-shirt and an NHL hat on backwards, the league's shield centered on his fore-head, he could have passed for a fan or just another player at the tables.

He was still scoping out all the cameras, microphones, and digital recorders pointed at him when he heard the first question over his shoulder.

"Alex, do you know who Stephen Strasburg is?"

A poker-faced response—Ovechkin said he didn't and seemed puzzled that in this celebration of all things hockey, where all the best and best-known NHLers had come together, an unfamiliar name would come up. A question about Crosby: he could have seen that coming. A question about Henrik Sedin, the other finalist for the Hart Trophy: he expected that as Sedin was sitting at the neighboring table with just a couple of reporters asking him about his first trip to the awards. But he had no idea about Strasburg.

When prompted about Strasburg's baseball connection and asked if there was room enough for both of them in D.C., though, Ovechkin smiled.

"I heard about him. I hope we fit good."

That Ovechkin wasn't up to speed on Strasburg was understandable. After losing Game 7 against the Canadiens, Ovechkin cleared out his stall in the dressing room, his equipment was packed by the training staff, and he headed to Germany for the World Hockey Championships. After that, he went to Turkey on vacation with Semin and a squad of beach bunnies. From there he went back to Moscow where he attended a friend's wedding and a mixed-martial arts event, where one trainer talked about getting Ovechkin into MMA training. His plan was to parachute into Vegas for the awards, fulfill an obligation to a sponsor by participating in a practice with a midget boys team near Toronto, and then beat it back to Moscow. With all this going on, it was no wonder he didn't get a chance to see the *Washington Post* or *USA Today* or *SI* or *Sportscenter.* He was a few weeks behind on the news in Washington and didn't realize that he didn't quite own the city's sports market like he had since the day he dropped his luggage in George McPhee's house five years before. It might not be a case of making room for Strasburg but rather leaving room for Ovechkin.

Strasburg had also been the No. 1 draft choice of a team that was a laughingstock, baseball's Washington Nationals. After starting the 2010 season in the minors, Strasburg had arrived in the big leagues and was soon mowing down batters like a modern-day Sandy Koufax. Nothing appeals to those who follow America's pastime like a flamethrower with a penchant for Ks, and Strasburg was that and more. In the short time that Ovechkin had been away, Strasburg had raised the profile of the Nationals higher than it had ever been and had himself become a national sensation, splashed across the pages of the *Post* and *USA Today*, featured on the cover of *SI*, and slotted at the lead of *Sportscenter*. Ovechkin's honeymoon was over. He now had competition in the market.

And it wasn't just Strasburg. Another follow-up question, out of earshot of Ovechkin, mentioned John Wall, who that week would be selected first overall in the NBA draft by the Washington Wizards. Another development while Ovechkin was away: Ted Leonsis had seized majority control of the Wizards after Abe Pollin's death. Washington is a city renowned for its playground hoops, where high schools like DeMatha had once built national profiles on the strength of their basketball programs, where Georgetown University brought home an NCAA title and the Wizards' forerunners, the Bullets, won an NBA championship. Wall was no Kobe, but the flashy new point guard in town resonated on the street. Even before Wall was selected by the Wizards, the 20-year-old had a $25-million deal with Reebok—with that single deal, and before he so much as dribbled a ball in the NBA, Wall was generating five times the endorsement money that Ovechkin was generating as hockey's most dynamic player.

Back when he did the fashion shoot in New York, back when IMG started drawing up his "mythology" and "iconography," these awards were supposed to be a victory lap, a chance for Ovechkin to revisit a glorious season. That was before Strasburg and before Wall and before the 2009–10 season. Then, he'd sat atop the hockey world. If he wasn't indisputably the best player in the world, he was solidly in the running, with few challengers. But the Olympics and the season had gone sideways. This wasn't a victory lap. It wasn't quite "Didn't you used to be Alexander Ovechkin?"—but it wasn't "Hail the Conquering Hero" either. He'd scored 50 goals and added 59 assists, numbers most NHLers would require two years to produce, yet his season was being widely viewed as incomplete.

Bad karma abounded. The Capitals had crashed and burned against Montreal but they fared better than Moscow Dynamo—Russia's oldest team, the team that set Ovechkin in the path to stardom, was folding. Nothing was going right. As he sat in front of the media, it was no wonder Ovechkin looked like he was back in his boyhood days in Moscow, being asked to read or do arithmetic when all he wanted to do was play hockey.

• • •

It was a small mercy that the reporters' attention at the awards was on the Olympics and the NHL season. Neither one had been a shining success, but each could be put into a forgiving perspective. In Vancouver, Russia had lost to the eventual gold-medal winners—and maybe that should have been expected. In the playoffs, the Capitals had not been outplayed, just ultimately undone by a goaltender on an amazing run—not the first time in league history that had happened. But as much as Russia's Olympic team and Ovechkin or the Capitals and Ovechkin could have won, the world championships were a different proposition. The Russians should have won in Cologne in May. They had won the previous two world championships. They brought back their Olympic lineup almost intact—all the frontline offensive talents, Ovechkin, Semin, Malkin, Kovalchuk, and Datsyuk, were on hand because their NHL teams were knocked out of the playoffs in the first two rounds. (In fact, Chicago would win the Stanley Cup without a Russian on the roster, the first time that had happened in a decade, and it would be the first Cup final since 1991 in which neither team had a Russian player.)

At the worlds, it looked like the Russians had averted disaster when they came back to beat their German hosts in a surprisingly tense semifinal. In the final, they were up against the Czech Republic and a lineup that featured only four NHL players, two of them goaltenders. The Russians had beaten a better Czech team in

Vancouver. The gold-medal game should have been a rout, but it didn't turn out that way.

For two periods, Jaromir Jagr was able to find some of his old game, not the one he had in Washington but the one he had back in Pittsburgh. On the first shift, just 20 seconds into the game, Jagr pounced on a turnover in the Russian end of the rink and passed the puck from behind the Russian net to Jakub Klepis, who was skating into the slot. Klepis one-timed the puck past Semyon Varlamov to give the Czechs the lead. For almost the next 40 minutes, the Russians dominated play but could not beat Czech goaltender Tomas Vokoun. Ovechkin showed flashes of his game, but the best play he made was a defensive one: coming from well back to break up a shorthanded two-on-one. Late in the second period, Ovechkin, as he did in Vancouver, leveled an aging star player. Unfortunately for Russia, it wasn't Jagr this time, but rather Ovechkin's teammate Sergei Fedorov. Ovechkin was taking a run at a Czech forward who bailed out and Fedorov took the full force of Ovechkin in fight. Unlike Jagr in Vancouver, Fedorov was knocked out of the game. Just as the Czechs had been stunned by the hit on their star in the Olympic contest, the Russians were taken off their game by the sight of Fedorov laying in pain on the ice. Karel Rachunek took the opportunity to fire a shot from the point. It went off the skate of Tomas Rolinek and by Varlamov, and the goal stood up after a replay. The Czechs, counterpunching all the way, had a 2–0 lead in a game that looked an awful lot like Washington's Game 7 against Montreal.

Ovechkin and the Russians tried to rally, but their bid to get back in the game was pretty well snuffed out when defenseman Alexei Yemelin undercut Jagr and was hit with a five-minute major for clipping midway through the third period. When Viktor Kozlov took a penalty for hooking just as Yemelin's major was running out, Ovechkin bowed his head. Just as in the seventh game against Montreal, Ovechkin's team picked up a late goal—in Cologne, Datsyuk scored with 30 seconds left in regulation—but a bid for a comeback ran out of time. Ovechkin had five goals in the tournament and in flashes, just as in the series against the Canadiens, he looked unstoppable. There just weren't enough of those flashes to get the Russians over the top. Once again, Ovechkin's team had underachieved and lost.

Afterwards, the IIHF officials rolled out the red carpet for the medal ceremony and the playing of the Czech anthem. Ovechkin's teammates stood on the blue line, leaning on their sticks and watching the unlikely champions celebrate, but Ovechkin was bent over on the bench—late in the game he had three teeth knocked out by a wayward high stick that wasn't called. It wasn't an image that IMG would have liked out there, but Ovechkin and the agency were lucky that the worlds fly under the North American radar— though important to the players involved and fans in Europe, the annual tournament is eclipsed by the Stanley Cup in the U.S. and Canada. The Russians did their best to dress up their silver medals as a significant achievement, rather than another international pratfall. Ovechkin, absent a few more teeth, repaired to Moscow. He brought home a souvenir: a new German shepherd puppy. You had to suppose he sought out some unconditional love.

• • •

Ovechkin sat behind the microphone and waited for more questions. Reporters were notified that he was going to be the star of a DVD next season and a couple asked him questions about it.

Q: *Whose idea was the DVD?*
A: "My agency, IMG, said the NHL is interested [in doing] a show . . . like a reality show."
Q: *What's the show about?* He made it sound like One Day in the Life of Alexander Ovechkin, but maybe more "show" than "reality."
A: "It's a pretty fun time. The NHL came to visit me in Moscow. It's good for fans [to know] not only Alexander Ovechkin hockey player [but] how he relaxes and what he's doing in Moscow."

Q: *Did he know that Crosby had done a show just like it?*
A: "No."

Ovechkin apparently didn't hear one reporter ask facetiously if his show was going to be more interesting than Crosby's. Or if he did hear the shot, he chose not to follow up, again showing that the wild-and-crazy-Ovie persona that was celebrated in IMG's New York war room wasn't coming out of retirement before the cameras rolled, if ever.

After that, the questions became more pointed about a season of highlight-reel moments and ultimate frustrations.

Q: *What did you learn about winning this season?*
A: "We didn't win."

Q: *What did you learn about what it takes to win?*
A: "It takes everything. It takes everything what you have. It's hard but it takes everything."

Q: *What will you have to do to be better going forward?*
A: "Right now, I'm taking my vacation, get ready for training camp, be in good shape, go to training camp and show the team, the fans we're ready."

Q: *Which award, the Hart or the Lindsay, would mean more to you?* For Ovechkin, this was like choosing between Jessica Alba and Megan Fox for *Men's Journal*.
A: "Both."

Q: *How are you different from the guy who won rookie of the year?*
A: "I am the same guy. I have more experience. English is getting better. Same fun. It's nice."

There was nothing in his demeanor that suggested this was any fun at all. Nor did it seem that he had drawn any life lessons from his losses in Vancouver, in the Stanley Cup playoffs, and in Cologne. He presented himself as living proof that the unexamined hockey life is still worth living.

What wasn't the same was Ovechkin's view on Sochi. When Russian Olympic officials designated him an official ambassador for the 2014 Winter Games, he told Russian news services that he was "honored," that he'd "do everything possible to help Russia win the hockey gold," and that he put all his "effort into providing organization of the highest level." At the Vancouver Games in February, he had been emphatic: "I'll go play the Olympic Games for my country. If somebody says to me you can't play, see ya."

However, at the press conference in Las Vegas, Ovechkin was noncommittal about 2014. It was, he said effectively, just something too far off to talk about. He had obviously listened to Leonsis cautioning him about future international commitments, and the worlds had underscored those warnings. Gary Bettman, it seemed, no longer needed to worry about having a rogue element in the league. The commissioner didn't have to put his foot down. With the league taking the lead in the production of Ovechkin's DVD, he could try to effect a rebel's style but he had to be a company man at the same time. Being rebellious had become more difficult the day the "C" was stitched on to his jersey in Washington. He fell in line with the boys at head office just like he had dutifully followed Bykov's marching orders in Vancouver. And as far as what the Russian team could do differently in Sochi than it had done in Vancouver and in Cologne, Ovechkin wasn't going to bite. He begged off talking about it because it didn't seem appropriate. "Right now we don't have a coach," he said. Bykov had been fired after the loss to the Czechs at the worlds, and Ovechkin didn't want to run the risk of appearing to bigfoot the incoming coach before he was named.

Ovechkin was at his most expansive when explaining why it was hard just answering questions. He claimed to be "mentally tired" even though it sounded more like emotional fatigue. "When you lose in the playoffs or a big tournament you don't want to talk about it," he said. "[You] just concentrate on next year. When you don't win you see how different teams, different guys win. It's a hard moment but it's life. Sometimes you're going up sometimes you're going down [and] every game can be your last game."

•   •   •

Ovechkin wasn't the only star in the room. Sitting at the table next to him was Henrik Sedin, who, with Crosby, represented Ovechkin's competition for the Hart Trophy. Crosby wasn't going to talk to the media at the same time as Ovechkin—less a matter of hard feelings than a practical consideration for reporters who couldn't be in two places at the same time. Mike Green, a finalist for the Norris, was a few steps away, waiting for reporters to ask him a few questions—he looked for them in vain, like he looked for teammates on those ill-advised solo rushes up the ice against the Canadiens in Game 7.

It seemed odd that just one player from the roster of the Chicago Blackhawks—the Stanley Cup champions—was among the awards finalists: defenseman Duncan Keith, who would win the Norris ahead of Green. Neither Jonathan Toews, the Conn Smythe winner as the Stanley Cup's most valuable player, or Patrick Kane, who scored the Cup-winning goal in overtime, quite made the cut this year, but it seemed likely that they were ready.

"I still feel young," the 24-year-old Ovechkin said, but the fact was that Toews and Kane were younger than him and already had their Stanley Cup rings on order. Toews also had his Olympic gold and Kane has Olympic silver. It was no longer a case of Ovechkin being measured against older, established stars. Now he was also competing with younger, emerging players like Toews, Kane, and Steven Stamkos, who shared the Art Ross Trophy with Crosby as the league's leading goal scorer, one ahead of Ovechkin. Moreover, Crosby's contract will be up in three years and Stamkos's sooner than that, leaving open the likelihood that Ovechkin, locked up until 2021, will find his contract surpassed. In fact, during the summer of 2010, there were rumours that his Russian Olympic teammate,

Kovalchuk, had been offered $15 million a year from a KHL team. Kovalchuk agreed in mid-July to a 17-year, $102 million deal with New Jersey that, from the third year to the seventh year, would have seen him draw an annual paycheque 15 per cent greater than that of Ovechkin. The league rejected the contract as an effort to circumvent the salary cap, but it again brought into sharp relief the questionable wisdom of the Washington captain agreeing to such a long-term contract with the Capitals. With the salary cap going up almost every year, and with any re-negotiation of his contract impossible under current collective bargaining rules, Ovechkin has left himself open to falling well down the NHL individual salary chart as he moved into his prime.

At 25 when the 2010–11 season starts, Ovechkin will be young but not so young and the same can be said for his team. He and his teammates and the staff believe that the Capitals are still on the upswing, that they'll be back and be better. Right after the season the Capitals signed Nicklas Backstrom to a 10-year contract worth $67 million to ensure that two-thirds of the first line was locked up for the long-term. Yet like all teams, the Capitals were in transition and there were going to be changes. Was Mike Knuble still going to ride shotgun beside Ovechkin and Backstrom at 38? Highly unlikely beyond next season. Would those who watched Game 7, David Steckel and Tomas Fleischmann, have roles in the organization? They might be more valuable to teams other than Washington. Was there going to be room under the salary cap to re-sign Alexander Semin, who had just a year left on his contract before unrestricted free agency? That seemed unlikely and the Capitals were planning to draft a talented Russian teenager, Evgeny Kuznetsov, who would offer the same sort of skill as Semin in a couple of years. McPhee was convinced that Ovechkin would serve as a magnet for young Russian prospects, who might otherwise be reluctant to leave the KHL for the NHL. The Capitals were going to have to wait a season or two for Kuznetsov but not for other changes. Young players from Hershey were going to step up and challenge veterans for spots.

John Carlson, a playoff surprise, seemed ready for a regular shift on the blue line. Others were already departing. Joe Corvo and Scott Walker, who had been imported at the trade deadline to make a difference but had not, would not be re-signed. Unproductive center Brendan Morrison, ostensibly Semin's setup man, was also cut loose.

One member of the Capitals who wasn't going to be back was in Las Vegas: Jose Theodore. He was pulled in Game 2 against Montreal and never played again for Washington. McPhee was up front about letting the 33-year-old Theodore walk away even though he'd impressed during the season. During one stretch, the Capitals didn't lose in regulation for 23 straight games with him in the net. But his salary of $4.5 million just didn't fit within the Washington payroll, and Varlamov and Michal Neuvirth, although unproven netminders, were ready for full-time NHL work. Theodore had a good run with Washington but was perceived, not necessarily rightly, as passenger rather than driver. Only the sentimental would hold on to the memory of Theodore stoning Crosby to keep the Capitals in the game late in the second period on Super Bowl Sunday, and NHL GMs can't afford to be sentimental. Even Jaroslav Halak's heroics in victory didn't win him the No. 1 job in Montreal and only made him a more marketable asset for the Canadiens when they traded him to St. Louis.

Theodore had won the Hart and Vezina Trophies with Montreal in 2002, but he was in Las Vegas as a finalist for the Masterton, the trophy that goes to the player who "best exemplifies the qualities of perseverance, sportsmanship, and dedication to ice hockey." Of any of the trophies that were up for a vote by NHL hockey writers, no one was a surer winner than Theodore. He wasn't being recognized just for playing through his grief after the death of his infant son. His nomination acknowledged his donation to the neonatal intensive care unit where Chace died and his help in raising funds for Children's Hospital. Theodore had blowouts with the media in

his days in Montreal—almost every Canadiens goaltender does—
but no one could hold a grudge in the wake of that tragedy and with
all his charitable work.

• • •

The finalists and other hockey celebrities walked the red carpet in
front of the Palms before the awards show. Because it was Pacific
time and the league needed to hit an Eastern Standard pre-prime-
time broadcast slot, those on the carpet sweltered in the 98-degree
heat at 4 p.m. Ovechkin wore a slate-gray striped suit and no tie, a
mix of high style and casual that made it look like he had walked out
of the pages of his *Men's Journal* fashion shoot. Crosby looked like
he was wearing his Sunday best to church. Steven Stamkos wore
a silver suit that almost reflected sunshine into the eyes of those
standing outside for the parade.

The NHL leaves room for a reasoned disagreement about the
identity of the game's most valuable player by making players eligible for two MVP awards—actually it's one league award, the Hart,
and one from the NHL Players' Association, the Ted Lindsay. The
former is a vote from the media and the latter is based on ballots
from NHL players. In earlier years, the NHLPA had delivered their
award—formerly called the Lester B. Pearson Trophy, but renamed
in 2010 in honor of Lindsay, a union pioneer—at a luncheon several
days before the larger NHL awards show. But the NHL had incor-
porated the Lindsay into the main show, seemingly undercutting
the value of the historic Hart, as player after player insisted they'd
prefer the support of their peers rather than that of voters from the
Professional Hockey Writers Association. For the most part, the
best player had been a matter so plainly evident that the same player
won both, as Ovechkin had.

In Las Vegas in June 2010, Ovechkin was looking to become
the first since Wayne Gretzky to win three consecutive votes of his

peers. Even though they don't like his stick-on-fire routine, even though many think that he plays recklessly and gets kid-glove treatment from NHL, even though some North Americans might cling to old-school hockey xenophobia, they understand what he does against them, and they understand how hard it is to do what he does. They had voted for Ovechkin in 2008 and 2009. And they did again in 2010.

Lindsay, a vigorous, well-scarred 84-year-old with hair the color of brown shoe polish, handed the trophy to Ovechkin, who seemed at a loss for words. He started with an affirmation of his bad-boy lifestyle by shouting out to his crew. "Thanks to Las Vegas for having good time here," he said. "It was a tough night last night, spent lots of time with my friends—Stas, Alex, whassup?" Then Ovechkin fell into the conventions of awards acceptances, recognizing the other finalists, Crosby and Sedin.

At this point, Ovechkin struggled for words to thank someone who never saw him play on hockey's greatest stages: Sergei. Toad was now a man of 24, the same age as Sergei was when he died. "I wish I could share this with my brother who passed away," he said. "It's all about him." He kissed his left index finger, looked skyward, right into the television lights, and raised his hand over his head.

The music then came up and Lindsay and others walked off stage, but Ovechkin stayed at the mike. Comedian Reese Waters came onto another part of the stage, but Ovechkin wasn't about to be rushed off and, drawing laughs, rhymed off a list of those he wanted to thank: his parents, brother Mikhail, the Capitals organization, Bruce Boudreau, and George McPhee. "What a life," he said as an exit line.

A few awards and only a couple of funny jokes later came the presentation of the Masterton. Theodore had been calm in the face of the league's best shooters for more than a decade, but when he took the stage he was visibly shaking, more so than Jaroslav Halak might have been in the opening round of the playoffs.

"This one is going to be tough," he said, going through his notes slowly. "I'm very touched by this award. I'm here because of a tragic loss that happened a year ago. On June 22 last year my son Chace was born but tonight instead of celebrating his first year I'm here accepting this beautiful award on his behalf . . ."

Here Theodore's voice cracked and he paused to collect himself.

". . . but all this would not be possible without my teammates. Thanks, guys, it was good being around you . . . and the Washington Capitals organization, they were very nice . . ."

The past tense was his way of waving good-bye to his now former teammates.

One by one, the awards were presented. Ryan Miller, the cerebral Buffalo goaltender identified by the NHL's Brian Jennings as the league's third most saleable player asset behind Ovechkin and Crosby, captured the Vezina Trophy as the league's best at his position. Miller was the second member of the Sabres to come away with an award—Tyler Myers, the towering defenseman who had neutralized Ovechkin in that first game after the Olympics, had been voted the league's top rookie.

At the end of the show, the three finalists for the Hart, Ovechkin, Crosby, and Sedin, gathered on the left of the stage before the winner's name was announced. In a small upset, Sedin, the league leader in points scored, was named winner and walked out to center stage after shaking Ovechkin's and Crosby's hands. The camera followed Sedin, and Ovechkin and Crosby were left to make their exits while the soft-spoken Swede made his speech.

The hockey writers voting for the award are, to be polite, unpredictable and, to be blunt, occasionally inexpert. The voting for the season's other awards was a case in point. One member of the hockey writers fraternity gave a first-place vote to Ovechkin in the balloting for the Selke Trophy, the award given to the league's best defensive forward. Wrongfully accused. Likewise, another writer voted for Ovechkin as the First All-Star team's *right* winger. You had to wonder if these two voters could have picked Ovechkin out of a lineup.

It later came out that the voting for the Hart was the closest voting in eight seasons, since Theodore edged Jarome Iginla for the award. Most of the working media at the awards show knew that votes had swung Sedin's way because of Ovechkin's suspensions—the hockey writers were seemingly more likely to claim the moral high ground than those who were endangered by Ovechkin's recklessness. The suspension for the hit on Brian Campbell had likely cost Ovechkin not only the goal-scoring title but also the Hart—and just maybe taken enough of an edge off his game to cost his team a series win over Montreal in the playoffs. Winning the Lindsay but losing the Hart was a kind of split decision for him, a referendum on his season that delivered no clear verdict. He was still quite obviously among the best, but no longer decisively the best. He was awash in challengers, both at home in D.C. and beyond.

Ovechkin would have given the post-awards media session a pass if he'd been shutout of the awards completely, but the Lindsay Trophy meant he had to put in an appearance. A small entourage of Russian friends waited for him while he spoke to reporters. If he had kept his answers short the previous day, he was even more curt after losing the Hart. He fielded questions like he had left his car running. A couple of minutes in, he became almost completely unresponsive. If he had joked that the *Men's Journal* was the most boring thing ever, it seemed he genuinely felt that way about this session.

"I couldn't hear your acceptance speech," one reporter said. "Did you say something about your brother? Did you say you were dedicating this to your brother or something like that?"

"No," Ovechkin told him.

"You didn't?" the reporter said, exasperated. The volume on the television in the media room had been turned down during Ovechkin's acceptance speech because other winners were being interviewed, but everyone in the scrum knew that Ovechkin had mentioned his brother—they just couldn't quite make out the words.

"Maybe," Ovechkin said, and he walked away from the microphone and towards the group of Russian friends waiting for him.

Before he could make a clean getaway and head off into the Vegas night, Ovechkin was stopped by Lisa Hillary, a television reporter for the Capitals' broadcasts on Comcast back in Washington. Ovechkin couldn't turn away a request from someone who'd covered him on a daily basis.

He seemed more comfortable away from questions shouted out from a crowd in front of him. He seemed more willing to open up in the one-on-one.

At the end of this long and ultimately frustrating season, at the end of an awards night when his own award felt like hollow consolation, Alexander Ovechkin was down and didn't try to hide it.

"You know you had a chance to win and you are a little disappointed and I am very disappointed by myself," he said.

Hillary then asked Ovechkin about Theodore. "You watched him accept an award that was very difficult," she said. "You can understand what he's going through because on a personal level you lost someone very close to you."

Ovechkin looked down at the floor, not at the microphone, not at Hillary. He waved his left hand in small circles, like he could find the right words hanging out in midair. He waved his hand like he was trying to find a good place to start. Neither the words nor a starting point were out there.

"I try . . . uh . . . I try," he said. "I sit . . . I sit in the stands . . . uh . . . I try to be fun but I know when he lose closest people to you it's very hard and you need the support and I tried to support him even when he is in the stands and I was . . . everybody . . . I still try to scream so . . . I say Jose . . . he is not alone over there."

Ovechkin bowed his head, chin to chest.

For a moment he drifted off, deep in the memories of his brother and his former coach who both were struck down far too young. He empathized with Theodore. He didn't just feel for him—he *understood*. There were defeats and there were *losses*. Sergei shouting from the stands, Vyacheslav Kirillov pushing him through drills, Anna Goruven reassuring and protecting him off the ice, and his grandfather telling him family stories. For a moment, it seemed their voices drowned out the noise around him. With all the neon and bustle, with the B-list celebrities filing by hoping in vain to get recognized, with the media clattering on their keyboards, with other television types doing their stand-ups, with players already in limos heading to clubs, it was easy to miss it—something rarer in Vegas than a royal flush on the flop: a moment of authenticity.

acknowledgments

THIS BOOK IS, PRIMARILY, the work of three creative impulses. In the fall of 2009, the authors were each engaged in their quirky, individual enterprises, one on what happens to a person when the bus of sports history runs them over, the other on the world of unthinkable strength, plus a Dickie Dunn-style novel/manuscript/screenplay. Fortuitously, both were rescued from their flights of fancy by Karen Milner, Wiley's senior editor, who suggested a book on hockey's top player, Alexander Ovechkin of the Washington Capitals. The initial answer was no. No thanks, actually. Then maybe it had merit. Then a phone call suggested a collaboration. Then off we went.

The original idea was that this book would, at the very least, include excerpts from lengthy interviews with Ovechkin himself. The title, the story and the concept changed substantially over the course of months. It was designed and imagined as an unauthorized biography, but the template left room for the subject to have his say. Unfortunately, that didn't happen. Months of negotiations between the authors, the publisher and the Ovechkin camp, primarily representatives of the International Management Group, were occasionally optimistic but ultimately fruitless. It was clear the Ovechkin family wasn't interested in giving their perspective, and we respected their position. Ovechkin is quoted extensively through his various public appearances, and the authors have relied on past interviews and other sources in an effort to deliver his point of view. We believe that in the end, the portrayal is both honest and fair.

The authors would like to thank the Washington Capitals for their extensive co-operation in this project, primarily general manager George McPhee, head coach Bruce Boudreau, team president Dick Patrick and owner Ted Leonsis. Not one roadblock was placed in our way over the course of months. McPhee immediately endorsed the concept when it was presented to him, Boudreau was unfailingly helpful even during the most pressure-packed moments of a long season and Leonsis, while engaged in a book process of his own, gave his time, his blessing and his stories. As well, a special thanks is owed to the crack Capitals media relations staff, the best in the business, and primarily to Nate Ewell. Nate had the difficult job of balancing his role as an Ovechkin confidante with his job of openly promoting the Capitals as one of the NHL's brightest and best franchises. He walked the tightrope beautifully, and without his patience and assistance this book would not be what it turned out to be. Thanks, Nate.

More than 100 interviews were conducted for this book over a period of six months, some by overseas cell phone, others in person, many more than once. Ovechkin's Washington teammates were most helpful, particularly Brooks Laich, Mike Knuble and Brian Pothier. Former teammates like Jamie Heward and Chris Clark helped fill out the picture. Slava Malamud of Moscow's Sport Express was invaluable for lending a Russian perspective. Dave Stiff, a resourceful producer at TSN, was most helpful in supplying video evidence of key moments in Ovechkin's career. Tarik El-Bashir of the Washington Post never once complained we were stomping all over his turf and selflessly provided stories and perspective. This was a book written with one foot in Canada, one in D.C. and one in Moscow, and the three-footed result is one that accurately portrays this hockey genius as a young man. hurtling towards his prime.

The authors would like to thank Wiley and Karen, mostly for sitting back, leaving us alone and gently suggesting that yes, there would have to be deadlines, and not minding when what started out as an ending chapter became the beginning, and vice versa. The story was a dynamic that changed over the course of the remarkable 2009–10 NHL season, and so did this book.

Finally, the authors wish to thank their families and primarily their life partners for not just patiently dealing with late night typing and early morning calls, but hastily organized road trips and unscheduled absences.

Now back to the quirkiness.

DC/GJ

index